Girt By Dirt

An Australian Adventure

By Phillip Butters

For my late father, Jack Butters

Co-founder of the Australian Society of Travel Writers.

He encouraged travel with a sense of hunger;
to pack a rumbling mind as part of our baggage to make the colours brighter, the shapes prettier and the people more interesting.
Whether travel is to broaden our minds is up to us and the attitude we take with us.

This trip, and this book, would not have happened without his influence and encouragement.

Table of Contents

1. The Beast Goes South

'Would youse like fries with that'?

And then we were underway, on a 35,000-kilometre odyssey around Australia's coasts and through its rugged red interior.

Who are 'we'? Well, Glen and I are a couple of 30-year-old Aussies who decided to give up the banking caper for a while, load up a new blue four-wheel drive and see as much of the country as possible. To look at, some might have seen us as Laurel and Hardy or Jake and Elwood, but many who knew us were doubtful that we would last so long together without doing harm to ourselves or each other, or at least giving up and coming home in frustration. To their surprise, our friendship survived intact, and we can still be seen reminiscing over a beer or two at the local pub.

Glen could best be described as *'a bloke'*. He likes his beer, steak, sport (as a spectator), cars, Cold Chisel and beer. But he also likes fine cheese, quality wine and the Corrs, and as I was to learn, also a great cook, especially with limited means. He's one of the most genuine and generous people I know. Just don't piss him off. I'm not too far different, but enjoy sport more as a participant than spectator. Oh, and I know a lot less about cars.

When I told Glen I was trying to shed some light to the reader on who we were, he offered these remarkably apt thumbnail appraisals:

'Me: An overweight, petrol headed, cigarette smoking boofhead who loves his wine and country. You: A short arsed, skinny butted dreamer who loves his wine and country.'

The trip was the culmination of a year's planning and research, from when we were chatting over a beer in a swish Sydney pub and finding that our dream to see the country was shared, to loading up the four-wheel drive and bidding farewell to anxious parents on a sunny autumn morning. When I say 'planning', I use the word loosely. Our only firm plan was to be back in Sydney before our scheduled return to work, and we intended to see as much of the country as possible in that time. We had a rough route mapped out, but essentially intended to go where our interests took us at the time.

Our course was to lead us south from Sydney to Melbourne, where we would load the car on a ferry and spend a few weeks exploring Tasmania, the south island of Australia. Back on the mainland, we would traverse coastal and inland Victoria, zig-zagging across several state borders on our way to Birdsville and its famous pub in Queensland's southwestern corner. Returning to the coast around Adelaide and the South Australian wine country, the Eyre Highway would take us west across the expansive Nullarbor Plain into Western Australia and to its capital, Perth. Bearing north along the western coast to Broome, an inland route would take us through the rugged outback Kimberley region and east to Darwin in the Northern Territory. To complete the trip, we would head south to the heart of Australia and then home through outback Queensland. It would be a fascinating and inspiring exploration of a diverse country, oozing with charming and rugged character and more than a few charming and rugged characters.

The car was pretty well stacked. The trusty little blue four-wheel drive two-door Holden Frontiera had the back seat folded down to fit our stuff, with the overflow strapped to a basket on the roof. We'd spent a few weekends shopping for containers (food, water and petrol), some dry food, cooking utensils, gas cooker and lanterns, safety and rescue equipment and other essentials. We'd get some extra four-wheel drive stuff, like another spare wheel and recovery equipment, closer to our real outback experience. We also had a few comforts and contraptions including CD stacker and 120 CDs, laptop computer with mobile phone connection to send and receive emails (on the rare occasions that we were in range), digital and other cameras, and more maps and guide books than we were likely to need.

After cramming an immense amount of stuff into and onto the car, and sharing our elation at finally getting under way, we were almost out of Sydney before we had succumbed to the lure of the Golden Arches. It wasn't an upmarket start, but we were confident it wouldn't become a habit.

We figured it would be in our interests to set a minimum allowable period between each fast food meal. We settled on five hours.

As we headed south out of Sydney, we decided the car needed a name. Discarding *Bouncing Betty* and *Outback Spice*, we considered *The Beast* to have the best ring to it for the journey on which it and we were embarking.

Just after that momentous decision, it began pouring with rain, so our waterproofing technique for the rooftop luggage was to be tested early. Ditto for my somewhat dubious knot tying ability. God knows how I got the knot-tying badge in cubs. Or the cooking one for that matter. They were undoubtedly the easiest of all to get. I'm a fan of quantity rather than quality when it comes to awards.

Out of the rain, we drove past a road kill patrol. What a thankless task it must be driving along the freeway scraping dead animals off the road without joining the pancake brigade yourself as a multicoloured blur of metal zooms past.

While we drove the more scenic coastal Princes Highway, the Hume Highway is the quickest route between Sydney and Melbourne. It is named after Hamilton Hume, born in Sydney's Parramatta in 1797. In his youth, he did quite a bit of exploration of the areas around Sydney and squatted on the land he discovered around now rural Yass. In 1824, Hume set out with William Hovell in a successful attempt to reach the southern coast along a route similar to that of the highway. After the expedition, they had a public brawl over who was the leader of the expedition. I assume Hume won, given that the Murray River, which they crossed, bore his name for some time, and the highway still does.

Explorers and early settlers seemed to like naming things after themselves, but none was better than New South Wales Governor Lachlan Macquarie. Macquarie was sent by Britain to Australia with his own troops to try to restore order following the coup against Governor William Bligh, led by prominent pastoralist John Macarthur in 1808 (more on that episode later). Among many achievements, Macquarie managed to name just about everything left to name after himself (or his wife Elizabeth), or encourage others to do so.

Welcome to the hilly and high Southern Highlands: famous for cricket legend Sir Donald Bradman and the movie Babe. It's also home to the *Tulip Time Festival,* although it didn't appear to be the right time for tulips as we passed through. *The House of Love Seafood Restaurant* was not able to draw us in, and the mind pictures weren't pretty anyway. We were tempted though by a shop offering Emu burgers. And we weren't even in the outback yet! In addition to its famous people and movies, the Southern Highlands is also known for its herbal lifestyles. The sign 'Live Naturally with Herbs' pretty much appeared to sum up some of the townsfolk. The locals don't eat meat and they smoke their greens in this part of the world.

Bodalla (once known as 'Boat Alley'), not far from our first night's destination of Narooma, is 'famous' for its cheese. In the same vein as the Big Banana in Coffs Harbour and the Big Marino in Goulburn, Bodalla has its Big Cheese. It actually looks more like a big tin can, but let's not take the wind out of their sails.

The drive through and around Kangaroo Valley is one of the most beautiful I have experienced. The road winds through the hills, crowded with tall stately eucalypts standing to attention as they reach up to the sky over lush green undergrowth. It's a quaint little town with several quaint little shops and a quaint little suspension bridge built in 1898, making it Australia's oldest surviving one. And quaintest. As we drove down the neighbouring mountains, a blanket of fluffy white cloud hung sleepily over the valley, and an eerie mist hung in the forest alongside the dewy road.

We made it to Narooma and tracked down our mate Tim, a former bank colleague who had enough of the rat race and went bush. We hit the local club for a few beers and a hearty and cheap feed. We all came up short in the meat raffle and, seemingly on a roll of bad luck, resisted the temptation to enter the crowded bingo hall.

On day two of the trip, the clear skies and warmish weather encouraged us to check out the sights of the Eurobodalla region from our base of Narooma. Narooma is an oyster town, which also has some very good fishing, and a great annual blues festival that the three of us had enjoyed the year before.

We travelled through Moruya, a dairy and oyster farming town, which intrigued us with its *Air Raid Tavern*. To my knowledge, the Japanese never flew this far south of Darwin. We ran the gauntlet safely. The town's claim to fame is supplying granite for the construction of the Sydney Harbour Bridge pylons, cenotaph and the GPO.

Mogo (or was it called *Historic Mogo*?) is a small town. It has at least three bakeries, a zoo and two confectionery shops. The zoo was our first stop. It had fewer than 20 different species of animals, so we were somewhat taken aback by the $10 entry fee. We had managed to arrive just as the otter feeding was about to begin. They had two very active otters named Dad and Dave and yes, they were father and son. And loud little buggers too. We also saw feeding of the lions, jaguars, Sumatran and Bengal tigers and a couple of big brown bears. Each feeding was accompanied by a talk about the species and the specific animals, most of which are endangered. We were told that there are only 400 Sumatran tigers left in the wild thanks to poachers chopping them into tiny bits and using them as ancient Viagra, among other things. The zoo was owned and managed by a dedicated and admirable couple who built it up from nothing over nine years. It participates in breeding programs on site in association with other Australian and international zoos, and contributes to conservation in the animals' natural environments.
Ok, so it was $10 well spent.

Driving back to downtown Mogo for a late lunch, we settled on Mogo Munchies, attracted by the flashing lights over its otherwise nondescript entrance. It boasted 99-cent award winning meat pies. The award was on display in the front window: 'First Prize, Sydney Royal Easter Show 1996, Class 38; Pie, meat'. And I must say it was a good pie, as pies go. In fact, we didn't know why it hadn't won since then. Glen thought that he should compare the quality of Mogo Munchies' pies with its competition. Luckily the shop next door offered steak & mushroom pies (for $2.50). Glen's verdict: the award was well deserved.

Mogo Munchies' other neighbour was Dragons 'n' Stuff. Intrigued, we paid a brief visit and found that it was mainly stuff and not much in the way of dragons. Just down the road was Bizarre Burgers, which tempted our pallets with *Skippy Burgers* but we were by that time full on pies. The remainder of Mogo is packed with antique and knick-knack shops including the alliterative but not very wittily named *Necessary Unnecessaries*. We resolved that visiting was unnecessary and hit the road.

From Mogo, we passed through several small coastal villages including Historic Broulee ('Village by the Sea'), Historic Mossey Point (neither of which provided us with the anticipated Kodak moments), Historic Potato Point and, what we assumed was Historic, Blackfellow Point. At the last stop we experienced our first contact with native wildlife on the trip – a mob of kangaroos and three wallabies slowly grazing their way to the beach as the sun set. I'd love to have known how the latter two places found their names, but it was late and the Air Raid Tavern was calling.

The next day we drove to another quaint town not far from Narooma. Historic Tilba is not far from Historic Tilba Tilba. I kid you not. The entire town has been classified by the National Trust as an 'unusual mountain village'. It didn't look particularly unusual to us. We bought the weekend papers and had lunch at a bakery, of which there are frequently multitudes in country towns. On the way home, we drove through Mystery Bay. How do these places get their names? Glen suggested that Mystery Bay got its name because it's a mystery why anyone would want to go there. Harsh.

Later in the afternoon, we had our first fishing outing of the trip. After a couple of hours of snagging the lines, and nearly being blown off the rocks upon which we were perched, Glen managed to land a barely legal leather jacket. The rest of the afternoon was spent feeding the fish, which were obviously attuned to snatching bait and leaving hooks unscathed. Glen cooked up the fish (with a supplement bought from the supermarket on the way home) into a great garlic chili onion fish pasta. An auspicious start in the culinary stakes (excluding the fast food experience).

After farewelling Narooma, we visited Bega, another town known for its cheese. Glen celebrated our arrival by cutting the cheese. The name Bega comes from the Aboriginal word *bika*, meaning beautiful. I gather it has changed a bit since then. We did the obligatory trip to the Cheese Centre and also went to a surprisingly good winery and lashed out on a few bottles to enjoy over the coming few days. I say surprisingly because the only other wine we tasted in the region was revolting, and the others that we didn't bother trying make only fruit or herbal wines.

While at Bega's Grevillea winery, we took the 30-minute walk through the vines and around a natural lagoon populated by dozens if not hundreds of birds of various species. I think if I were a birdwatcher I would have been very impressed. Alas, I am not, although it was a pleasant walk and the multitude of birds busily preening and feeding were pretty cool.

Bega is a relatively large town for the area, and is different to other places we had passed through, in that a majority of the population appeared to be permanent rather than holidaymakers. And they are very proud of their cheese. Our *Let's Go* guide book says that apart from the cheese, Bega is 'otherwise utterly dull'. A bit rough but I wouldn't make a special trip.

Falling short of our intended destination of Mallacoota in Victoria, we stopped at the coastal town of Merimbula ('City without a jingoistic phrase after its name, nor does it overtly claim to be historic'). A profusion of people was mingling there, with school holidays lingering on and on. We stayed at a youth hostel, the owner of which was taking a break and left some sketchy guy, who had been staying there for a week, in charge. A few backpacking Poms were in residence and were the friendliest. The others weren't interested in talking to anyone else.

Before dining and settling in for the night, we drove to the nearby town of Pambula. This area provides Sydney with many of their oysters when the season is right, and on the way back to the hostel, we had the opportunity to buy three dozen oysters for $8.50. Since Glen doesn't eat the 'snot-like creatures', we stuck with our planned pizza for dinner and gave the oysters a miss, to my later regret.

When staying in hostels, our preference was for a twin room rather than dorm accommodation, partly for privacy, but mainly to secure the laptop and other valuables. On the down side, Glen is a snorer and I am a light sleeper so I travelled with earplugs for such circumstances. When we camped, we could pitch our tents on either side of the car to buffer the din. Glen also has an amazing ability to fall asleep in bed while reading and somehow manages to keep holding his book up in the air.

Further down the coast, we set off to explore Eden and the Ben Boyd National Park. Eden has some great whale watching, but our timing wasn't quite right so there was not a whale to be seen. Its cemetery is built right on the water's edge with spectacular views over Twofold

Bay. It's a shame the residents can't enjoy the view. We both enjoyed a stroll through the old weather-stained gravestones, reading the intriguing epitaphs. Many of them were children and several died in the nineteenth century. One chap, relatively new to the afterlife, had a great inscription on his gravestone: 'Remember me with laughter, not with tears'. I think I would like to have that as my epitaph.

After taking advantage of a few Kodak Moments, we headed back to the surprisingly interesting Killer Whale Museum. Eden was built on the back of whaling and logging, neither of which is now in vogue, although logging continues, evidenced by the numerous log and woodchip trucks roaring past us.

My favourite part of the museum was the story of the bloke whose whaling boat was smashed apart by a whale upset at being harpooned. This guy and one other were presumed dead. After several hours, the whale finally died and came to the surface. When he was dragged ashore and sliced open, one of the missing men was supposedly found in the whale's stomach. The man was alive, although his hair and skin were bleached and he was in a stupor. It wasn't until 18 years later that he finally kicked the bucket. I wonder if he is buried in the cemetery.

South of Eden is Boydtown, founded by Benjamin Boyd, a wealthy banker, stockbroker, whaler and pastoralist. Boyd arrived in the area in 1843 and soon became one of its largest landholders, at one stage second only to the Crown. His vision was for his town to rival Sydney and even become the capital of Australia. It didn't take long for his ostentatious plans (including a bank whose shareholders were £80,000 in debt) to crash like the waves against the red rocks surrounding Twofold Bay. He abandoned Australia in 1849, left for the Californian goldfields and disappeared in the Solomon Islands on the return trip in

1851. An expedition sent in search of him returned with a skull which was optimistically presumed to be Boyd's but is now thought to have belonged to a female Melanesian.

From Eden, we took a few rough tracks through the Ben Boyd National Park. One led to the Boyd Tower, used by Mr Boyd's whaling company to spot whales before his competition got to them. The ocean view from ground level was spectacular, which was a good thing as there was no ladder to get to the top of the tower. We also went to a small house and what's left of a whaling station used by Boyd & Co. The rocks along the coastline jut out from under the thickly vegetated cliff tops into the churning water, are amazingly red and seem to attract a lot of fishermen. We assumed it was the fish that attracted them rather than the colour of the rocks.

There were a few people driving around the rough narrow roads in the park, but how they got some of their cars there I don't know. Glen drove back from the end of the road and shifted into four-wheel drive for the first time on the trip. If Glen had bought his dream car, the Holden Suburban ('The Ultimate Urban Assault Vehicle'), I'm sure it would have got wedged between some of the trees straddling the narrow track. The forest was very dense, and there were signs everywhere telling us how long ago each little pocket of land had been logged.

Our target stop for that evening was Mallacoota, just over the border into Victoria.
Mallacoota Inlet is lucky enough to have two town mottoes: 'Victoria's best kept secret', and 'The natural choice'. For a best kept secret, the campground we chose was positively huge, and in most areas was packed. It had over 600 camp/caravan sites, and that was after some had been removed to cater for an expansion of the unused soccer field.

Our spacious campsite was only a few steps away from an amazingly beautiful and serene beach. Another amazing thing is how frequently caravan parks have the best locations in town on the South Coast. A short walk through some coastal vegetation took us to the empty beach. Several sandbars radiated out from the beach, and pelicans floated peacefully on the water. The tree-lined beach provided a buffer from the campground and a haven for birds and tourists seeking solitude.

So we set up camp, cooked up dinner and enjoyed our first night of camping under a fine still sky. We boiled the billy for the first time and the gas light burnt bright. This is what we'd been waiting for. What a life!

Mallacoota is the main town for the northeast region (the Gippsland Coast) of Victoria and a popular tourist destination. Its main industries are fishing and abalone diving and it is surrounded by the picturesque Croajingolong National Park, a diverse area stretching 100 kilometres along the coast with great beaches and forest walks and home to more than 300 species of birds.

One's whole schedule is changed when camping. When it gets dark early and you've got nothing better to do, you make dinner, eat and go to bed. So by nine o'clock I was snug in my sleeping bag listening to Glen burping, farting and snoring the night away in his spacious but no doubt pungent tent.

Following the early night, we both rose early and while Glen braved the shower block, I went for a wander along the shore. The location's beauty and peacefulness captivated me. The plethora of birds and the brilliant red rocks along the coast, shadowed by thick forest, created a very tranquil setting so distant from the hustle and bustle of Sydney.

Back on the road for a short drive, we visited Genoa, a small town just off the Princes Highway. It had a characteristic single lane wooden bridge and that was about all. The bridge was dedicated to all those who 'fought bureaucracy' to save it and have it restored. Apparently they won, and as far as bridges go it is quite attractive, held together with a mesh of chunky white wooden beams spanning its plank deck.

On our way back to the campground, we discovered that Mallacoota was blessed with not two, but three mottoes, the third being 'Jewel of the Wilderness Coast'. How nice.

We thought it was about time to do some washing, so we tracked down the local laundromat. Glen planned to get a haircut, but 'A Cut Above' was (amazingly) booked out.
They may have been a cut above the rest, but as far as we could tell, there was no other hairdresser in town.

More bad luck at the laundromat: the guy from the shop next door (a combined travel agent, tourist information, sports shop and real estate agent) said that there was a blackout in the town so we wouldn't be able to use the washers and dryers. We tried calling people to arrange a fishing trip in the afternoon, but none of the town's public phones was working, and on top of that, we couldn't get any money out of the ATM. We went to the local youth hostel to pre-book the hostel in Melbourne for the weekend and the bloke didn't know how, so he told us to come back after 4:30. We did, and were told by the girl who was supposed to know how to do the booking, to come back after five so we went to the bar and watched *Wheel of Fortune* over a beer. I was the Wheel champ and I didn't even need to buy a vowel. Eventually we found someone who knew how to pre-book the hostel although we weren't convinced we'd have beds waiting when we rolled into

Melbourne. The travails of spur-of-the-moment travel can be many and tend to come in clusters.

Driving back to tent city we managed to rack up our first 1,000 kilometres for the trip. We decided to polish off the day with a bit of fishing. Glen caught two fish that were to a legal size what Tasmania is to the Australian mainland. Some bloke came along and started talking to us. As soon as we said we were from Sydney, he said that he hated Sydney. Not long after, he asked if he could have some of our bait. I said he could have some if he agreed that he didn't really hate Sydney, to which he agreed that indeed, he didn't really hate Sydney. In fact, it was Sydney people that he hated. Great much better. Take some bait and fuck off.

Glen whipped up a mean satay chicken dish for dinner while intermittently setting the grass on fire, and proceeded to let off a fart that could have brought down the Genoa bridge. He advised that it was caused by lunch and that dinner was still to follow. Thank God for separate tents.

Again in camping mode, the next day we got off to an early start. Our packing technique was improving by the day, but needed more refinement if we were to be able to use the rear vision mirror. After stopping at a service station for air and breakfast, we decided to head for the inland town of Buchan ('Gateway to Snowy River Country'). We'd heard about this place for a while and were attracted by the limestone caves through which the Victorian Parks folks shuffle herds of tourists on a half-hourly basis at ten bucks a throw.

From Mallacoota, we headed back along the Princes Highway, both taking the helm. The road was full of holidaymakers heading back to Melbourne with their caravans, boats and kids. It amazed us how bad the drivers were. I was particularly enthralled by the dozens of cars and motorbikes overtaking across the double lines and around corners. We were waiting to become witnesses to something bad.

We took a scenic tourist drive up an occasionally sealed road to get away from the drivers hell bent on getting back to Melbourne as fast as possible. The road took us though a couple of small villages and along a coast road with scrubby coastal vegetation (surprise!) and some great views over narrow inlets, deserted beaches and a rough ocean. This region is known as East Gippsland. It's not a big agricultural area (although there are some cattle farms) but logging (or 'commercial thinning' as the industry calls it) of the spectacular forests seems to be the main industry other than tourism. Although commonly attributed to Strzelecki who crossed and named Gippsland (after Governor Sir George Gipps), Angus McMillan was the first European in the area when he traversed it in 1839.

We eventually hit the town of Orbost, stopped briefly for directions, and on our way out we immediately got lost and inadvertently ended up back into town; the road that we thought would get us to Buchan took us back to Orbost in a not so scenic loop. We went to the tourist information centre and tried to decipher the directions they gave us earlier, while listening to meditation music and inhaling a pungent incense. Orbost means 'winged island' in Gaelic and was named after Orbost on the Isle of Skye. Definitely above average on the scale of interesting town names, but our version bares little resemblance to an island, let alone a winged one.

The road from Orbost to Buchan is about 55 kilometres of very twisted and narrow but sealed road. We knew we were in the country when we came across a herd of cattle wandering around the road. It took a while to pass them but eventually we made it through without damaging anything, and finally started getting closer to our destination, rather than further away.

We arrived at Buchan in the early afternoon and headed straight for the caves, where we booked into a 'mystery tour' of the Federal cave. We were a bit late for lunch at the overpriced kiosk, but were able to score a couple of meat pies (again). I'd lost track of how many pies I'd eaten thus far, and we were only a few days into the trip! It's disgusting really. Glen decided (much to my surprise) after having a sausage roll for breakfast and meat pie for lunch, that he would prefer a vegetarian dinner, or at least something remotely healthy. I said that I'd believe it when I saw it.

The name Buchan comes from an Aboriginal term meaning 'place of rocks with holes in them'. You've gotta give it to the original Australians for telling it like it is. In terms of white settlement, Buchan is one of Victoria's oldest settlements and is surrounded by the Alpine and Snowy River National Parks. We thought that as a result of this it would be freezing but it's only 100 metres above sea level and the temperature was quite mild.

The town seemed to be a great community, with various sports teams (the Buchan football club was premier of its league in the previous year). According to our host at the Buchan Lodge backpackers, while a lot of country towns were in decay, Buchan was growing. Slowly, but growing nonetheless. The Buchan General Store was licensed to sell ammunition but we weren't sure where you'd use it - there were 'no shooting' signs up all over the place.

I was hoping for a hot spring near the cave entrances, but since the water comes down from the Snowy Mountains, it wasn't to be. A multitude of very tame kangaroos were hanging around outside the caves, virtually ignoring the throngs of tourists ogling at them and recording them on megabytes of memory.

After we ogled at the kangaroos, took a few photos and made a few Skippy pie jokes, we headed to the cave tour.

The limestone caves were originally reserved in 1887 and date back 300-400 million years. There are two lit caves – the Royal and Fairy – but we did an unlit cave and had to wear miners' helmets with lights on the top. Very attractive it was, but with evidence throughout the cave of years of tourism. There had once been lights and some of the globes, fittings, electrical tubes and switch boxes were still there rusting away. Several of the amazing white stalactites had been broken off, which is upsetting but, I suppose, inevitable. It's an amazingly fragile environment, with stalagmites, stalactites, sheets and blankets of sediment cascading down the cave walls and long hanging formations as thin as straws hundreds or thousands of years old dangling before our faces. It was tempting to reach out and grab one, but we all resisted the urge, unlike some before us.

After the tour, we headed back to town and had a couple of beers in the Buchan pub, chatted to the barman and some Europeans who had walked two hours from the farm at which they were staying and working. After our fill of chit chat and cricket on the TV, we made our way to Buchan Lodge. I love the way they call hostels 'lodges'. Unlike others we'd seen this one did actually have a lodge feel to it; I'm not sure why but I think it was because it was a big wooden farmhouse surrounded by a dilapidated wooden fence and nestled in a small green valley. It just felt lodgey. It was run by an old bloke, Dick, who moved from Melbourne several years before and built it from scratch. There was only one other guest while we were there, a girl from Canada, and locals popped in and out throughout the day. It was clearly a town with a laid-back lifestyle. We stayed up chatting with Dick and hearing about his proud days as a supervisor at the ship engine building factory in Melbourne and then as a driving instructor. After too many ports we collapsed into our spacious dorm room.

After recovering from the night before, Dick took us on a journey to find a cave he hadn't yet seen. A slow and painful drive with a lot of gate opening and closing led us to a clearing near the river we were to traverse. Huge red boulders lined the riverbed and canyon walls were exposed by the lack of water – a common sight in most of the places we drove though in Victoria. I'm sure that changes when the snow melts in the alpine country.

The purpose of our trip was to get to a cave that feeds water into the river. Dick had never been there so he wasn't quite sure what to look for. We stumbled for over an hour along the rugged riverbed – the river looked like it would be much larger in full flow than the small trickle we walked beside - and through the scrub along the riverbank, in awe at the landscape and beautiful red rock gorge walls. We eventually found the *Sub Aqua* cave and it did indeed feed water into the river. No one thought to bring a torch, so we couldn't see into the cave, and being an aquatic cave with freezing water, no one was feeling adventurous enough to explore too far inside. Apparently it's 150 metres long with a massive chamber 35 metres tall. I guess we'll have to come back some day.

The riverbed was wide in places, with huge piles of dead trees and the odd tyre that the river had dumped. On one side, mottled high cliffs loomed over the river, and atop the hollow mountain, chunks of pink granite protruded through the surface to form pyramid-shaped features a few metres high. They had been creatively named *the Pyramids* by earlier travellers.

Back at the lodge, we managed to score an invitation from a local to a birthday party that night. Glen was too stuffed from the walk so I went solo, which gave me a good opportunity to meet some of the locals. The proximity of the party to the police station didn't seem to deter anyone from smoking enough pot to fly to the moon and back. There seemed to be a lot of people from out of town who lived a rather 'herbal' lifestyle and they had come into town for the special occasion. A nearby town called W Tree was home to many of them. There were several guitars, a couple of drums, a flute and a didgeridoo for entertainment. I spent some time with the didge player, who was telling me that a recent severe hail storm in Sydney was caused by a weather control experiment carried out by the Americans in their push for global dominance. Then he took another puff and told a fascinating traditional story with the didgeridoo. The sixties tunes were the order of the night though, and I even managed to strum a few chords on a few of them. I also played some solo tunes later in the evening when everyone was seriously stoned. They loved it. Well, they swayed a lot anyway. I was in with the groovy W Tree hippies, but out of my mind.

While studying the map before our departure the next day, we spotted a place that had to be visited simply because of its name. It was quite a diversion but what the hell. It took a while to find, and after driving through Historic Bruthen and a place called Red Knob, we found the road we were looking for. The dirt track took us right up to Mount Little Dick. Not only that, it took us to Little Dick Range Road, and then Little Dick Tower, a bushfire spotting tower atop Mount Little Dick. Our efforts were rewarded with great views of undulating green mountains and some entertaining photos.

Onward to Melbourne, we passed through the towns of Garfield, Robin Hood and several others with names too weird to remember.

Eventually we got to the big city and found ourselves a cheap and loud (but surprisingly pre-booked) hostel for the few hours before we needed to get up to catch the ferry to Tasmania. The sooner we got out of the big loud hostel and the big loud city the better.

2. South Island Sojourn

A very early start got us to Port Melbourne in time to drive the car onto the huge double-hulled *Devil Cat* for its last run to Tasmania before sailing off to battle the notorious Cook Strait between New Zealand's north and south islands.

After parking the car in one of the neatly packed vehicle decks, we settled in upstairs by a window for the six-and-a-half-hour cruise across Bass Strait. We departed on the comfortable cruise at 7:30am and arrived at Very Historic George Town at about 2pm with little idea of where to go. After the immigration people commandeered all of our fruit and vegies to ensure compliance with the strict interstate pest control regulations, we spent roughly 30 seconds driving through town. We tracked down the local youth hostel, which turned out to be a quaint historic house loaded with character and with a quiet and friendly atmosphere, in contrast to the boisterous and impersonal version of the previous night. The only other guests were a pleasant couple from Germany.

Tasmania's population of fewer than half a million is concentrated on the north and southeast coasts of the upside-down triangle-shaped island state, plus a few more on some of the 20 surrounding islands. Native forest covers about half of its land and more than 30 per cent is listed as a UNESCO World Heritage area, including more than 150 national parks and reserves. The *Webster's Encyclopaedia of Australia* notes that Tasmania has been described as the most thoroughly mountainous island on the planet and its inhabitants enjoy the cleanest air in the inhabited world.

It was only about 13,000 years ago that Tasmania was cut off from the mainland by the last post-ice age thaw, stranding the chilly Aboriginal tribes of the region. They lived in isolated peace until 1642 when Dutch explorer Abel Tasman came along while looking for a southern passage to America. He stepped ashore and named what he saw Van Diemen's Land after the governor general of the Dutch East Indies. After doing a bit of mapping and missing most of the country, he moved on to discover New Zealand (which he thought was part of Australia). A little more attention to detail might have enlightened the Dutch about the make up of this corner of the world.

Throughout the 18th century, numerous Europeans, including Cook and Bligh, visited Van Diemen's Land, mostly believing it was part of the mainland. In 1798, Lieutenant Matthew Flinders circumnavigated the island, thereby proving it to be one, and named the stretch of water between the mainland and Tasmania after the ship's surgeon and future explorer, George Bass.

Towards the end of the 18th century, Governor King of New South Wales decided that a second Australian convict colony was called for and in 1804, Hobart was established. From day one, Van Diemen's Land became the most feared penal colony in the British Empire. In 1824, the fierce Sir George Arthur was appointed Lieutenant Governor of Van Diemen's Land and in the following year, the colony became independent of New South Wales.

As the colony grew, the settlers fenced off increasing tracts of fertile land to establish farms. The Aborigines, who were shorter than their mainland counterparts and didn't have the advantages of such effective tools as the boomerang and woomera, struggled to defend their homelands. The level of violence was absolutely shocking, particularly on the part of the new Australians. Abduction of children, rape of women, shootings, stabbings, poisoning and trapping were commonplace. In 1828, Governor Arthur declared martial law and gave solders the right to arrest or shoot any Aborigine found trespassing on 'European land'. In 1830, an attempt was made to remove the remaining natives from the island's settlements across a border known as the *Black Line'* in a costly and unsuccessful exercise. Two thousand men spent seven weeks to catch just one woman and a boy. An attempt was then made to relocate the natives to Flinders Island to be civilised and taught about the Christian God. Of the original estimated population of 2,000 sent there, only 47 survived and were transferred to Oyster Cove in 1847. At the same time, a new Aboriginal community emerged on the Furneaux islands, keeping the race alive, albeit with a European influence. It is from this group that many of today's Tasmanian Aborigines descend. Almost 4,000 Aborigines were killed in the first generation of European occupation in Tasmania.

George Town sits at the mouth of the Tamar River and is scattered with historic buildings dating back to the early 19th century. It was named by Governor Macquarie after George III and founded in 1811 as the main settlement for the area until Launceston took over in 1824. It claims to be Australia's oldest town, despite Sydney and Hobart being settled earlier. Don't ask me to explain; I don't understand either.

One thing about George Town is that they love their hedges and manicure them into boxes squarer than Buddy Holly, above and around white picket fences. Rows of amazing pines with very thick layered foliage line many of the streets.

We should have filled up with petrol in Melbourne rather than get whacked for an extra 15 cents a litre in George Town. A taste of things to come. We chatted with the young girl pumping the gas; she complained at length about all her friends leaving Tassie for Melbourne, Sydney or Brisbane in search of a warmer climate, more exciting lifestyle and better job opportunities, but she assured us that she wanted to stay put in George Town and pump gas. Would that there were more like her, contented with their lot down south.

After checking in at the hostel and dumping loads of stuff in our room, we set off exploring the area. A short drive north of the town is Low Head. Its two highlights from my perspective were the Pilot Station and the fairy penguins traipsing up the beach at dusk.

The Pilot Station is a compound of about eight strikingly bright white buildings topped with gleaming red-painted corrugated iron roofs. It now accommodates a few private residences and an interesting little maritime museum housing seafaring memorabilia covering its 200 years of helping ships navigate through the treacherous harbour en route to Launceston. It appears that this mission was not always successful, judging by all of the shipwreck displays. The station still operates in its traditional role, and is therefore (and proud to announce) Australia's oldest continuously running pilot station.

We killed some time being tourists and stopping for a cuppa before heading back to Low Head to gawk at the Fairy Penguins waddling up the beach like lots of miniature cloned Charlie Chaplins. At the reserve, we were led up to a viewing platform by a couple of women who ran the private penguin gawking tours (overseen by National Parks rangers). It was bloody freezing; evidently, winter had arrived that day. As we waited anxiously in the chilly twilight, dozens of the little buggers waddled up the beach – apparently several more than in previous days. Firstly, you hear them bark like small dogs, and then they start appearing just above the shoreline to preen themselves. They have an oil duct near their butts where they retrieve oil to waterproof their feathers. After several minutes, they began making their awkward way up from the water to snooze in their burrows. Some chose the easy route along the sand and some clambered over the rocks to get to where they were going. Most of the other tourists gave up early because of the cold and/or nagging kids, so by the end we had our own private tour wandering through the reserve looking at the penguins, none of which seemed terribly interested in us.

We were disappointed that we still hadn't seen a Tassie Devil, but they tend to eat penguins so it was probably a good thing. We returned to the hostel for a vegetarian pasta.

Things didn't start well when we set out the next day to explore the wine regions – it was cold, raining and the first winery we went to was closed. Two of Tasmania's main wine regions, the Tamar Valley and Pipers River, are conveniently (for us) a short drive from George Town. Pipers River is suited to various whites (particularly sparkling) and Pinot Noir while the Tamar Valley produces more reds and some good Chardonnays. It covers a large area but was well marked by 'Wine Route' signs.

The next winery along the way was open so we indulged. Dalrymple is a small family winery that at the time produced five wines, four of which were white. It was established in 1987 and had its first vintage in 1991. Dalrymple was fronted by an aggressive former PR exec who seemed quite offended that the other visitors there didn't care much for any of her wine. We enjoyed a couple of their styles and made a purchase or two.

The next stop was the large marketing-aware and publicly listed Pipers Brook, which boasted pristine vineyards and an immaculate winery, through which we took a self-guided tour. The winery, established in 1974, produces the high-quality Pipers Brook and good, but more moderately priced, Ninth Island. We tasted a few of each and Pipers clearly stood out as excellent wines, although a Ninth Island dry white appealed to both of us. We couldn't resist a few more purchases.

Our final tasting before deciding we'd done our dash and didn't want to be tempted any more was an even smaller family-run place called Brook Eden, at the opposite end of the scale to Pipers Brook. The wife of the winemaker came out to greet us and took us into the tasting room, which was in fact their kitchen. They only had three wines for tasting – wooded and unwooded Chardonnay and a Pinot Noir. All of them were excellent and we stayed for at least half an hour talking about Tassie and its wine industry. We accepted some very good cheese and a taste of the grapes that went into each of their wines – both endearing personal touches to the tasting experience. We each bought a bottle or two before we were escorted to the car and we bade farewell to a fine day of tasting.

After searching through the drizzle for an open café, we headed back to George Town via places called '*Glen*' and '*The Glen*'. Glen was chuffed. We drove through, and got lost in, a major forestry operation and were intrigued by a pedestrian crossing sign stuck in the middle of the carnage. It looked like a war zone. I guess some would say it was. The dirt road passed by a huge expanse of charred land littered with remnants of huge tress rotting under an increasingly overcast (and seemingly appropriate) sky. Also along the road from the wine route was a farm shed with 'Happy 1975' painted in large letters on its side. The paint looked fresh.

Glen finally saw a Tasmanian Devil. Sadly, it was flat as a pancake by the side of the road. These days cars aren't the only major threat to Devils. The world's largest carnivorous marsupial is being decimated by a mystery facial cancer. Some areas have seen a 90 per cent decline in adult numbers. Scientists are working on it and hopefully these little critters won't go the same way as the elusive Tasmanian tiger.

Next stop was Bridport (*'Village by the Sea'*), a village by the sea, which is thought to be named after Bridport in Dorset, England. It is about 20 kilometres north of Scottsdale, the major town of the top right hand corner of the state, a pleasant place with a beach and several coastal walks. Fishing and tourism are the town's mainstays, exporting scallops and crayfish as do so many coastal Tasmanian towns, and a few tourist dollars backing up their haul. We spent a while at the servo getting drinks and listening to the friendly attendant telling us all about the east coast's attractions. The town didn't have too much to offer, except for a great scene by the water where a procession of old wooden pier pylons stretched out about 50 metres from the shore through the beautifully clear turquoise water.

We continued north to the coastal Waterhouse Protected Area and stopped at Waterhouse Point to whip up a couple of tuna and cheese sandwiches and christen the thermos with a comforting cuppa by the ocean. Tea by the sea may sound odd but it was cold enough that warming from the inside was a welcome panacea. After lunch, we drove around a few dirt tracks, stopping briefly and freezing our butts off for the occasional photo of the reserve's several beaches and a series of kinetic sand dunes.

All around us the trees slanted in the same direction, some at almost 45 degrees to the ground, from fierce winds off Bass Strait. The uniform slant to the landscape made it look like a cartoon scene and played havoc with the senses. It wasn't surprising though – the wind batters the coast with an almost continuous force. Why anyone would sail a yacht across Bass Strait for fun is beyond me. This place was supposed to be a popular camping destination, but only for thrill seekers with strong tent pegs. We didn't see another soul during our visit.

Back on the main road we landed in Gladstone, an old tin mining town, again with not much, in fact nothing that we could see, to offer the sightseer. The main intersection featured a service station that was also the post office, bank, general store and vendor of ammunition. We filled up the tank and cleaned multitudes of dead, sticky, gooey bugs off the windows. Eight kilometres south of town the attractions picked up with a magnificent blue lake, a flooded former tin mine appropriately called Blue Lake, coloured by lingering pyrites.

Our next stop turned out to be our last for the day. Mount William National Park is at the isolated north-eastern tip of Tasmania and is full of wildlife, particularly Forester kangaroos, Bennett's wallabies, wombats, possums and birds. Animals have right of way throughout the park and a good thing too, because they choose the split second before you drive near them to cross the road. And boy, does Tasmania have a lot of road kill. After driving though the four Stumpy's Bay campsites, we chose *number one* to pitch. The sheltered site was only a few metres from the beach and popular with the wallabies, who wandered around us caring not a jot. Thankfully it wasn't popular with tourists at that chilly time of year and there was only one other group far enough away that they didn't bother us.

Despite being sheltered from the wind by a thick mesh of coastal vegetation, it was still icy but the unspoilt beauty and serenity of the place was overpowering. We pitched our tents in a small cleared inlet to take advantage of the ocean view through a gap in the trees. We pumped some bore water into one of our ten litre containers. When we took a whiff, we decided that not even boiling would make it drinkable. It took months to get rid of the stench of that water from our jug, and then to get rid of the pine disinfectant aroma. It wasn't until later that I read advice to bring in one's own drinking water to the park.

Glen whipped up a warming soup for dinner, which we enjoyed with a bottle of just purchased pinot noir that we were challenged to keep from freezing. After dinner and while we were washing up, our backs were turned to the table upon which our supplies were stacked, and a rather rotund possum pulled off the lid of one of our food containers. The commotion attracted our attention but the beast wasn't phased by us walking right up to it with our torches and telling it sternly to bugger off. It eventually got the message, and we relaxed with hot chocolates in front of the log fire before retiring to the tents and an eventually warm sleeping bag, listening to the breeze filter through the trees, and to the patter of furry feet through the campground.

We started the following day walking to the summit of Mt William, partly to thaw the bones and blood. I like saying summit because it makes the effort sound grander than it really was (it's only 216 metres high). It adds a certain Everestesque quality to the 'climb'. It was only an hour's walk and not too steep in most parts, but with a great view of the entire National Park and out to Bass Strait and the Furneaux Islands.

Exhilarated and back at sea level, our next adventure awaited. In one of our many guidebooks, we had seen a picture of an enticingly steep corkscrew road called Jacob's Ladder in the Ben Lomond National Park. It was back inland, not far from Launceston, and was begging to be conquered by Glen, Phil and The Beast. On the way, we drove through some really pleasant and pretty little country towns and very attractive natural forest scenery, marked by as yet uncut massive native trees and that sense of clear fresh wilderness.

Derby is a small historic town in a large valley about half way between Mt William and Ben Lomond, yet another tin mining town with a European history dating back to 1870. It was once home to the largest and deepest hydraulic tin mine in the Southern Hemisphere until the dam broke and flooded the mine and the town, killing several of the residents. Not surprisingly, there's a mining museum. Apparently the annual Derby River Derby is a big event for the locals. The Bank House (c1888) is the oldest timber bank building in Tasmania. Wow.

As we drove down from the mountain into the town, we passed a lush green cricket pitch on which a small herd of brown cattle was grazing. Not much further along the road, a large fish-shaped rock protruding from the mountainside. We weren't the first to notice: the rock had been creatively painted to resemble a colourful fish. It was quite impressive.

Just about everywhere we had driven in Tasmania so far had shown evidence of logging. Much of the countryside is a patchwork of old growth forest, newly planted pine trees and bare ground piled with burnt scraps left by the loggers. All over the place logging roads make driving off the main roads tricky, and big logging trucks seem to be everywhere, most often coming straight at you. Much of it is no longer the pleasant landscape it once must have been. It's a disappointing sight, but it's easy to be disappointed if the trees don't provide your livelihood.

Most towns and villages seemed to have timber mills, but many also seemed to have old long-vacated and dilapidated shops. Some entire villages looked to have become ghost towns, including several built on the back of the tin mining boom in the nineteenth century. One place had a service station with the leaded pump on one side of the road and the unleaded pump on the other side. The countryside away from the loggers' saws is beautiful and frequently quite distinctive from the mainland.

Our map reading abilities – which we both thought were reasonably proficient - were put to the test in searching for Ben Lomond. In fact, the map we were using seemed to bear little resemblance to reality. As a result, we inadvertently ended up near the base of Mount Barrow. After driving along a dirt road for a while we caught a spectacular view of the prominent mountain range and decided to see how close we could get. The mountain is a long monolith, a dark igneous escarpment on the top third with massive rock falls below. The rock formations are like giant black crystals that give the mountain a cathedral-like appearance caused by centuries of faulting and freeze-thaw cycles.

We kept driving and discovered a road right up the mountainside. The final few kilometres of the drive were along a very steep and narrow unsealed corkscrew road, not unlike the one we had been heading for at Ben Lomond. The shabby fence provided little confidence that it would actually prevent a disaster. The road was very slippery, even with four-wheel drive engaged. All up it was quite a hair-raising experience but well worth the effort and fear. From the top of the mountain we could see back to the sea and all around the surrounding national park. Spectacular stuff. Most amazing of all was that two mini buses full of school kids had made it up that road for a look around.

Among the rocks was a variety of tightly packed grasses and low bushy shrubs, with small pools of water between tufts. You've got to give it to them for survival – it was literally freezing and extremely windy up there, yet they seemed to flourish. In most places the water had turned to ice, and there were small patches of snow lying around the place. It was the kind of cold that hurts, especially our ears, which were glowing red. The gale force wind had taken its toll on an undistinguishable bird, which had strayed up to the peak and was mashed into a wire fence.

We followed the mini buses back down the track but somehow they left us in their wake. Struggling to find the road we needed, we stopped at a camping ground to ask the proprietor for directions. Maybe she was upset that we woke her from her afternoon nap, but she said the road we were looking for didn't exist. Minutes after leaving the empty campground, we proved her wrong and found it.

After driving for most of the day, we finally made it to Ben Lomond National Park, only to be greeted by a sign telling us that our goal, Jacobs Ladder, was closed due to 'remedial roadworks', which seemed a good idea but really pissed us off after the effort we'd made to get there. We decided to drive on and see how far we could get. As luck would have it, we were there at 4pm, which must have been knock-off time for the workers, so we were able to drive all the way to the ski village at the top. The road was almost as hair-raising as that to Mt Barrow, but the roadworks had obviously greatly improved the condition and there were sturdy-looking safety barriers, a wider road and work done to avoid rock falls from the fractured ancient dolerite walls above.

The view wasn't as spectacular as Mt Barrow so we drove on to the ski village. We could see several lifts and numerous weathered wooden chalets, but no sign of life, save for a couple of brave and probably freezing wallabies hopping around through the ice and snow. We briefly got out of the car to take photos but – surprise - the second highest peak in Tasmania was painfully cold. Some of the more interestingly, if contradictorily, named parts of the national park include Misery Bluff, the Plains of Heaven and Little Hell.

It was getting late and had been a long day, so we made our way to Launceston for the night. After trying a few nondescript motels that wanted to charge over $70 a night for a crummy room, we opted for the Centennial Hotel, an old pub on the fringe of the CBD. We took a room each for $30 and gratefully settled in for the evening.

After enjoying our first shower for a couple of days, we wolfed down a huge dinner. Our hearty meal was taken under the watchful eyes of several deer heads mounted on the walls. They almost made us feel uneasy about enjoying our mixed grills so much. Almost.

Beer in Tasmania is served in '6s', '8s' or '10s', reflecting the volume of each glass in ounces. Tens come with or without a handle. I can't imagine why you'd bother ordering a 6 of beer. It's hardly worth the effort. These Tasmanians have some strange habits but they are incredibly friendly and courteous to strangers. Everywhere we went (except the camp ground), we were offered friendly advice. We would stop at a service station and be stuck there for 15 minutes talking about our trip and finding out about the must-see locations in the region and elsewhere in the state. Occasionally I almost wished someone would just tell us to fuck off while rolling their eyes and sighing, just to make us feel at home.

Launceston was founded by Lieutenant-Colonel William Paterson in 1804 after lengthy deliberations over the site for the state's northern capital. It was part of an ambitious expansion strategy of NSW Governor King. The mix of ex-convicts, pastoralists and natives made for a far from harmonious environment in and around Launceston. Originally called Patersonia after its founder, it is now Australia's 16th largest city. There is a rivalry between Launceston and Hobart, the state capital, similar to that between Sydney and

Melbourne but this one primarily based on beer. The northerners drink Boags, while Cascade is the beverage of choice down south.

William Paterson lived though and was intimately involved in a tumultuous period of Australia's history. He wrote numerous letters back to London from New South Wales complaining about revolutionary and prohibitionist Governor King, a first fleet veteran. Despite Paterson's opinion of King, he refused to join other insurgents (particularly activist and pastoralist John Macarthur) in boycotting King. In the midst of the controversy he held a duel with Macarthur (who took great joy in removing governors from office) in which Paterson was seriously injured. In 1804, Paterson was instructed by his superiors to sail south to establish the Van Diemen's Land settlement, where he stayed until returning to Sydney five years later to take over Bligh's governorship until the arrival of Lachlan Macquarie one year later. Having played a prominent role in early Australia, Paterson soon set sail for England but died at sea.

The influential, aggressive and colourful Macarthur was sent back to England by King in 1801 to be court martialled but en route the case documents vanished and after resigning his commission, Macarthur returned to Sydney a free man. While Paterson was down south, Macarthur played a leading role in overthrowing Governor Bligh in what became known as the Rum Rebellion. Macarthur became de facto governor for a short time before being dispatched back to England until 1817. While there, he studied wool development and trading and his wife stayed behind to build up the family's pastoral interests. He returned to build a wool empire, got involved in banking, and continued to dally with politics until he was accused of being a 'lunatic' in 1832, two years before his death. The Macarthur dynasty lives on in Australia's pastoral landscape.

With a somewhat more peaceful intent, we drove ten minutes to Cataract Gorge Reserve, a pristine area surprisingly close to downtown Launceston. Heavily forested high rock walls flank the river, but the slope is gentle enough to allow plenty of sunlight to reach the sparkling South Esk River, which ends near the park's entrance in a large lake, over which the world's longest single span chairlift takes tourists too lazy to walk to the other side.

We walked away from the developed entrance up the river through the less civilized gorge to the old vacated Duck Reach Power Station, originally commissioned by the Launceston City Council as long ago as 1895, the largest hydro-electric scheme of its day. The area is well marked with historical information and photos, and a few remnants from the early electricity generating days of the late nineteenth and early twentieth centuries. The suspension bridge leading to the old station has been washed away by massive floods twice since being built in 1896, but one of the pylons still remains and supports the latest and strongest (we hoped) version of the bridge. We were surprised to find that Tassie played a ground-breaking role in early power generation technology on the world scene.

Parking at the gorge cost $1 for up to four hours or $2 for up to 8 hours. Take note Sydney City Council!

We spent a couple of hours in the afternoon wandering around downtown Launceston. It's kind of a cross between a small city and a large country town. No building was more than three storeys tall, and there never seemed to be many people on the streets, even over lunch hours. Perhaps the locals are smarter and stay inside away from the cold. Both nights that we stayed in Launceston, the temperature bottomed out at one below zero. By far the biggest congregations of people were at the few ATMs in town.

Launceston reminded me a little of San Francisco on a much smaller scale because of the hills leading out of the city. We drove down a narrow twisted hillside road which was windier and narrower than San Francisco's famous Lombard Street, but much less touristy. We noticed at the other end that it was one way in the opposite direction to the way we drove it, but we didn't see any sign and pleaded ignorance as dumb tourists.

Back at the hotel, we had another dinner under the watchful gaze of those bloody deer. Glen had venison.

The following day we veered back to the coast, not really knowing where we were heading. It was one of those days where we decided to drive until we found something of interest. We swapped drivers at the town of Mathinna, a little town (but once Tasmania's third largest when gold mining peaked) named after an Aboriginal girl befriended by Tasmanian Governor Franklin and his wife when visiting the Flinders Island Aboriginal community. The Franklins raised her as their daughter until their return to England when she was left behind in an orphanage. This pushed her into a life of prostitution and drinking and she was found dead in a creek, her roller coaster life ending tragically early.

The small town had a large empty sports field and some insightful black and white photos from the early 19th century on the local information board by the side of the road. Did many people stop to look around this otherwise nondescript village and wonder about life out here, whether today or in times long since past? Thankfully, we had the time to soak it in for a while.

Many of the small rural towns we drove though had at least one pub, a post office which doubled a bank agency and acted on behalf of several other organisations, a public toilet (often a hole in the ground), occasionally a service station with one or two pumps, several churches, a phone booth, and a general store, usually licensed to sell ammunition. It passed time spotting the similarities and differences between the towns. Most common were a dog and several utes outside the pub and neighbours chatting over fences and gazing at the Beast as it rolled through town, as though it was the highlight of their day. Mostly they waved. Theirs is a lifestyle far removed from that of we city folk, with a different assortment of challenges and rewards. We worked at being part of their world but no matter how much we interacted, we were essentially and understandably aliens.

Along the road were hundreds of massive trees that must have been scores of years old. Huge specimens, mainly eucalypts, fat, tall and bushy. Minutes after pondering how they had escaped the loggers' axe or chainsaw, we passed the devastating sight of a previously similar area cut to the ground, as usual with tonnes of scrap wood left behind to be burnt and later replanted with tightly packed pine trees. One can be driving through beautiful untouched countryside and then get a view of hills and valleys, a patchwork of stripped land, burned land and pasture; little of the original environment.

While the huge scale of Tasmania's logging industry is concerning when you see these old growth forests being stripped, we also saw dozens of tree plantations in various stages of development. Still, it is heartening to know that more than 30 per cent of Tasmania is heritage listed and cannot be logged. The logging industry has built and maintained so many of the state's country towns but we hoped that the industry could be focussed on more sustainable and less destructive methods that leave old growth forests and their sensitive ecosystems for future generations to experience.

From Mathinna, we went to St Marys, about ten kilometres from the coast, for lunch. I went healthy with a sandwich and Glen had a gross-looking hamburger and chips. Eavesdropping on the various conversations of the locals with the shop proprietors provided a brief insight into their lives. Everyone knows what everyone else is doing, and if a school kid has dared to take the day off school and shout himself to a burger or chips and someone he knows should walk in, watch out. Everyone seems to walk in and start their conversation with, 'did you hear that such and such…'. Country town gossip is fearsome and ubiquitous.

We made our way up the coast from St Marys to Scamander, which is lined with beautiful long beaches and dunes contained in narrow coastal reserves. We continued northward to the east coast's biggest town, St Helens, for the night. Originally settled in 1834 to house convicts, it became an important tin mining and whaling town. We settled on a sparsely populated caravan park with a big camping area at the back of the property. Numerous caravan & camping parks tell you to go to number x camp site and you're crammed in between other allotted campers, but the best ones have a big grassy area and you park it where you want. This was one of those.

There was a place near the campground called Humbug Point. If there isn't one already, I'd like to open a pub there – Bar Humbug. Beerbarrel Beach happens to be across the bay as well. Further north is the Bay of Fires Coastal Reserve, named by explorer Captain Tobias Furneaux in 1773 because of all the fires lit by the natives as he sailed past.

We decided to do a bit of fishing and buy some prawns to barbecue over the fire for dinner. It was amazing that in one of Tasmania's biggest fishing towns, we couldn't buy fresh prawns, and there was only one place to buy a limited variety of fresh fish (unless we were missing something). This turned out to be the case in so many fishing towns around the country. Our fishing excursion was completely unsuccessful as usual so we tried to buy some veal. Neither of the supermarket butchers had veal, and the butcher said that I was only the second person to ask for it in six months. We gave up and just threw together a pasta with the ingredients we had in the car, and cooked them over the fire at a painfully slow pace. We vowed next time to use the fire to warm ourselves and cook with gas.

The freezing temperature drove me to bed early but Glen stayed up soaking up the atmosphere and a beer or two around the fire until the wee hours. He told me the next morning that there was ice on the tents when he went to bed. It wouldn't surprise me – it was definitely our coldest night out in the open.

The following morning had us starting very lethargically while waiting for the moisture to evaporate from our tents. We eventually retraced our tracks and went further south along the coast to Bicheno. On the way, we drove past a place amusingly called Piccaninny Point. Pick a what? Actually, the word means Aboriginal child.

Bicheno (formerly called Old Fishery) was named after a Colonial Secretary of Van Diemens Land and started its life as a coal-mining town (and perhaps fishing, based on its earlier name) until the gold rush in Victoria cleared the place out. In the 1940s, it picked up as a fishing and tourist centre. There's a fair bit to do in Bicheno and two national parks are not far away. One of our guidebooks told us that we could go down to 'The Gulch' where the fishing boats come in and that we could buy fresh seafood straight from the boats. Our taste buds were fired up and we asked at the information centre where to go at what time. They told us it was apocryphal and had never been the case and the guy was sick of people asking. So we went to the friendly pub and enjoyed a very good $5 fish and chips, washed down with a couple of local ales.

We checked into a caravan park and got an on-site van for $28. The camping area was closed because 'no one was stupid enough to camp at this time of year'. Plain talkers these Taswegians. We were allocated a massive caravan that you'd need a semi trailer to pull and contained all of what had become luxuries to us, like beds and cooking facilities, not to mention a solid roof.

I tried to buy a radio in town, but to no avail. You really miss hearing something other than each other or caravan park staff, so we agreed that a radio would be a good idea. Yes mum, I know you said I should bring one and you were right again. We also lashed out and bought a tea towel at last. It only took 16 days, but we thought it was about time; a minor oversight at the planning stage.

The water all along the coast was smooth as glass, unlike the ferociously rough western side of Tasmania, and the sky was a rich blue, without a cloud in sight. Most of the seaside route is lined with beautiful white sandy beaches flanked by rocky outcrops at their points. It was curious seeing so many enticing beaches without a soul on them, but it *was* winter after all and presumably no one was game enough to camp at that time of year. It was frosty enough on land so the water temperature must have been cold enough to kill, without a good wetsuit.

From Bicheno, we took a short drive south to the tourist town of Coles Bay, which is the gateway to Freycinet National Park. On the way, we drove past a place curiously called Friendly Beaches. We stayed at a very ordinary backpacker hostel about 3 kilometres north of town. Some hostels are real downers, without discernible ambiance and friendliness. This one fit that description.

Freycinet covers 11,000 hectares with spectacular pink and red granite cliffs and amazingly white beaches. It was named in 1802 by Captain Nicolas Boudin - who was leading a French scientific expedition around the south-east coast of Tasmania - after his cartographer Henri Freycinet. The closely packed mountain peaks which shadow Freycinet are individually named, but are together known as 'The Hazards' after Captain Albert Hazard who ironically lost his whaling ship, *The Promise*, in Hazard Bay. He swam to the beach and climbed to a settlement to get help for his stranded crew. Coles Bay was named after Silas Cole, an early settler who industriously burnt sea shells to make lime.

We started with a short walk to Sleepy Bay, a peaceful and aptly named little inlet surrounded by massive jutting boulders. We then drove up to a lighthouse at Cape Tourville (both inside the park) where we had great views all around the park. We decided that as a quick diversion before lunch and before we did the main walk we would drive down a four-wheel drive track to Bluestone Bay. When we got almost to the end of the very rough and unmaintained track, we came across a thrill-seeker who had gone down the '4WD only' track in an old beat up 2WD station wagon. His wheels had become stuck in two deep gullies with the car's belly firmly beached on the hardened sand that characterised the area. We tried pushing while he drove, pulling with one of our nylon ropes, which snapped, tried digging the wheels out and tried calling the ranger on the CB, all of which failed. Finally, we used our long rope, using several lengths between the two cars, and pulled him out. We decided that at the next four-wheel drive shop we saw, we'd invest in a snatch strap, a long strap of elastic material used for such circumstances. We didn't intend to, but we might be in that predicament somewhere along the journey and the Beast was a heavy bugger.

Glen was too stressed out to continue right away and the road was even worse from then, so I wandered down to the beach myself – only a couple of hundred metres – and Glen had a smoke and checked the car for damage (there was none). We then drove back to Coles Bay for the novelty of a fresh crayfish sandwich before heading back to the park (only one kilometre away) to do the Wineglass Bay walk.

The walk's first stop after ascending a moderate mountain trail is the Wineglass lookout, which offers a great view down to the twin back-to-back bays of pristine white beaches and beautiful water which form the wineglass shape. Again, the water is a 'tropical' turquoise. The mountainous terrain that covers the land within sight of the lookout is heavily wooded, against a misty green blanket rising from the icy water. The tops of the mountains were intermittently shrouded in thin cloud, with the sun striving to shine though. We continued along the trail to the beach and then returned to the car a little over two hours later. The track is well maintained and very popular, especially on a long weekend, which we happened to have struck. It has hundreds of stairs and the knees were feeling the strain, although I was feeling much better than after our first walk back in Buchan. Glen struggled but made it to the end, and both of us have tightened our belts one notch since starting the trip. It was a great feeling not working, having a fantastic time soaking in some marvellous country and getting the right balance of exercise, food and sleep. For us, a rare and valuable experience.

As we approached the car, Glen, muttered, 'I've had enough of this Rocky Mountain High John Denver bullshit', but I think he enjoyed the walk and the vague and unaccustomed feeling of fitness. He celebrated with a smoke. The views and scenery were again spectacular and are thus included in just about every tourist brochure about Tassie.

When we got back to the hostel, I opened a box of six fresh oysters I had bought in great anticipation at Coles Bay on the way, only to find a couple of sea worms wriggling around in the shells. Glen challenged me to eat not only the oysters, but also the worms. I declined both challenges and we grilled up some hot dogs for dinner.

3. Convict Country

There had been hints at convict pasts throughout our journey thus far, but we were about to hit the heart of the most brutal corner of Australia's history.

The first scheduled stop on the convict trail was Maria (*Mar-eye-ah*) Island, and for that we needed to catch a ferry from the east coast town of Triabunna. En route, we stopped at Spiky Bridge, a convict-built stone bridge from the 1840s. The sides of the solidly built bridge are crowned with spiked rocks but the motive is a mystery. Probably the whim of some convict-driving soldier who wanted to leave his mark. Also on the drive, we spotted a huge wedge-tailed eagle gracefully gliding over the road. I had no idea that these massive elegant creatures were found in Australia at all, let alone in the abundance we were lucky enough to sight.

Triabunna ('native hen') didn't appeal (but hey, they produce sodium alginate from seaweed which is used as a food thickener) so we drove on to nearby Orford. They couldn't offer any accommodation in our modest price range, so we came back to Triabunna. We searched for the YHA and eventually went to the information office where the attendant thought the hostel had closed for winter. We decided on $25 for a caravan, but had to call the caravan park at Orford to get someone to come and take our money and give us the key. Quite an effort for one night's basic lodging. We would have settled on a campsite if it weren't so damned cold and wet.

When everything was finally sorted out, we did some grocery shopping so we wouldn't have to unpack the roof basket in the rain. We roughed it when we felt like it but on this occasion, we didn't. We just wanted the incessant rain to stop. We sat in the caravan with the rain falling loudly on the roof, watching game shows on TV and gorging ourselves on various cheeses. As I said, we weren't in the mood to rough it. Or be healthy.

While taking advantage of the bargain-priced laundry, I got chatting to some Tasmanian caravanners who spent ages telling me all about Bruny Island and Port Arthur and giving us maps and ferry timetables etc. These people are just too nice. Fellow travellers are generally sociable but these Tassies are the ultimate.

Strong wind warnings were issued for the east coast of Tasmania with winds whipping up from Antarctica, and we heard that the ferry probably wouldn't be running, so we reluctantly decided to give the Island tour a miss. Despite that, I'll tell you a bit about it because I reckon it's pretty interesting.

Abel Tasman spotted the island in 1642 and named it after Maria, wife of Anthony Van Diemen, the supporter of many southern explorations including that of Abel Tasman. The island sits 16 kilometres from the Tasmanian east coast and is made up of two rugged chunks of land, one three or four times larger than the other, and joined together by a narrow isthmus. Between 1825 and 1852 the 260 square kilometres island was used as a penal colony, producing shoes and woollen cloth before Port Arthur took over. It seems to be best known for the number of convicts who managed to escape across the water. Several of the original buildings still stand at the settlement of Darlington, although I'd be surprised if they survived the rotten weather that seemed to be following us. It wasn't until 1972 that Maria Island was proclaimed a national park. It is now uninhabited by people and cars but is home to numerous species of animal and a few irate ghosts. Apparently, they're really good at holding a grudge.

After yet another lethargic departure, we hit the long-beaten path to Port Arthur. Thankfully, the trip was more comfortable than that endured by its first visitors who had a dangerous and uncomfortable journey to an even more miserable existence of servitude.

Port Arthur sits on Maingon Bay on the sizeable Tasman Peninsula, a mangled piece of land jutting south from the east coast of Tasmania. Abel Tasman stopped at Storm Bay, sailed southeast and in a fit of creativity named the southern tip South Cape. It was later renamed Cape Pillar.

The narrow stretch of land keeping the Peninsula attached to the mainland is called Eaglehawk Neck, another location infamous for its connections with our convict history (more about that later). We checked out the Eaglehawk Neck hostel there where Terry, the proprietor of 20 years, gave us a tour that included his preserved tiger snake, a rather stunted Huon Pine (this is far from Huon Pine territory, but he wanted to experiment), and gave us a full rundown of the region. He loves the place and its history and it shows. The passion was infectious.

Despite being Tassie's biggest tourist drawcard, we saw surprisingly little in the way of tacky exploitation of Port Arthur's dubious history, although we did drive past the Convict Country Bakery on our way in and got a bit worried. The recently rebuilt visitors centre had an excellent display, a cafeteria and, not surprisingly, a large shop with the predictable balls and chains, books, beer coolers, tea towels, spoons, thimbles and patches, most with the broad arrow convict symbol emblazoned on every available surface.

Before checking out the sights, we checked into the hostel overlooking the historic compound. Everything was open but the office was unattended until five, so we donned our rain jackets and cameras and hit the tourist trail.

Port Arthur was established as a convict timber station in 1830, and was named by Governor Sir George Arthur after himself. Arthur was appointed Governor of Van Diemen's Land after its administrative separation from NSW. In 1830, he decided to move the colony's penal settlement from Macquarie Harbour on the west coast to the 'natural penitentiary' (so called because of the narrow isthmus connecting it to the rest of Tasmania) of Port Arthur on the other side of the colony.

Port Arthur initially manufactured material mainly for government projects. It became a prison settlement for male convicts and was intended to provide severe punishment for repeat offenders. Crimes committed by the convicts included, theft, murder, highway robbery 'skulking without permission' and 'gross filthiness'. Good thing for Glen he wasn't around then. By 1840, there were more than 2,000 convicts and staff at the town. It became a major industrial centre, the convict slave labour producing ships and boats, timber, clothing, footwear, bricks, furniture, vegetables, church bells and more.

The last transportation of convicts was in 1852, when the Lords of the Empire decided that giving people free passage to one of the biggest gold rushes in the world was not an ideal punishment. Port Arthur continued to function as a penal settlement, but the industrial output fell considerably as the population grew older and less mentally stable.

More appropriate facilities had to be built for the aging cons, including a lunatic asylum. In 1871, the British Empire decided that the cost of maintaining Port Arthur was no longer justified, and they flogged it (pun intended) to the Tasmanian Government, which used it as a gaol until 1877, by which time about 12,000 sentences had been served there.

Unfortunately, over the next 20 years, several of the buildings were pulled down or destroyed by fire, and in 1884, the name of the settlement was changed to Carnarvon in an effort to wipe out the 'convict stain' and encourage people to settle there. The name Port Arthur was reinstated in 1927.

It wasn't until 1970 that the whole site was passed to the National Parks and Wildlife Service. The area is divided into precincts: convict; military, administration and early settlement; health and welfare; dockyard; agricultural; civilian; religious; commandants; waterfront; and harbour, plus the Isle of the Dead and the Point Puer adolescent prison.

We decided that it was too fascinating a place not to go the whole hog and do just about everything. Our first adventure was the ferry trip out to the small and eerie Isle of the Dead, selected by a minister of the settlement as its burial place in 1833. It is believed that more than 1,000 people were buried there (convicts, civilians and military), the youngest only a few hours old and the oldest being 92. Many of the headstones are still legible thanks to an annual restoration project. Unfortunately, all but one of the graves run north-south rather than the traditional east-west direction, exposing them to some rough weather which has taken its toll, just like the punishment in times gone by.

Our appropriately Cockney guide told the stories of several of the 'residents', convicts and military alike. One convict's father reported him to the police for stealing a couple of his mother's possessions. Dad thought he'd just teach his son a lesson rather than send him to Hell on Earth and eventually his death. It's believed that the old man had a guilt trip and forked out for one of the most elaborate grave stones on the island. Another large tabletop gravesite is for Benjamin Horne, a headmaster of the school at the juvenile prison, a man admired by his pupils and peers, but who was struck down by TB in his thirties. His epitaph reads, 'sincerely regretted by all who knew him'. I think we know what they meant to say. Many of the elaborate engravings feature some atrocious spelling, reflecting the literacy level of convict stonemasons and the very poor socioeconomic conditions of their era.

The return trip on the ferry took us past Point Puer, the site of the experimental boys' prison established in 1834 to separate the 'impressionable boys' from the hardened crims. Discipline was tough, but they were spared the floggings which were commonplace just up the road. There was a school on the island and they also produced various goods. There are stories of kids jumping to their deaths to escape the nightmare, but not much in the way of evidence to support the stories.

Upon our return to the visitors' centre we toured the Interpretation Gallery. At the entrance, we were given a card containing the identity and crimes of a real convict and followed his journey to and through Port Arthur. My crim was 25-year-old Robert Goldspick, who was transported to the colony for 14 years in 1822 for housebreaking. He was moved to Port Arthur for the crime of theft. He was a shoemaker, which offered a sense of connection because of my history as a department store shoe salesman to get me through university.

I also learnt there that Marcus Clarke's famous semi-fictional historical convict novel *For the Term of His Natural Life* (which I was midway through) was loathed by Tasmanians at the time of its printing because of the brutal image it portrayed. There was a scathing attack in the local newspaper, but the rest of the world seemed to lap it up.

After whipping up a couple of bowls of soup back at the hostel, we wandered down to the much-anticipated evening Port Arthur ghost tour through the haunting settlement. The two-hour tour was excellent and pretty darn spooky. In the light rain and mist, with only the light of three candles, the stage was set for a night of terror.

Our heavily bearded local guide took us to several of the settlement's buildings and told stories of people who had died in each. Then of course we heard stories of their ghosts coming back to haunt the original residents, and staff and visitors from then until now.

The colony's parsonage is supposed to be the third most haunted house in Australia. Our guide told us some rather convincing stories, including one recent one of a small team of builders who were staying there while they worked on the building. One by one the builders were spooked by various apparitions. They tried to act tough when talking of their fellow inhabitants, but each one refused to return.

We also were told frightening stories of people who died during the building of the now roofless grand church. Deals were struck between convicts wanting to escape the horror of Port Arthur where it was common for one convict to kill another (at the request of the victim) so that both could escape by death, one instantly and one as punishment.

We were led to a basement dissection room of the doctor's residence where the dead were cut up in the name of research. The guide did a good job of scaring the shit out of all present. I won't tell you how, but it involved a skull.

The worst of all sites was the 'Separate Prison' with its solitary confinement cells. The large crucifix-shaped building is mostly intact, with dozens of small cells where brutal punishments were administered. One room is separated from the corridor by four doors to ensure that the convict could not hear or see anything. If he was taken out of the cell, a bag was placed over his head so that he didn't have the luxury of sight. The floor used to be carpeted and soldiers wore soft shoes so that nothing could be heard by their guests. So many men went mad there that they had to build a lunatic asylum (now an insightful museum).

I'm not sure if I could work at Port Arthur and lock up at night. Indeed, some staff refuse, and who can blame them? It was bad enough that Glen and I had to walk back across the settlement through a misty drizzle to get to our hostel. We made it, but it took a while to get to sleep.

It takes hours to wander through the well-preserved settlement, which we did in the safety of broad daylight the next day. There are several buildings that can be explored and most have a guide to tell stories of their pasts.

Governor Arthur was an absolute tyrant and was proud of his little hell. He likened Port Arthur to a mill that ground men to rehabilitation. Arthur was a firm believer in severely punishing those who did not conform, but 'rewarded' those who did, with various privileges such as a small tobacco ration or less exhausting labour. He is reported to have said, 'the most unceasing labour is to be extracted from the convicts...and the most harassing vigilance over them is to be observed'.

Other than the Separate Prison, the primary form of punishment was the cat of nine tails, or 'the cat'. It was a sturdy handle with nine thin cords tied to it, each with nine knots tied in them. Before use, the cat was soaked in salt water and then dried to ensure maximum stinging pain. One convict noted that after it had been used a few times the dried blood made it feel like razor blades. After only a few lashes, the back could be turned into a bloody jelly-like mess. Often a pool of blood and chunks of flesh had to be cleaned from below the wooden gallows to which the offender had been bound. And if you dared collapse while being flogged, you were thrown into a pool of salt water and once revived, you were usually strapped up and the flogging resumed. In order to inflict maximum pain, a flogging was occasionally postponed mid way through to allow the back to begin healing before resuming the punishment. After hearing and reading all that, I was surprised that only one person was ever flogged to death at Port Arthur.

The place was quite haunting. After reading all information at the site and hearing what the guides had had to say, and from the detailed narrative in *For the Term of His Natural Life*, I can imagine what the scene would have been like at Port Arthur: officers would wander about treating convicts like dirt, ladies would look over their manicured English gardens as they took tea, and gangs of convicts chained together carrying huge logs or manufacturing something would show pain and anguish in their tormented faces. There was possibly the occasional scream from the triangles or the asylum, although many of the convicts were silent while being flogged to maintain the respect of their peers. Ships and whaling boats would come and go in the harbour. I expect that one of the prevalent sounds was that of clanking irons as convicts, clad in their yellow and black uniforms printed with their ID number and with several stereotypical broad arrows, moved about the compound. The grounds, buildings and setting are so comely and peaceful now; it's difficult to comprehend what a diabolical place this was.

In the early afternoon, we attended the service of comfort, marking an anniversary of the random shooting of 35 tourists and staff at Port Arthur in April 1996. The service was held in the roofless sandstone church. The church was designed by a convict mason but never consecrated because two murders were committed during its construction. It was a most sombre and upsetting experience, not only wondering with difficulty what it would have been like when gunfire rained around this now peaceful and beautiful place, but also observing those who were obviously closely involved with the tragedy and had lost loved ones.

The incident clearly dampened the spirit of the close-knit community. There were reminders of that day, including the remains of the bullet-ridden café, and a small discretely placed information brochure which understandably requested visitors to refrain from asking questions of staff about the tragedy. It was a sobering reminder of our fragility.

Afterwards I went to look at the flowers that had been laid at the memorial cross by the water. One was from the people of Dunblane, Scotland, which was shocked by a similarly horrific tragedy at a school around the same time of the Port Arthur tragedy.

After the service and sombre stroll through the rest of the settlement, we drove back to the hostel at Eaglehawk Neck. The Neck is less than 100m wide from shore to shore and was one of the main reasons why Arthur thought of the peninsula as a natural location for his convict settlement. In his day, the Neck was lined with sentries, vicious dogs and lights to ensure no escapees could get through, and it was emphasised to the convicts that the waters were full of sharks. Martin

Cash was one of the few prisoners to survive the gauntlet, and one of Australia's most famous convicts.

Cash was born to a wealthy family in Ireland in 1810 and transported to Sydney in 1828 after shooting a man during an argument over a woman. When he was released, he got hitched and went to Tasmania but was soon found guilty of theft and was sentenced to seven years. He escaped from a road gang, was captured and sent to Port Arthur.

Somehow he managed to escape twice from Port Arthur, the second time with two New South Wales bushrangers, Kavanagh and Jones. The three operated a successful bushranging existence, including the capture of 23 men in one raid. He met up with his missus, Bessie, again and she was caught stealing dresses in Hobart. Cash sent a threatening letter to Governor Franklin and Bessie was released in the hope that she would lead the authorities to Cash. When freed, she found herself another man and police caught a jealous Cash as he tried to track his absent wife. He killed a policeman in the fracas but somehow got his sentence reduced from death to life on Norfolk Island, and was released for good behaviour after 12 years. He married again in Hobart and became caretaker of the Government House gardens and bought himself an orchard to make a few extra bob. He died a respected citizen and his autobiography, published in 1870, was a best seller and used extensively by Marcus Clarke in his research for *For the Term of His Natural Life*.

Near the Neck is the town named Doo Town (yes, really), which boasts some interesting natural formations and a corny name for most of the houses in the small village, such as Doo Mee, Doo Drop in (there had to be at least one), Thistle Doo Me, Dr Doo Little, Gunna Doo, Doodle Doo, What'll I Doo, Yabba Dabba Doo, Kakadoo, Doo Nothing, Doo

Write, Doo Us, Doo Us Too, Much A Doo, Didgeri Doo, Sheil Doo, AF 2 Doo and Love Me Doo.

Other curious attractions in Doo Town included the Tasman Arch (a huge red rock arch battered by the raging ocean below), the less interesting Devil's Kitchen (a high walled narrow inlet with churning water thrashing around at the base), and the blowhole which isn't really a blow hole, or wasn't when we were there.

The Tasman Peninsula has other smaller former convict settlements, including the Coal Mines Historic Site, Australia's first operational mine. For our visit, the site had few information signs, no guides and not many tourists. The main settlement housed the ruins of about six buildings in various states of decay, the most interesting being the solitary cells and separate 'apartments'. These cells are below ground and very small. Being above ground would have been enough of a nightmare, but below ground with no light would be unspeakable. During our visit a restoration project was underway to save what little was left of the structures.

When an outcrop of coal was discovered along the coast in 1833, immediate plans were made by the government to mine the area. Apart from producing coal (which was considered to be of poor quality), the mines were thought by the hard-nosed Arthur to be good punishment for the convicts. This was the punishment station for repeat offenders 'of the worst class'. The coal was used in households and government offices for heating.

Reportedly, the incidence of homosexuality among the convicts was a concern at the station. The dark recesses of the underground workings were believed to be 'sinkholes of vice and infamy'. In an effort to curb such behaviour, additional lighting and irregular patrols by soldiers were instituted. Success of this strategy was limited. Let's not forget that the soldiers were lonely young men as well.

Allegations of inefficiency and bad management led to closure of the mine in 1848 on both moral and financial grounds, although coal continued to be mined there privately, with limited success, until 1877.

While at one of the Coal Mines sites along the shore, we collected a few dozen mussels and two oysters and later cooked them up for dinner in a rip snorter of a chowder. It is an amazing sense of satisfaction finding one's own dinner in the wild and cooking it up into something edible. It's especially pleasing to wash it down with a refreshing Tasmanian chardonnay.

The next morning, we continued driving to the small coastal town of White Beach, where the sand is more off-white than white, and where we wondered what the locals actually do there. I suppose some of them run the few shops in town, some are school teachers and some are retirees. Several must travel to Port Arthur, which isn't really that far, to tell the same tales over and over to the quarter of a million visitors annually. God knows how these people manage to appear interested in giving the same blurb ad nauseam, but they do it well.

We also visited nearby Remarkable Cave, a large chute into which water pounds at each wave (not unlike the blowhole in Doo Town), and Palmers Hill lookout, which seems to be privately set up and is surrounded by a menagerie of garden gnomes. Some peoples' obsession with gnomes is truly disturbing.

Before leaving Eaglehawk Neck the next day, we checked out the Tessellated Pavement natural attraction, a flat area of rock at sea level that looks like a man-made pavement of stones, complete with mortar.

I took a photo of a chilly Glen looking like a hoodlum in his beanie and well-worn jumper over reflections of the deceptively blue sky in small pools of water.

Heading off the Tasman Peninsula, we drove north to the town of Copping. There isn't much to it, except a small museum on the main road, outside of which tourists are flagged down by a mechanical arm-waving policeman (or should I say cop). From a distance, we thought he was really pulling people over. Willing to oblige, we pulled over and decided to try our luck with the middle-of-nowhere museum. We were initially surprised at the $5 entry fee because the place appeared to be a big shed full of junk. But after being assured by the intriguing and enthusiastic attendant at the door that we didn't have to pay unless we thought it was worth it, we took the punt and were pleasantly surprised that the place was, in fact, a big shed full of junk. But this junk dated back to convict times and included several convict punishment devices, ancient sewing machines, gardening equipment, pianos, phonographs, and thousands of other objects and interesting (and uninteresting) inventions that never appeared to have got off the ground. Other highlights were animated life-sized models of people using some of these implements, and the oldest car in Tasmania. We ended up spending quite a while checking everything out. As it happens, Australia is full of places like this, and you can only handle seeing so much old junk, but this first of many on our journey was one of the more interesting.

Our next scheduled stop was the very historic town of Richmond, which boasts the oldest Catholic Church in Australia, the oldest bridge (and one of the most photographed), and the oldest gaol. This fact is boldly proclaimed by a sign at the office, which notes that the gaol is five years older than Port Arthur. A fact that is not so proudly broadcast is that there were so many breakouts that they shut the place down in

1856. The self-guided tour through the gaol was interesting enough and further enforced the notion of brutality shown by the British Empire against suspected criminals and innocent Aborigines. The 1820s building is remarkably well preserved and still displays prisoners' names carved into window shutters and draughtboards cut into the floor. Like Port Arthur, floggings were common, although the Magistrate could only order a maximum of 36 lashes. Administrators of the floggings, know as flagellators, were usually ex-convicts and were paid an annual wage equivalent to $37 for their services. One of the particularly vicious flagellators was murdered by being thrown from the parapet of the Richmond Bridge one night, presumably by a disgruntled floggee.

After downing another meat pie and tasting some products of the apple-based Richmond distillery we headed south past Hobart to Bruny Island. En route, we travelled through the curiously named towns of Tinderbox (near which we struggled to find a very ordinary blowhole) and Snug. I'd love to live in a place called Snug, but I'd think twice about Tinderbox.

4. Way Down South

The open deck ferry to Bruny Island is thankfully a quick trip. 'Thankfully' because the car next to us was a ute with a full load of manure and we were downwind. The ferry crossed D'Entrecasteaux Channel to drop us off at Roberts Point on North Bruny. We settled in at the welcoming Lumeah Hostel in Adventure Bay, which had a very friendly host and a big inviting log fire. It also had the best-equipped kitchen we'd experienced thus far, a notable point to weary travellers.

Bruny is almost two islands connected by a narrow isthmus of sand dunes. The island stretches for 56 kilometres and agriculture and tourism are its livelihood these days. Bruny was named after French Admiral Bruni D'Entrecasteaux who surveyed the Tasmanian coast in the late 18th century. Abel Tasman had earlier passed by the island in 1642 with little interest, although it was the first part of Tasmania he saw. Cook, Bligh (a few times) and Furneaux were some of its earliest European visitors. It is believed that a botanist on Bligh's ship began Tasmania's apple industry here. In 1773, Furneaux anchored in a bay that he named after his ship, HMS *Adventure*.

Tasmania's last full-blooded Aborigine is thought to have come from Bruny. Her name was Truganini and she died back in 1876. You might have heard Midnight Oil sing about her.
The early sealers, whalers and loggers killed many of the Island's natives. In the 1830s, Truganini and her hubby mustered together most of the survivors with George Robinson who established the Flinders Island settlement. Robinson was a bricklayer and Methodist lay preacher employed as a guardian of Aborigines. Robinson tried teaching Christianity and the European way of life. Sadly, but not surprisingly, most of the Aborigines died. In 1838, Robinson and

63

Truganini went to Port Phillip, Victoria, where another attempt was made to set up a safe haven for Aborigines. Again, it failed. Truganini tried to rebel, but was captured and sent back to Flinders Island. She and a few other survivors were shipped off to Oyster Bay in 1856. By 1873, she was the sole survivor and died three years later. Her skeleton was displayed at the Tasmanian Museum for a few years in the early 1900s. Robinson lost his job and his failures drove him back to England in 1852.

The island is sparsely populated – only about 500 – so most of it is a peaceful sanctuary for a variety of birds (including fairy penguins), echidnas, reptiles and even a mob of albino wallabies. And of course, tourists. There's heaps of sightseeing to be done, whether from the car, boat or on foot on the beaches or the forested inland. Both sides of the isthmus are populated by hundreds of birds. We saw dozens of swans with their heads dunked in the water, and overhead a kookaburra was watchfully perched on the power line whenever we drove past. I don't think a day went by on our entire trip when we didn't see a kookaburra on a power line looking cool and sophisticated.

Thankfully, tourism hasn't overtaken the island. If anything, the agriculture and forestry have taken care of that. Visitor facilities are limited, which is pleasant. A small Bligh Museum of Pacific Exploration is at Adventure Bay offering a history of the island, but never seemed to be open when we drove past. Of course, there's a lighthouse as well. It's a good one, as lighthouses go (and we're fast becoming experts), and claims to be Australia's second oldest at 153 years.

On our second day, we headed up into the hills of the larger and surprisingly mountainous South Island. The road was quite muddy and steep and the weather had a cold bite. We kept bumping into the same people all day, and later chanced to see them on the Tassie mainland. That's one of the fun things about this sort of travel (provided you're not trying to avoid them). After hopping from lookout to lookout, we stopped for a bite at a general store in the middle of nowhere. Lunch was a very good home-made veggie burger that rather surprisingly, Glen also enjoyed.

After lunch, it was low tide time and we had to get to North Bruny to collect dinner. Our host, Simon, had told us of a bay where mussels and oysters were plentiful. It was a crustaceous gold mine. Unfortunately, I was the sucker who brought the sandals so I was the one who had to wade into the freezing water to collect the big juicy mussels. When my feet went numb, I trudged up to the beach, where Glen was opening oysters to keep me going. These were mammoth oysters and tasted like no other oysters I have ever had. Man, they were good. But then again, you don't usually get them this fresh. After I'd thrown down about a dozen heavyweight oysters and we'd collected a bag full of generously sized mussels, we headed back to the hostel via another spot recommended by Simon. It was now late afternoon, just as kangaroos and wallabies come out to play. But Bruny has something a little different and we managed to see one of their ghostly albino wallabies in the wild. Several of them lived there, but seeing one grazing on the lush grass was pretty special.

Back at the hostel, we sat in front of the fire and enjoyed a ripper of a mussel chowder and a beautiful Tasmanian sauvignon blanc. Unfortunately, some of the wine ended up on the keyboard of my notebook computer after dinner so I was forced to use more old-fashioned means of recording my diary until I could find someone to fix it.

After completely repacking the car, trying (unsuccessfully) to isolate and stop an annoying noise, we caught the ferry back to the Tassie mainland and drove up the Channel Highway towards Huonville. It was a very indirect route to our target destination of Lune River, but unfortunately, the wide Huon River is unbridged until Huonville.

The road to Huonville is beside a long narrow island that sits in the middle of the River. The spear shaped island looks to be well vegetated and would be great to explore, but as usual, time was against us. It's an interesting formation, and for some reason it is known as Egg Island. We also drove past a place called Woodstock. Peace, brother.

While stopping at Huonville for lunch, we noticed that the local pub's coming attraction was *Mr Ugg and the Bionic Budgie*. We were sorry to be missing that one.

Huonville sits at the heart of Tasmanian apple country, but obviously started out as a logging town, shipping Huon Pine to England from 1829. The apple industry kicked off in the mid 1800s.

A long day of driving through the rain got us way down south to the hamlet of Lune River, home to Australia's most southerly post office. As with so many places around southeast Tassie, Lune River was named by the French. The name has something to do with the moon but despite our inquisitive efforts, no one seemed to know the actual story, not that there were many people to ask. At the hostel, we contacted the proprietor over a two-way radio stuck to the wall to arrange the night's lodging. Chatting with some other guests, we soon learnt that we were one night late for the hostel's full moon festival, which sounded like quite an event for guests and locals alike so we were sorry to have missed it. We were told that they cook wood fired pizzas and sit around the fire, either outside or inside the massive tepee out the back and eat, drink and sing until they are as full as the moon.

A few kilometres further south of the hostel is the Ida Bay Railway. The lanky ocker train driver was obviously looking forward to going home rather than taking the scheduled 4pm train trip, especially for only two tourists with a YHA discount. Nonetheless, he fired up the old diesel engine and we were shuddering down the line a few minutes later. The narrow-gauge rail traverses 16 kilometres of southern Tasmanian bushland to Deep Hole Bay. The trip was 40 minutes' return with a break half way, where the driver had a whinge about National Parks and how they conduct burn offs and send all the railway sleepers up in smoke. Over a fag, he told us about the women he could have made it with down there at the end of the line by the water, and a couple of other stories which contained much more information about his medical conditions than we would have liked. We jumped back on the train and froze our butts off on the trip back to Ida Bay Station.

On the next day, rain dissuaded us from taking the four-hour return walk to what we thought was Tasmania's southernmost point. We were disappointed to find how far from the actual southern tip of Tassie the walk takes you so our enthusiasm was not great anyway. We started driving down the unsealed road to see how far south we could get, but decided it was too rough and too wet so we chucked a youey and started our journey north.

Not only is there a beer battle in Tasmania, but judging by the radio advertisements, the meat pie market is also fiercely contested. It's National Pies ('Meet the meat on the first bite') versus Mrs Mac's. Based on extensive research, Mrs Mac is our preference.

Considering we'd been in the Apple Isle for a couple of weeks, we were surprised not to have seen a single apple orchard thus far. That was about to change, and could be expected from the names on the map. We drove through Apple Valley near a town called Grove. It is home to the Apple and Heritage Museum. Not resisting the temptation, we forked out the admission and were immediately given an apple each, cored and peeled by an antique apple peeler/corer. It was an interesting contraption which I think was invented in America and was quite popular in ye olde days. Tasty apple too. The museum had artefacts from the early apple growing days, displays, photos, equipment, and 500 different apple varieties on show. A few were missing (hungry staff?), but several were lined up in row after row, including the Climax, the Geeveston Fanny, Dr Hogg and dozens with French names which my four years of high school French couldn't help me translate. Pomme something...

We continued north through the outskirts of Hobart, Australia's most southerly and second oldest city. In 1798, Bass and Flinders strolled through the area and seemed to like it, particularly the harbour and Derwent River. The first European settlement was at Risdon Cove, just north of what is now Hobart. Half a year later, the governor of Van Diemen's Land got sick of running out of water and went for a sail up the Derwent. He quite liked the Derwent River estuary area and settled Hobart Town as the new capital. Two thirds of the original population of 262 was made up of the first of thousands of convicts to be sent there. Now our smallest state capital city has 185,000 inhabitants, only a few of whom are convicts.

I'm sure Hobart's a great place, but neither of us was keen to spend precious time in another city, so we kept driving. Sorry Hobart.

Instead, we drove up Mt Wellington (1,270m) to get a bird's eye view of the city and surrounds. As it happened, the only birds up there were dead and reduced to bone and a few feathers. It was barren, numbingly cold and windy. The view was spectacular though, covering the large green-rimmed city perched on the edge of the bay's ragged shore.

After taking a few photos of the panorama, we ran back to the car before frostbite set in. The sound of the wind was shattering. Gusts regularly reach 150 kilometres per hour and the clouds whiz by as if you're driving past a herd of big fluffy sheep really fast. We tried to spot a McDonald's for lunch from the lookout but couldn't see any arches peeking up from the concrete jungle.

After descending the mountain, we spotted a sign to Maccas in Bridgewater, just over the Derwent River. It was time for lunch. And a big one. I realise it sounds like we constantly ate junk, but most of the time we were actually eating well; it's just that the fast food outings seem to feature more than their share in this chronicle.

Back on the track inland following the Derwent, New Norfolk is not far up the road. It was settled when people from Norfolk Island were moved to Tasmania in 1808 and granted four acres for each acre they owned back home. Not only that, they were given a year's worth of rations. The first boat brought 34 islanders and within a year, more than 500 others had taken up the attractive settlement offer. Governor Macquarie originally named the place Elizabeth Town after his wife, but the settlers preferred to name it after their island home. In 1825, the town was doing so well it was recommended that it become the new capital of the colony. Apparently the civil servants couldn't muster up travel allowances (oh how times have changed) to get there so the plan was trashed. The National Trust now classifies the entire town, which is claimed to have the oldest continuously licensed hotel in Australia, the Bush Inn (1815) and the oldest church still standing in Tasmania (from the same year – a coincidence?).

The pub was built by Mrs Ann Bridger and was designed by and named after D.W. Bush, clerk to the colony's first Chaplain. Don't tell me the clergy didn't know a good drop. My dinner placemat gave a brief history of the pub: In 1830, it housed a butcher shop, operated by the owner's son, and five years later the tap room was used by Methodist preachers in from Hobart. The Christening Font still resides in the Hotel. In 1888, the first telephone trunk call in the Commonwealth was made from the hotel. The hotel's phone number was simply '1', right up until the 1970s.

After stopping in New Norfolk town for supplies and cash, we headed down to the caravan park by the river and scored an on-site van for the cold night. Our main interest in New Norfolk was the Oast House Hops museum, which contrary to the opening hours signs, was closed and was likely to be closed the next day as well. Unfortunately, it doubled as the town's information centre. Lucky the caravan park people were so friendly and full of information that it didn't matter. We went for a short drive up a hill for an unspectacular view back to the town and of all the high voltage power lines radiating out of the landscape like a big green pincushion.

Another long day was looming so we got an early start to Mt Field National Park and Gordon Dam. Along the way we passed through Plenty, a very small hamlet that couldn't be said to live up to its name, in size at least. One of the biggest industries around here is the growing of hops. The hops fields were studded with hundreds of two-metre tall posts sticking up all over the place with twine strung between them. The Derwent Valley, in which New Norfolk sits, grows hops to flavour billions of stubbies of beer. I'd like to able to say more about it, but unhelpfully, the visitors' bureau was still closed.

The plethora of road kill was becoming less prominent, but there seemed to be an awful lot of empty beer bottles by the road. Better than dead wild animals in a national park I suppose, if less biodegradable.

We passed a golf course of note. The sign outside told us it was the last one for 25,000 kilometres. That's assuming you're heading south.

Mount Field is Tasmania's oldest national park, declared in 1916. Its 16,000 hectares were formed by glaciers slicing through the land thousands of years ago, and it sits in lower central Tasmania. It has a huge variety of environments, from eucalypt forests to ferny rainforest to snow gums and alpine moorland at the higher altitudes. Among the flora is the panadani, the tallest heath in the world. I think my mate Heath is taller, but I won't rain on their parade. The park is also home to one of Tasmania's two ski fields. A menagerie of little furry animals was hopping around, including pademelons, Bennett's wallabies and probably a lot more after sundown.

We walked through the park for a couple of hours. The trees were huge and no doubt ancient, having escaped the loggers' saw. Even the tree ferns were an amazing size, but the eucalypts were staggering, dozens with trunks broader than the length of our spread arms. As Glen said, even the small trees were huge. These trees are second in size only to the giant redwoods of California (but not nearly as touristy). Several of the massive gums had fallen, taking large clumps of earth with them, which supported completely new ecosystems.

The winter environment is damp below the thick canopy that shades the forest floor, although the sun shoots sharply through an occasional break where an old sentinel has fallen. This leads the way for several smaller trees to fight for the light and race to the canopy for survival. The dampness has also spawned moss, fungi and lichen in abundance all over everything. Most of it is your common looking bright green stuff, but with plenty of light green stringy growth hanging like cobwebs from the trees, and the occasional bright patch of orange or purple. Glen was pleased to find several mushrooms to satisfy his interest in fungus. Almost every corner we turned we came across one or two small Rufus Wallabies feeding along the trail, unconcerned about our intrusion. Along the walking trail is Russell Falls, one of the park's main attractions. It is a beautiful, very high tiered waterfall cascading down the rock face shrouded in rich vegetation and well worth another Kodak Moment.

After the wander, we drove up Mt Field only to find that you can't actually drive to the top. We didn't have enough time to walk to anything interesting so we drove back down again and on to Gordon Dam. Along the mountainous road, distant peaks were barely visible through the haze. The environment is very rocky and the rock is white, giving it the appearance of being snow-covered in many places (it felt cold enough) and was obviously used in construction of the noticeably pale coloured road.

In 1972, one of Australia's most heated environmental battles was fought over the flooding of Lake Pedder in south-west Tasmania. The area had been a national park since 1955, but in 1971, the Tasmanian government approved construction of the $100 million hydroelectric scheme. The intense protestations of environmentalists led to the formation of the first green political party in the world, the United Tasmanian Group. The Gordon River Power Development (which includes four dams) created Australia's largest water storage, equivalent to about 27 times the volume of water in Sydney Harbour and began generating in 1978.

At the end of the long drive, we had missed the only dam tour for the day and were just in time to look at the visitors' centre before it closed at 3pm. We both walked down the steep steel steps to the dam wall and walked along the top to the other side looking out over the huge expanse of water on one side and the relative trickle on the other. We thought about the pressure against the wall, wondered what would happen if the wall broke, and walked swiftly back up to the car.

The next destination was one of the places I most wanted to visit – Strahan. Again we drove through a broad variety of environments: from rainforest, to pine forest to eucalypt to low scrub to completely barren. Along the road, we passed a shop with the original name of *Spuds are us*. We also passed through the town of Ouse, which sits on the Ouse River. We looked for a lonely 'H' lying around somewhere, but with no luck, so we drove on. Several power stations are strung along the road to the west coast and a number of lakes, many man-made behind dams to supply the power stations.

We made the monumental achievement of reaching the geographic centre of Tasmania, marked by a bunch of rocks with a stick rising from them. Not exactly a big tourist drawcard, emphasised by the dilapidated picnic area, but the milestone gave us a sense of achievement, albeit negligible.

The roads through this mountainous part of the world were particularly corkscrew-like and there was plenty of road kill to feed the scavengers.

En Route to Strahan we reached the Cradle Mountain - Lake St Clair National Park which houses, not surprisingly, Lake St Clair, the deepest freshwater lake in Australia (167m) and Cradle Mountain. The two attractions are at opposite ends of the giant park and we entered at the southern end, beside the glacial lake. The 17-kilometre-long lake is the source of Tasmania's longest river, the Derwent. The Aborigines called it *Leeawuleena*, meaning 'sleeping water'. I like it. In addition to the serene lake, the area boasts Tasmania's oldest rocks. Discovery of the lake by Europeans is unclear, but Surveyor General George

Frankland named it in 1835 after the St Clair family of Loch Lomond, Scotland.

From the new visitors' centre at Cynthia Bay we walked along the lake shore and met up with the Overland Track. This walking trail between the lake and Cradle Mountain takes six days from start to finish and is renowned around the world as one of the best long distance walking tracks, despite very unpredictable weather. We opted out of the six-day hike and strolled to a place called Platypus Bay and unsuccessfully looked for a platypus. I convinced Glen to return to the visitors' centre and car park via a slightly longer nature trail. Much of the track was a narrow boardwalk, making it dry and smooth. I felt like I was following the yellow brick road, not that Glen bore any resemblance to Toto or a Munchkin or me to Dorothy. There were so many huge dead old, but still standing, trees that I was driven to inquire about them at the ranger station. The ranger told me that bush fires in the sixties and seventies were the main cause, resulting in most of the existing trees being around the same height. Glen marked the discovery with a smoke as we prepared for another journey through our convict past.

5. Convict Country Part II

As if Port Arthur wasn't bad enough, the west cost of Tasmania was as brutal with convicts as its weather is for unwary seafarers.

Back on the trail westward we were surprised by the number of beehives beside the road. Every now and then, we passed a small clearing containing 20 or so hives, but we were forewarned by hundreds of the buggers flying into our windscreen. Apiary and highways clearly don't mix.

On the way into Strahan, the road winds through Queenstown. It's not the quaint English town surrounded by forest that we had naively expected. It more closely resembles nuclear fallout. Queen Victoria, for whom the town was named, would turn in her grave if saw the environmental rape of the land that has occurred over the last 100 years. Some distance out from the town we hit this stark, incredibly barren landscape. It came as quite a shock. The environment around Queenstown is littered with grey and orange rock and there is scarcely any vegetation in sight. The town is nestled in the valley, surrounded by mountainous wasteland.

In 1883, mining for gold began in the area and continued for ten years when it was found that copper could also be profitable in this area. The Mt Lyell Mining Company's smelter was established on site and the surrounding rainforest was stripped to fuel the smelter. Any vegetation left was killed by the sulphur emission, which also efficiently poisoned the soil. Water then washed over and through the soil, polluting the Queen River. The smelters finally closed in 1969, leaving the area decimated. It appears that the vegetation has only recently begun to struggle through the adverse conditions. The townsfolk also adapt to their environment; the Queenstown football field is gravel (*you* try growing grass here).

The road into the valley where the town is nestled was the most contorted we'd been on, winding through the mountainous moonscape. With barely any vegetation to keep the mountain together above or below the road, it wasn't the most comfortable driving experience. We were still too much in shock at the scenery to worry about the comfort factor anyway.

It had already been a long day so we didn't stop in Queenstown and kept going to Strahan on the western coast of Tasmania, and a pleasant, if rowdy, hostel. We got a takeaway pizza and sneaked a couple of much needed beers into the common room. Despite paying the highest hostel rate so far, a bunch of supposed greenies kept us up all night. How about preserving my environment?

Strahan is the gateway to the unforgiving Macquarie Harbour (we rarely pass through a town that isn't a gateway to, or hub of, something and of course historic). A village was settled here in 1877 and the town proclaimed in 1892. It was named after Major Sir George Strahan, Governor of Tasmania in the late 19th century. It started out as a Huon Pine timber-milling town and was helped along by the Queenstown mining industry. It is also the nearest port of call to the infamous Sarah Island penal settlement in Macquarie Harbour. More about that shortly.

Huon Pine, native to Tasmania, is one of the world's longest living organisms. According to Forestry Tasmania, trees older than 2,000 years have been dated and they reckon there are some living trees in south-west Tasmania that could be over 5,000 years old. Now that's an old tree! Just stop and think about what was going on in the world 5,000 years ago. Generally, the trees are about 25 metres tall and are notable by their hanging feathery foliage, not unlike a cypress. When Huon pine was discovered in the rainforests of western Tasmania, the logging industry took off, and Strahan was the heart. After more than 100 years of destruction, most remaining stands of Huon pine are preserved in World Heritage Areas. How anyone can chop down a one or two-thousand-year-old tree these days is incomprehensible. There is still high demand for the aromatic wood, and much of the supply is salvaged from hydroelectric water storages.

We were awakened early on our second day in Strahan by our friends the self-proclaimed environmentalists, but needed to get up early anyway to take the cruise around Macquarie Harbour and up the Gordon River.

We boarded one of several tourist boats and headed out from Strahan into Macquarie Harbour. The water of the harbour was a murky, frothy brown yet very reflective. Tannins washed into rivers from grasses cause the effect.

James Kelly discovered Macquarie Harbour in 1815 when he circumnavigated Tasmania in a whaleboat. He named it after the governor of New South Wales to add to the long list of namesakes. The harbour's Aboriginal name is Parralaongateck. No wonder he changed it.

Our first attraction on the tour was to cruise through Hell's Gates, the narrow passage guarding the Harbour from the violent ocean outside. The convicts thought of Sarah Island as Hell, and passing through the narrow jagged heads is still known as running Hells Gates. It was with mixed emotions that the men and few women onboard the convict ships sailed into the harbour. After months of sailing they would finally be on land (those who survived the journey), but their torturous lifestyle of slavery and punishment was only about to begin.

We then berthed at Sarah Island, possibly the most brutal and feared penal colony of convict times. When the first convict ship came to Macquarie Harbour, it was packed to the hilt mostly with male convicts, but there were also about eight women on board. While the men worked on construction in buildings of Sarah Island, the women were dumped in a cave on a tiny nearby island to avoid fraternisation. Eventually the authorities ended up sending them to Hobart.

Few remnants of the past are left on Sarah Island, which operated as a prison for 11 years from 1822. At least one of the buildings was destroyed by a bomb planted by a local who was ashamed of the area's convict past, as were so many before the age of appreciation and the prospect of employment on the tourist trail dawned on the local people. About 1,200 men and women were sent to Sarah Island, most of them having committed offences while already incarcerated elsewhere.

Our towering guide was a very theatrical and enthusiastic local character who had obviously done his homework. He bounded about the site with a strong, rrrrrrrrrolling voice telling us about the history of what are now piles of rubble. After the formal half-hour tour, we were invited to stroll down to the shipyards where our guide would meet us after donning his wetsuit. There was much rumbling in the audience and everyone moved down to the waterside. Sure enough, our man arrives in wetsuit and jumps into the freezing waters of Macquarie Harbour to demonstrate depth and inform us what used to be where, and tell a few more interesting yarns about some of the island's past residents.

As with many other convict settlements around the state, Sarah Island was an industrious camp, harvesting the water-resistant Huon Pine and Celery Tops to build ships, which they reputedly did very well. In all, 121 ships were built during its twelve-year existence as a penal colony. The first commandant of the island was Lieutenant Cuthbertson, a war hero from the Napoleonic Wars, but who was described as a 'sadistic bully with peculiar tendencies'. God knows what that means, and I don't want to guess. Anyway, he drowned and had to be replaced with a no doubt equally sadistic ruler.

There were two methods of escape from Sarah Island, as with Port Arthur: physically running (or swimming) away, or death. My guidebook says that one event provided a dramatic turning point in the story of Sarah Island. In 1827, nine men on Grummett Rock (a small island where the acutely nasty convicts were chained to a rock) drowned a constable in full view of four others whom they had bound and gagged to ensure witnesses. The nine men were taken to Hobart for trial and hanged. It was, in fact, a mass suicide, or escape. Repentance would see them escape to a better life. One of the murderers was George Lacey, who had originally escaped in 1824 with Matthew Brady and twelve others. Brady was hanged in 1826, but Lacey landed back at Sarah Island. Before Brady, the 'gentleman bushranger', was caught, Governor Arthur posted a 25-guinea reward for information leading to the convict's capture. In response, Brady offered a reward of 25 gallons of rum for information leading to the capture of Governor Arthur! Unfortunately for Brady, Arthur's reward must have been more enticing or at least been taken more seriously.

Another one of Sarah Island's residents was Matt Gabbitt. Somehow, he managed to escape and, with his gang, raided settlers and travellers in the area. Unfortunately, they ran out of people to rob so he began eating members of his gang. He continued until he was the last one left! Perhaps a sandwich short of a picnic, Gabbitt returned to the penal settlement to give himself up, complete with uneaten arm sticking out of his kit.

For me, Sarah Island and the hour we spent there was a tremendous highlight, but highlights were piling up already.

We briefly visited an aquaculture farm (not much to see from above the water; just a circular pattern of buoys), and then the boat cruised up the Gordon River through yet another beautiful part of the world. We were very lucky to have a clear sunny day with smooth water reflecting the lush green hills on either side of the river. There was a thin mist hanging peacefully over the still water. The boat pulled up at a small jetty in the middle of nowhere for us to do a short walk through the forest, the highlight being a 2000-year-old Huon Pine. The bonus was an assortment of colourful fungi for Glen to photograph.

Also, hidden in the bush was a small hut with seven beds, generator, lights, fridge and stove that was set up by fishermen years ago, and was still maintained. Anyone could use it but there were no booking facilities so you had to take your chance, especially in the busy fishing season. We picked up a kayaker who had been staying in the huts for a few nights with a drug-taking Dutch backpacker. He had some interesting stories to tell.

While cruising the Gordon, we heard the story of the Gordon below Franklin dam saga of the early 1980s. This was probably Australia's most hard-fought environmental battle and was eventually won by the greenies. In 1979, the Tasmanian Hydro Electricity Commission proposed damming the Gordon, Franklin and King rivers for the purpose of power generation. In answer to the fierce environmental backlash, the government held a referendum asking voters where they wanted the dam, not if they wanted one at all. Forty-seven per cent of people voted to put the dam on the Gordon River below the Franklin River. A massive 45 per cent of people voted informally, many of them simply writing 'No Dams' on their ballot forms.

In 1982, the Franklin and Lower Gordon Rivers were nominated for World Heritage listing, obligating the government to protect them. Despite that, work was ready to proceed, and people came from around the world to protest the construction of the dam, including the famous botanist David Bellamy and Dr Bob Brown, leader of the anti-dam movement and more recently leader of the Australian Green Party. In fact, so many people came to the construction site and were arrested that the police and courts couldn't keep up. The magistrate involved, in an attempt to streamline the process, offered arrested protesters an option to avoid a lengthy and costly legal process: the greenies could sign a form promising not to go back to the site or they would be sent to gaol. Not surprisingly, those that did sign the document and were set free headed straight back to the site and chained themselves to trees. Those that refused to sign were locked up.

Well, the gaol system wasn't big enough to cope with all these people and they soon ran out of beds, so the inmates had to bring their own sleeping bags and bedding. The Federal Government didn't really want anything to do with the controversy, but in 1983, Malcolm Fraser came to Tasmania and offered the Tasmanian Government $500 million to stop construction of the dam. The Tassies said no thanks and kept going, much to the disgust of many of its citizens. Then the Federal Labor Government swept to power on the back of a promise to block construction of the dam, which it did. It forked out about half the $500 million originally offered. The greenies were happy, and two other dams were built instead of the Gordon below Franklin and now generate about the same amount of electricity that the Gordon below Franklin would have produced. I certainly don't remember any protests about their construction and apparently there was little fuss, with the exception of some controversy over the unfortunate flooding of some Aboriginal sacred sites. There's now talk of geothermal (underground heat) power generation, which would make all of the existing power stations in Tasmania obsolete.

After the cruise, we did the dreaded washing back at the hostel, and I went to a play at the visitors' centre back in town. The play, *The Ship that Never Was*, not surprisingly written and directed by, and starring our friendly guide from Sarah Island, had been running in various forms and places since 1984. The cast seemed to consist of as many actors as were available on the day. There were about 12 characters and on the night I was there, only two actors showed up. Consequently, significant audience participation was required. The play was the true story (with corny comic acting) of an escape from Sarah Island in 1834 and was ten bucks well spent.

Our friends the greenies woke us up at six again the next day, and we were gone by eight – a record departure. We drove further beyond Strahan to check out the small, brightly coloured corrugated iron shacks of Lettes Bay which I had seen featured in an *Australian Geographic* magazine. The bright colours contrasted well in this small and rather eccentric village. There was a roughly painted 'shack for sale' sign in front of one of them with street frontage. I'd love to see the agent's description...'Very blue with short walk to water. Great for first shack owner.'

On the way north and away from the coast, we filled up the petrol tank across the road from a woodcarver's gallery called *Tut's Whittle Wonders*, proudly displaying a five-metre tall wooden kangaroo outside. Smaller versions were available for purchase inside but we had some serious travelling to do to get to the north coast and had neither the time nor the inclination to dally with wooden marsupials.

6. Full Circle

We had breakfast at Zeehan, a shortish roller-coaster ride north of Strahan over the mountainous terrain. The takeaway shop, as in so many other rural towns, had a couple of notice boards outside advertising everything from babysitting to bush dances to houses. On offer was a two-bedroom house for $15,000 and three-bedroom for $22,000. What a bargain! At the other end of town was a sign advising that there was no petrol for 169 kilometres. As we were to learn, there wasn't *anything* other than high winds and winding road for 169 kilometres.

Bass and Flinders named Zeehan after Abel Tasman's ship in which he was travelling when he saw a lofty mountain, also now named after the ship. Silver was first discovered in the area in 1882 and it became a very prosperous mining town – the third largest in Tasmania - with 10,000 people and 26 hotels. Twenty-five years later, the mines began to fail and the town shrunk to about 600. In the 1960s, the tin mine was reopened and the town experienced a bit of a revival, now up to a population of about 1,100 and classified by the National Trust in recognition of its heritage value. There are several quaint old buildings to check out, a diverse museum, the 1,000 seat Gaiety Theatre and not far away is the state's highest waterfall, Montezuma Falls, thought to be named after one of the area's early mining companies.

We had decided to take the challenge of the rugged western road that winds north not far from the coast. It was a long rough ride. Numerous signs warn of the steep cliff (upon which the road sits), the road's isolation and various other potential calamities. As with the Gordon Dam area, the ground is formed of white rock and most of the area we drove through along the coast was sparsely vegetated, although we had go through some forested (and deforested) areas. At the tiny village of Corinna, we had to page a punt to come and pick us up for the 20 metre $10 river crossing. Also along the highway, we were confronted with the biggest warning sign I've ever seen. The road was unsealed, narrow, winding, rocky and there was no mobile coverage (nothing new for us). We were really out in the middle of nowhere. We passed a few other cars; mainly four-wheel drives but not many for a minor 'highway'.

After continuing up the coast, Glen 'I never get sick of dirt roads' was sick of dirt roads so we bypassed the final bone-jarring northern loop and cut through to the relatively large town of Smithton for a late lunch, which was fine with me. We were not far from our destination of Stanley, a small town that juts out into Bass Strait from the north coast.

The weather report for the next day was not good, so we decided to take in Stanley's main attraction, 'the Nut', straight away.

The town rests at the base of the Nut, a large flattop monolith looming over Bass Strait. Stanley was discovered by Bass and Flinders in 1798 and was the first settlement in northwest Tasmania. It was then the home of the Van Diemen's Land Company, established in 1825 for the high-quality merino wool industry. It was also a whaling port in its day but now caters for crayfish and other fishing boats, and a bit of tourism.

Schoolteacher Joseph Lyons was born here. He was Australia's only Tasmanian Prime Minister and held office in the 1930s, but died in office. He was in the Scullin Labor Party but left to lead the United Australia Party, which later formed a coalition with the Country Party. Not surprisingly, Stanley is yet another historic town and was the first Tasmanian community to win the Tidy Towns competition.

Tidy Towns competitions are state-based programs run to support local communities in their efforts to manage their public facilities and environments. They've been going for years and have been a great success story for isolated and not so isolated country towns in providing inspiration to improve and maintain aesthetic standards. Most towns we passed through proudly proclaimed some form of tidy town notoriety.

The walk up the 12.5 million-year-old Nut is steep but takes only 15 or 20 minutes at a moderate pace. Alternatively, a chairlift can take the less energetic to the top for the 40minute walk around the plateau. Glen opted for the chairlift and I struggled up the very steep path, unable to walk with my wobbly legs by the time I got to the top. While I laboured along the trail in the gale force wind, Glen sprained his ankle in a hole left by one of the many creatures inhabiting the rock. At one of the lookouts overlooking the water we saw tangled in the fence the sprawled bare skeleton of a bird with a feather barely attached to each wingtip. Did I say it was windy?

I scurried back down to the base of the Nut and Glen met me at the bottom of the chairlift. Not surprisingly, we had a quiet evening in a caravan park on-site van while Glen iced his ankle, courtesy of a very friendly proprietor.

I did all the driving on day 30 – sprained ankles and clutches don't mix. Ordinarily we'd swap over every two or three hours, depending on how long the day's drive was.

We drove though the relative civilisation of Wynyard and Burnie, the amusingly named town of Cooee, and splurged with a KFC lunch. We didn't have far to travel so we did some side-trips on the way. As soon as we hit mobile range, the phones went off so I pulled over to the shoulder of the road. Unfortunately it wasn't quite as level as the cut grass made it appear. I suppose it could have been described as a ditch. At least Glen was as surprised as me as we sat there tilted to 45 degrees. Glen took control and got us out admirably. We continued on to a spectacular lookout at Table Cape, made some calls, soaked up the views, and headed south to Cradle Mountain at the northern end of the giant Cradle Mountain-Lake St Claire National Park.

As soon as we got to the national park we drove up to Dove Lake, shadowed by the famous chest-shaped mountain which features in so many posters, postcards and books, not to mention photo albums at homes around the world. The day we were there was certainly different to the ones when the poster, postcard and book photographers visited. The temperature and the rain were freezing (not uncommon here) and the mountain was truncated by a layer of cloud, but enhanced by a rainbow radiating from the lake. We took some photos and headed back to the hostel to warm up. For such a painfully cold place, the toilet block was a long way from the hostel, but the fire in the common room was very welcoming. We chatted to some Poms, Irish and the bloke who kayaked the Gordon River, and I whipped up my mum's famous beef stroganoff. Mr Kayak was about to embark on the Overland Track to Cynthia Bay with amazingly little preparation. He had one candle, no watch and hardly any food. We wondered if we would read about him being rescued in subsequent days (we didn't).

As much as we were looking forward to exploring Cradle Mountain, the weather continued to be bad and showed no sign of improvement so we decided to head back to Launceston for our last two nights in Tassie. On the way, we explored some spectacular limestone caves not far from a small isolated town called Mole Creek. The first was the King Solomon Cave, a smaller dry cave with some amazing reflective crystals known as 'King Solomon's diamonds'. There were only two other people on the tour and our National Parks guide was excellent. His booming and enthusiastic voice was made for the job and he was great at telling a yarn. He called all the stalagmites and stalactites 'him': 'Look at him over there...'. The Marakoopa Cave (Aboriginal for 'handsome') was an outstanding huge feature with a couple of streams running through its massive 'rooms'. It also turned on an impressive glow-worm display.

Instead of Launceston, we decided to stay at Deloraine, half an hour out of Launceston, and went straight to the YHA hostel. The office was closed when we got there and we started chatting to a Victorian couple who were incredibly boring and, frankly, a little strange. We escaped by going into town. Neither of us was too keen to stay at the hostel so we booked in at *Ye Olde British Hotel* for the night. We spent much of the afternoon chatting to the friendly publican. It seems that so many country pubs are struggling to stay alive because of tightening drink-driving laws, not to mention people moving to the cities. Despite having his regulars, business for him or his few remaining competitors wasn't what it used to be so we were happy to keep him company. I don't think there is much better way to get a feel for a place – publicans tend to know everything and everyone in a country town.

Deloraine is Tasmania's largest inland town (population around 2,200), half way between Launceston and Devonport. It was settled in the 1820s and was named by surveyor Thomas Scott after a character in the poem The Lady of the Last Minstrel by his relative Sir Walter Scott. It is yet another historic town and many of its Georgian and Victorian buildings have been restored. Not only that, it's home to the Big Coffee Pot, a fact we sadly learned after we'd departed.

On to Launceston, and the hotel had stuffed up our booking so we booked into another pub. The stomach bug which was to knock me out for the next week kicked in but didn't get really bad until the 14-hour trip across Bass Strait a couple of days later. We spent most of our time in the city wandering around and catching a movie or two. It was good to relax after our exhilarating but exhausting travel schedule. Strolling back to the hotel we came across the warm and eclectic *Foggy Mountain Music Shop*. The proprietor, Chris, spent two hours very enthusiastically playing us mostly Australian blues and discussing the Aussie blues scene. After telling him that I planned to mention the store in a Sydney Blues Society article, we left with several well-priced CDs of some excellent Australian blues.

I noticed while we were wandering that Tasmania's two number plate slogans are 'Holiday Isle' and 'Your Natural State'. There must be one including apples as well. Everything else does.

Having most of our final day to kill, we drove up to West Head, across the harbour from George Town. After exploring for a while and stopping at a couple of historical sites, we headed to Devonport for our departure. The Devil Cat had stopped running so we were on the larger and much slower Spirit of Tasmania for the overnight return trip to Melbourne. We were able to board the boat at 2:30, which we did, and I spent most of the afternoon in bed. I struggled up to dinner, but didn't get much down before returning to bed. As soon as I reached the dorm, which was right down in the guts of the ship, I thought I heard my name paged so I went back to the slowest lift in the Southern Hemisphere, looking and feeling half-dead. It turns out that it *was* me being paged. The first officer had seen our car in the hold and wanted to ask me about it as he had just bought one. After comparing notes, I headed back down to bed and slept terribly. Crossing Bass Strait when you're healthy is bad enough, but it really sucks when you're already sick. At least I had the last three weeks of non-stop spectacular and thought- provoking Tasmanian travels to run through my head as we pitched and rolled back to the mainland.

7. Victorian Vistas

The ferry from Tasmania pulled into Port Melbourne early in the morning after the fourteen-hour voyage. Thankfully, the frequently choppy trip was rather sedate; my already troubled insides wouldn't have coped well with a rougher journey. Having chosen the cheapest dorm-style beds on the boat, sleeping wasn't easy, with a high volume of nearby human traffic in various states of sobriety.

From Port Melbourne, the Beast battled the trams and strange hook-turns and stopped off in downtown Melbourne to drop off my wine-soaked computer for repair.

Over the next few days, Glen stayed with relatives and I stayed with friends. Neither of us did much. My friends back in Sydney couldn't understand why we needed a rest after a month of holidays, but four weeks of non-stop sightseeing can be very wearing.

The Melbourne weather was living up to its reputation; the temperature was six degrees at midday, the coldest May day since 1977. We were hoping for more luck with the weather as we continued around the country.

Despite the weather, Melbourne is a great place to be. Being from Sydney I'm not supposed to admit that, but it's true. Melbourne was named 'the world's most liveable city' in 1990. I'm not sure why it was so special back then, but I assume it has only got better since. The first thing that hits you is the trams and tram cables criss-crossing the city and suburbs. Then there's the groovy cafes, multitude of restaurants, huge sporting venues including the famous Melbourne Cricket Ground ('the 'G"), prominent casino, and the bizarre hook manoeuvre to turn right from the left lane on the city streets. It's a mecca for sports fans, shoppers, caffeine addicts and the beautiful people strutting their stuff on ritzy Chapel Street.

Melbourne, Australia's second largest city (over 3.5 million people), was settled by Europeans in 1835 when John Batman decided that it would be 'a good place for a village'. Batman was born in what is now Parramatta, New South Wales. It's satisfying to know that a Sydneysider settled Melbourne. The son of a convict, Batman shot to fame when he secured the surrender of the infamous bushranger Matthew Brady. He 'found' Melbourne while searching for decent grazing land, bartered with the local Aborigines for land and settled in 1836 with the wife and kids. He seemed unconcerned that the British government preferred to confine and control settlement. Batman was one of the more native-friendly settlers, even earning commendation from Governor Arthur (of all people) for humane handling of Tasmanian Aborigines. Plus, he had black and white servants.

Just before the Batmans settled, an ex-convict by the name of John Fawkner decided to settle in the area as well. Initially the two parties clashed, but eventually amalgamated to form one settlement. Consequently, both men are credited with establishing the town. Unfortunately, Batman dropped dead soon after and Fawkner was left to take the kudos in the place named in 1837 after the British Prime Minister, Lord Melbourne.

The discovery of gold in Victoria in the 1850s greatly boosted Melbourne's population and status. At the same time, some parts of the city were almost completely deserted as eager prospectors upped shovels and headed north to find their fortune in the soil and rocky riverbeds. Melbourne nearly lost its status to nearby Geelong, which was closer to the goldfields but devised tactics such as printing inaccurate maps to bring people back to the great city. They needn't have bothered – the gold rush brought fame and fortune to few, and the miners came back to Melbourne either to spend their booty or look for a job.

Late in the 19th century, a series of bank failures led to a collapse in the city and it wasn't until Federation in 1901 that the economy got back on track. Melbourne challenged Sydney as the site of the country's new capital and even hosted the first sitting of Federal Parliament. Both cities ended up losing out to the now pristine Canberra which at that stage was not much more than a bunch of trees. Melbourne battled on and in 1956 hosted the Olympic Games, helping to satisfy sports mad inhabitants and giving the country a boost. It has continued to grow and improve since then and, as I said, I have to admit to quite enjoying it.

After a few days of R&R, catching up with friends and getting my computer fixed, it was time to head south for some sightseeing. Wilsons Promontory National Park, known as 'The Prom', was first reserved as a National Park in 1898. Its European discoverer was George Bass who declared it, with a nice sense of drama, 'the cornerstone of this continent'. The Prom is the most southerly part of the mainland and once connected mainland Australia with Tasmania. In 1982, the United Nations Educational, Scientific and Cultural Organisation (UNESCO) declared The Prom a Biosphere Reserve, a designation assigning the land's use for conservation, research and ecologically and culturally sustainable development, one of twelve so gazetted in Australia. The diverse range of environments, including a rugged high range going through the guts of the park, which is bordered by beaches and a Marine Park and Reserve around the shore. The park has more than 100 kilometres of walking tracks, a fraction of which we intended to explore. We stayed on the west coast in a small two-bunk cabin at a place called Tidal River. The only settlement in the park, it started life during World War II as a commando training facility.

We had planned for significantly more camping than we seemed to be doing, but it was cold and windy around the coast of Victoria at that time of year and the fully decked out $40 cabins by Tidal River were too good to miss out on. We were surprised that you have to book the huts at least six months ahead in peak season. Demand appeared to be a lot lower when the Antarctic wind shoots over Bass Strait to the Prom.

Our first walk for the day was a short drive away. Lilli Pilli Gully is a rainforesty five kilometre track winding through some very tall tree ferns, and not surprisingly, some tall lilli pilli trees. Some of the lilli pillies had engulfed the tree ferns but both seemed to survive comfortably together. Despite large displays in the information centre that got Glen excited, we couldn't find much in the way of fungi for him to photograph along the trail. The thick canopy kept low vegetation to a minimum it seemed, almost as though the forest floor had been vacuumed. As usual, we saw a wallaby or two along the way and plenty of birds. The track soon steepened and opened out into a eucalypt forest. The track just kept going up and up. Glen's comment: 'Doesn't Victoria go downhill'? It eventually did and we arrived back at the car after about one and a half hours, rather than the two to three suggested by the sign at the beginning of the track.

We drove back to Tidal River and went for a stroll along the beach and up the river. We saw how the river got its name – the water seemed to be flowing faster upstream than down. We were both starving and decided to have a BBQ lunch with the chops and corn we had intended to cook for dinner. While cooking away, we heard a massive crash in the forest across the river as a tree fell and obviously took several others with it. We certainly heard that one fall. Thankfully, such an event is a rarity these days and isn't caused by a long-bladed saw. Anyway, lunch was a ripsnorter.

Neither of us could be bothered doing anything more after lunch so we set up our folding chairs by the river and spent much of the afternoon reading and soaking in the riverside beauty. It was so peaceful (with only an occasional passing tourist) and relaxing. There's abundant birdlife in the Park: kookaburras, seagulls, rosellas, ducks, wrens and more, most of which were quite tame. It was the first time either of us had seen seagulls foraging for food other than discarded fish and chips. Their behaviour was also a little odd: they stamped the sand very rapidly just below the water line like they were on hot coals. Were they looking for food, looking for a mate or just having a dance?

When the mosquitoes became too much to bear, we went for a drive and found a good beach for sunset photos. It was a great call of Glen's to stop there with the cameras – the sunset stained the darkening sky with colour, advancing through shades of red and orange to a very rich pink. It's always great to stumble upon such a spectacular place. I love that feeling of discovery, as if no one else knew about it.

The next morning, on the way out of the National Park, we passed several large mobs of kangaroos and emus. They seem to graze happily together and generally in large numbers. We drove through a few small coastal towns to San Remo, looking forward to some of the supposedly excellent fish and chips. Someone lied. They were very ordinary. Along the way, we stopped at Port Welshpool, once the departure point for the Devil Cat to Tasmania, and now I imagine a lot quieter. We walked to the end of Welshpool's tourist highlight, a very long jetty.

Unfortunately, we bypassed Korumburra ('blowfly' to the original inhabitants) which is home to the giant Gippsland earthworm, and, of course, to the annual giant earthworm festival. Further east, Wonthaggi didn't appear to have much going for it apart from a funny name.

San Remo is another one of those towns that have no historical significance that we could determine, and little interest of their own (other than ordinary fish and chips), but whose claim to fame is being the gateway to somewhere else. San Remo is the gateway to Phillip Island.

Other than motorcycle racing, Phillip Island is about penguins and the penguin parade, and boy is exploitation rife. Huge grandstands flank the area where the little creatures wander up the beach every evening at dusk. Not for us thanks. We did penguins on a much more intimate scale at George Town in Tassie. The penguins at Phillip Island, numbering up to 2,000 a night, waddle up Summerlands beach to what is purportedly the second most popular tourist attraction in the whole country. Wild koalas also are supposed to live on the island but we couldn't find any and got sore necks trying.

We drove past the penguin parade ground to Seal Rocks at the south-western corner of the island. With visibility distorted by rain, I peered through my nifty little binoculars at the seal colony several dozen metres from the shore. I saw a bunch of seals on some rocks mysteriously called '*The Nobbies*' and got very wet. A Seal Centre at the shoreline had a live video transmission from the seal colony, but the $15 admission was too rich for our blood, so we headed to the hostel into which we had booked.

The hostel was inside a caravan park and wasn't much chop. The room we were assigned didn't lock so we complained and were put in an on-site van. Well, we thought we were in a van (and a big one too), but we were in a temporary-looking structure stuck to the side of it (the van was securely locked). It came complete with flimsy walls, mould, and ants, but the mother of all heaters. The beds consisted of saggy foam so I slept on my camping mat on the floor. The guest book was full of complaints about ants, mould and uncomfortable beds, among other things.

On the following day while we were stocking up on our standard list of supplies at the local supermarket, we discovered the first major scratch on the car. It appeared to have been caused ignominiously by a shopping trolley rather than any rugged trailblazing. Glen was livid.

The Australian Dairy Centre was our first stop and, frankly, it was a bit of a letdown. There were tastings of only a few cheeses, none of which we liked. The smoked cheese wasn't even smoked – it was 'smoke flavoured'!

Our cheesy visit was brief and the Phillip Island Vineyard and Winery wasn't open until 11 so we had some time to kill. Glen, being the petrol head that he is, wanted to go to the Phillip Island race track visitors centre and museum, and I was happy to tag along. It was surprisingly interesting and I took longer to go through the museum than Glen did. He was very disappointed that racing legend Peter Brock's car ('the Great Man' according to Glen; also known as the 'King of the Mountain') was not on show.

The winery was enjoyable, with a good range of reds and whites. We thought the $5 tasting fee was a bit steep, but the friendly lady serving us didn't charge it when we bought a few bottles for the next stage of the journey. We couldn't be expected to travel and exert ourselves without good wine and cheese.

Nine kilometres east of San Remo is the Wildlife Wonderland, which is home to the world-famous Wombat World. We had a vague curiosity to see this enticing site, but not quite enough to stop. Also on the way to the Peninsula, we drove through Koo-wee-rup which is not only the centre of Australia's largest asparagus growing district and has the weirdest name, but proudly hosts the Potato Festival on the third Saturday of March.

Long before our visit to Mornington Peninsula, the first white visitor was John Murray, closely followed by Matthew Flinders. Murray named the Peninsula after Mornington in Ireland and landed at what is now Sorrento where he raised the Union Jack to claim the land in the name of King George III. One year later, they hustled in a bunch of convicts, soldiers and civilians to establish Victoria's first white settlement and to deter the French from settling. The settlement lasted less than a year, when lack of water, poor farming land and substandard leadership drove the settlers elsewhere. These days, the Peninsula is very popular with holidaying Melbournites who swarm to the numerous beaches in summer.

We decided to stay in a town called Flinders on the eastern side of the boot-shaped peninsula to avoid what we suspected was the more touristy and populated west coast. As usual, after checking in we went for an exploration of the town and surrounds. We found it generally worthwhile to get a bit of a feel for the places we visited rather than simply passing through or concentrating on tourist traps. We stopped at the town jetty, chatted to a fisherman with several outrageously big fishing rods and watched a swag of fish being sold straight from a boat all for the bargain price of $10. It was a brief negotiation.

As we were walking back to the car, along the beach we found our first bit of bush tucker that we had seen the Bush Tucker Man talk about on TV: the bush tomato. Naturally, we picked one and 'cut 'im open'. He's no good to eat, but definitely smells like your common tomato, but smaller and yellow. The Aborigines of Central Australia ate a similar variety but neither of us was game to test out which variety this one was. Les would have been proud. Or maybe not.

The next stop was Mornington Peninsula National Park, which stretches along much of the southwest-facing ocean coast of the Peninsula, the sole of the 'boot', and on to the big toe, called Point Nepean. You park at the car park and walk past an expanse of military land littered with unexploded shells. Signs warned us that objects picked up might explode and kill us. I was not aware that there was so much military presence here now or in the past. It is not surprising really, as the Point is a prime spot from which to protect Port Phillip, upon which Melbourne sits. In fact, the National Park was a military reserve until 1988. The maximum number of 600 people allowed into the park at any time highlights its environmental fragility, although this seemed a little at odds with hosting a military base and bombing range.

The walk through the park took us past a couple of old forts, which are still in reasonable condition despite their 100-year-plus age. One of the outpost's cannons fired the first official shot of the British Empire in World War I, and the same gun fired Australia's first shot in World War II. Fort Nepean was built in the 1880's to protect the colony from the feared Russian invasion. We doubted they did much damage to enemies on the other side of the world. Despite its crumbling state, we could still make out a few signs and numbered gun racks. I don't think it would have won any architectural awards and can't have been an enjoyable place to live thanks to the cold, wet and windy weather, not to mention a perceived and perhaps paranoid threat of invasion.

It was quite an interesting two or three-hour walk, which also included a good view of the beach where Australian Prime Minister Harold 'The Fish' Holt supposedly drowned or was taken by a shark or a Russian submarine back in 1967. It's a very rocky beach with rough surf even on a calm day, so you wouldn't catch me swimming there. So why was he swimming there? And how does a country just lose their leader? It's not like misplacing some change between the couch cushions or forgetting where you left your keys. It remains a staggering mystery.

After the walk, we visited the posh seaside towns of Portsea and Sorrento and continued further up the coast to Mornington and Frankston. George Coppin, an entrepreneur in theatre among other things, who contributed significantly to the area's development, named Sorrento after the Italian city in 1868. For more than a century it has been the holiday destination of Melbourne's well heeled, who appear to have been enamoured with its ornate Victorian architecture, or at least its beaches and certainly its lifestyle. They say that Victoria's first white child was born here with a silver spoon in its screaming mouth.

All along the coast are hundreds of small brightly coloured beach huts. They look quaint and are part of the whole holiday tradition when the hordes of Melbournians flock to the Peninsula in summer.

We were again reminded about Melbournian driving habits, including overtaking around corners and over the crests of hills, and a complete lack of interest in staying within any one lane. At least they don't tailgate like the Tasmanians. Of all people to tailgate, you'd think the laid-back Tasmanians would never be in a hurry to get anywhere, but a definite trend was clear.

By the time we were ready to push off at 10am the next day, we had missed the morning ferry across Port Phillip Bay to Queenscliff. Rather than wait two hours for the next one we drove around Port Phillip via Melbourne and probably arrived at the Great Ocean Road at the same time as if we'd waited for the noon ferry. We were both anxious to get to the famed coastal road, but concerned about its ability to live up to its lofty reputation. We need not have worried.

8. Greatest Ocean Road

The appropriately named Great Ocean Road is as spectacular as we could have hoped. The stunning turquoise, crystal clear ocean can be seen from much of the drive. The narrow road twists and creeps along the shoreline for more than 300 kilometres from Torquay to Warrnambool. It was built over 14 years and financed by a bunch of enterprising citizens to provide 3,000 returned diggers from World War I with a job through the Great Depression. In 1936, the road was given to the State of Victoria as a memorial to solders.

The tourist trail starts at the tourist and surf town of Torquay. It has the state's largest surf lifesaving club, a surfing museum and more than enough surf shops. I looked for a hotel called Fawlty Towers to no avail ('What do you expect to see out of a Torquay hotel bedroom window?'). Not far up the road we stopped at the famous surfie hangout, Bells Beach. The waves were touted to reach six metres in height, but the surf was flat as a pancake for our brief visit. Despite this disappointment, several waxheads were trying to catch what little waves rolled past. We called a surf-mad mate back in Sydney and I have to admit that we enhanced the truth a little about how good it was. He was suitably jealous.

Further up the road is Anglesea, another popular little resort town with an eclectic mix of residents and visitors, and a large mob of kangaroos which frequent the golf course (just spectators; they're not very good golfers). Its population is reputed to be artistic; a few galleries are around to check out if you're that way inclined. There's also plenty for the nature lover, with numerous walks around the Anglesea River.

Little towns dot the winding road down to Lorne, a fashionable tourist destination before and since the construction of the Great Ocean Road.

It's been around since 1871 so I think you could say it's not a passing fad. Not being fashionable tourists, we kept driving. It didn't seem the place to relax during school holidays.

After one of the most spectacular stretches of road, we stopped for the night at Apollo Bay. It was another long but impressive day of driving, the kind when it's a pity one person has to watch the road instead of the view. Apollo Bay is a pleasantly laid-back little seaside town shadowed by the Otway Ranges. It started life as a whaling town and was quite an important port to the region. When the harbour filled up with silt, its importance as a trading port waned. It is still a fishing town though - for both seafood and tourists. If you're into seashells, there's a museum full of them.

We did the usual stroll through town and wandered out to the end of the breakwater. Of course it started raining while we were at the furthest point from the car at the end of the breakwater. Somewhat dampened, we continued exploring.

Not far from Apollo Bay is the Otway National Park and Cape Otway, a mixture of heavily wooded area, fern forests, and coastal bush and grassland with an amazing array of birds, bats, reptiles, glow worms and even a rare carnivorous snail. That, I'd like to see - from a distance. We planned to drive to the Cape, but found that to get to the lighthouse (and therefore the tip of the cape) you have to pay. Neither of us was really fussed. We'd seen so many lighthouses, and let's face it, there's not much architectural diversity in lighthouse construction. Another walk in the rain didn't appeal, so we left.

Further on up the road is Castle Cove. A line-up of cars at the roadside car park enticed us to check it out. Most of the cars belonged to surfers catching waves far below the cliff top lookout, and a throng of tourists watched them get dumped. Several of the surfers were hanging around what looked to be very rocky ends of the beach where the waves looked good, but the rocks didn't. Perhaps they'd been dumped a few too many times.

This part of the coast is known for three things: the picturesque coastline, whales and shipwrecks. Unfortunately, we were a few weeks early for the calving of the Southern Right Whales (so named because they were 'right' to hunt – slow, swam close to the surface, floated when harpooned and yielded large quantities of oil and whalebone) and it was too wet to walk to any of the shipwrecks. They reckon more than 160 ships have met with disaster in the area, so the '*Shipwreck Coast*' tag seems appropriate.

The highlight of the drive and the major attraction of the Great Ocean Road is the Twelve Apostles. The Apostles of Victoria are huge fingers of layered sandy-coloured limestone rock sticking up from the shallow water, the survivors of thousands of years of pounding by the waters of the Southern Ocean. Despite the rain, the 50-metre-tall 12 A's are as impressive as advertised and endlessly photographed. So many of these sorts of attractions are a bit of a letdown when you finally get there after a long build-up, but these handsome remnants lived up to their lofty reputation.

Other natural attractions along the road are the impressive Loch Ard Gorge, the not so impressive London Bridge (fallen down), and the spectacular and strangely underadvertised Bay of Islands.

The deep and steep Loch Ard Gorge that empties into the ocean is named after a ship wrecked there in 1878 with only two survivors out of the 54 on board. They sailed for three months from England to get to Melbourne, and held a party the night before their expected arrival to celebrate the occasion. All were below deck, except for Captain

Gibb, who was concerned about the thick mist that enveloped the ship. Early the next morning, the watch spotted rocks ahead. Despite desperate attempts to turn the ship, it crashed into the jagged outcrop, waves smashed over the deck and the ship crumbled. The two survivors were only 18 years old: Irish immigrant Eva Carmichael and ship's apprentice Tom Pearce. Eva's parents and five siblings didn't make it, but Eva survived by clinging to a piece of the ship. Tom made it to safety but returned to the churning waters to rescue Eva. He dragged her into a cave in the gorge and reputedly revived her with some brandy from the wreckage. Tom climbed out of the gorge and found two stockmen who organised a rescue party. Only four bodies were recovered and a small amount of cargo. The media whipped itself into a frenzy as ferocious as the ocean that took the lives of the 52 people on board (ok, maybe that's a bit dramatic but it would certainly be true today) and Tom became a hero. He received 1,000 pounds from the Government of Victoria, a gold watch, an award and other gifts from all sorts of people. It was reported that Tom proposed to Eva, but her experience was too much and she jumped aboard a ship back to Ireland and married some less chivalrous suitor. Tom later returned to England and became Master of Steamships, surviving many more wrecks. Almost a fairy tale, but not quite.

Several days after the Loch Ard sank, a wooden crate washed ashore. Inside the crate was a full-sized porcelain peacock that was to be exhibited at the Melbourne Exhibition of 1880. It is now on display at the Flagstaff Hill Maritime Village in Warrnambool. The Loch Ard was the last passenger ship to founder en route to Australia.

Not far from Loch Ard Gorge, London Bridge used to be a massive natural double arch rock structure stretching out into the sea, until 1990 when two tourists were stranded as the land side arch collapsed. You can get a postcard with before and after pictures.

The Bay of Islands, further on up the road, is a stretch of the coast dotted with small and large rock formations jutting out of the water, similar to the Apostles, but slightly less dramatic. Unfortunately, the rain was pelting down, but if we'd been able to better appreciate the view, I think the spectacle would rival the 12 A's. Surprisingly, we had read nothing about them.

We decided to continue through the large coastal town of Warrnambool and smaller town of Port Fairy to Portland. Although used by whalers for many years before, Warrnambool was properly settled in 1839. Its name is derived from an Aboriginal word meaning 'plenty of water', and that it has. It was a major entry point for immigrants, with the exception of Russians. Gun emplacements were built to keep *them* out. As with many of the towns around here, shipwrecks played a substantial role in its history.

Portland claims to be Victoria's first permanent settlement, established by the Henty family in 1834. Lieutenant James Grant named it in 1800 after the Duke of Portland, although he didn't trouble himself with entering the bay. I'm not sure if that's a reflection on the Lieutenant or the Duke. Portland is only 75 kilometres from the South Australian border and is the only deep-water port between Melbourne and Adelaide. It's the point where we were to leave the coast, turn right, and head north. The first caravan park we tried gave us an entire two-bedroom *house* for $40. A kitchen, good shower and a night of sleep without the need for ear plugs! Bliss.

We decided to lap up the luxury for another night and took it easy for a day before heading into the rugged inland. We did nothing in the morning but cook up some bacon and eggs and watch some TV. Regional TV stations again proved risible, if not annoying. The ads are generally bad and most seem to be for car yards or livestock drench, and the majority are done by company proprietors who can't act but who try anyway. As if that wasn't bad enough, the TV shows we saw were between one episode and an entire season behind Melbourne. We were getting used to life without TV and were happy to leave it behind for a while.

When we eventually got moving, we stumbled upon some intriguing natural attractions at a place called Cape Bridgewater. First, we wandered through a petrified forest. Although not technically a petrified forest because of the chemical makeup of the 'trees', it's near enough, so that's what they call it. It covers a huge area stretching atop cliffs that hang out high over the churning sea and crashing waves. The creamy-coloured landscape looks kind of lunar, but more rugged than I imagine the moon's surface to be. *And* with more tourists. The 'trees' of the forest are more like stumps than trees, but impressive nonetheless, and they populated the terrain as far as we could see.

A long stretch of the area is known as *'The Blowholes'*. At first, we were disappointed because we couldn't see the holes themselves, but we were satisfied when confronted with huge plumes of water gushing up over the cliff through an unsighted fissure. The Southern Ocean batters the cliff faces with shattering energy. The rocks are fascinating. Mostly jet-black volcanic basalt, they provide a stark contrast with the foamy white water. The very rocky shoreline whips up the water like a gigantic washing machine. The water gushes up and over the black rocks and is sucked back down into the next wave. Sometimes big waves are reflected back off the cliff and smash into the oncoming waves with spectacular effect. I'm glad I wasn't down there, but watching and listening to it was mesmerising.

We walked along the coast for half an hour until it began raining, and as we came back the weather started getting rougher and the spray of water higher and more and more spectacular. It's no wonder this place is called the shipwreck coast. I am surprised it's not a more publicised tourist attraction.

We spent the afternoon being blokey – watching Tony Lockett trying to kick his 1,300th AFL goal (unsuccessfully) and listening to HG & Roy's This Sporting Life on JJJ radio. Departing from the blokey atmosphere Glen cooked up soup and vegies for dinner at the house, just in time for Australia to play Pakistan in the World Cup Cricket. A most relaxing day before changing tack and heading north after a restful night.

9. Taste of the Outback

Refreshed, we changed tack for our northerly run early the next morning. Up the Henty Highway, we drove through the town of Hamilton, evidently known as 'the wool capital of the world' (by whom?). Not surprisingly, there's a wool museum in the shape of a bunch of wool bales. It's called the Woolbales. The town's annual festivities include the Beef Expo, and Sheepvention, featuring sheep and wool inventions and sheepdog demonstrations. We'd hit the bush, big time.

'This is really the life', I wrote in my diary on my rejuvenated laptop computer. 'It's late in the afternoon and we've set up camp in the Grampians National Park. The spacious campground is a former pine plantation on the edge of the mountainous park. Despite its size, we're the only ones here. We even have the luxuries of toilets and tap water but we're really out in the middle of nowhere. All I can hear is the songs of a multitude of birds and the hum of my laptop. Right now there are four kangaroos within ten metres of me, caring not a jot about our invasion of their home'.

The kangaroos had no qualms about coming right up to us for a sniff and to beg for food. Their tameness suggested that thoughtless campers, despite requests by rangers not to do so, frequently fed them. The roos knew they could get food by coming up to humans and looking cute, as they do. We resisted.

Much of the day was spent getting to the Grampians, although we did stop for a short walk at Silver Band Falls. It wasn't the most impressive waterfall, but interesting in that the water vanished into the ground and emerged again from the ground into a river later on. Nature's plumbing.

We drove into the park through Dunkeld – 'The Southern Gateway to the Grampians'. It's not even the only gateway, but every town needs something to cling to. Surprisingly, it has been around since 1851. It was named after Dunkeld, Scotland by someone who liked and/or came from Dunkeld, Scotland.

The Grampians (or 'Gariwerd' in local Aboriginal parlance) National Park protects an amazing array of flora and fauna. Thomas Mitchell named the Grampians in 1836 after Grampians, Scotland. Perhaps he was responsible for Dunkeld as well.

Major Sir Thomas Livingstone Mitchell (1792-1855) appears to have been one of the most incompetent people to ever walk the harsh face of this country. He was somehow appointed Surveyor-General of NSW after arriving in Australia from Scotland in 1827. All I can find to his credit is that he solved the problem of the course of western rivers, a quandary that had puzzled many in the colony before him. After extensive exploration of eastern Australia, he returned to England to publish his diaries, receive a knighthood and get a promotion to Lieutenant-Colonel. He has the dubious distinction of being a participant in the last recorded duel in the colony - against Stuart Donaldson in 1851, who later went on to become the first Premier of NSW. Donaldson set up an enquiry into
Mitchell's running of the office of the Surveyor-General and it wasn't very complimentary.

In 1836, Mitchell grudgingly confirmed Sturt's theory (which he didn't previously believe) that the inland rivers of eastern Australia were part of the Murray-Darling system. Unlike Sturt (whom he disliked) Mitchell didn't think it was necessary to establish relationships with the Aboriginal tribes he met throughout his explorations, although he did make use of Aboriginal guides because of the gross incompetence of his travelling colleagues. Explorers before him, particularly Sturt, wrote copious descriptions of environment and events, but much of the time Mitchell (and several other explorers of his era) chose to ignore their predecessors' lessons and fell into the same or worse predicaments. Elements of Mitchell's diaries are a comical insight into his party's lack of understanding of their task. I thought Glen and I had over-packed, but the inventory of some of Mitchell's journeys is remarkable. He would plan to take so many animals (for transport and food) and so many people, that he had to get more people to come along just to run things. Everything he did was ridiculously military, right down to uniform and sword. He even took tables and lace tablecloths on his expeditions! It really is incomprehensible how naïve and arrogant these people were and the lack of regard they showed for the dangers of the outback. How they survived (those who did), remains a mystery. Sadly, people like that are still out there today getting stuck and occasionally dying, unprepared in the middle of nowhere.

Anyway, back to the Grampians. The National Park protects more than 1,000 species of wildflowers, some unique to the area, and more than 4,000 rock art paintings – 80 per cent of Victoria's native gallery. Animals there include more than 200 bird species, kangaroos, platypuses, koalas and red deer. Accommodation alternatives in and near the park are wide and plentiful, with those inside centred on Halls Gap. Some 160 kilometres of walking tracks in the park lead to several of the most breathtaking spots we saw on the whole trip. Unfortunately, the rain would keep us from that realisation for 24 hours.

Shortly before sunset, an old bloke in a beat up four-wheel drive drove up and started chatting to us at the campground. In only a few minutes we found out that he lived in nearby Stawell, loved coming to the Grampians, had a full (and rather odd) life story, and was having a hernia operation the next day. The prospect of him camping near us was a little worrisome, but he continued on.

Mr Hernia would have been nothing compared to the busload of raucous kids that turned up just before sunset and shattered the tranquillity of our campground.

The serenity in the plantation campground was indeed fractured by the recalcitrant youths, who also managed to scare off all the wildlife. Thankfully, the kids took off early the next morning and the wildlife returned almost immediately. Glen had a sleep-in and it was raining so I was happy to start a new book in my tent, listening to light rain falling on and around the tent, the whooshing of birds flying overhead and kangaroos hopping nearby.

After rising I was eating an apple which a hungry looking kangaroo tried to snatch from me. They're very cute and it was hard to resist the temptation, but I did, much to the dismay of our friend (we named him 'Plugger') who hopped away in disgust.

Moments later, a ranger came up to us for a chat. She told us we should have got the mobile phones out and called the Halls Gap police to come and shut up the loudmouth youngsters. Not much else to do as a police officer in the middle of a national park I suppose.

We packed up the tents and paraphernalia in the rain and headed to the ranger station and Koori centre, a bit of a let down as far as its displays went. We strolled through it in minutes, but were attracted by the café menu that included crocodile salad, emu and roo burgers and emu kababs. Unfortunately, we'd just had a couple of 'King Kong' sausage rolls and cappuccinos for breakfast. While eating, we tried to spot the local koala that reputedly hangs around Halls Gap like the town drunk after a big night scoffing fermented eucalyptus leaves, but he didn't show.

Deciding against walking in the rain, which didn't look like it was going anywhere, we set course for the wineries of nearby Great Western. We ended up taking the long way there via the town of Ararat. As usual, we tuned the radio in to the local tourist station playing a continuous five-minute recording of what there is to do in the area. The most interesting and striking offering of Ararat was the *World Rabbit Skinning Championships*. Sadly, we were too late in the year to catch it, but I will have to remember it for future holidays; what a great event for the kiddies.

Ararat also has a *gaol for the criminally insane* tour to entice the tourists, but as we had seen the country's best down in Tassie, we gave this one a miss. In fact, we talked about the things we were missing as we journeyed our way through the outback. If we had come directly to Ararat from home we probably would have stopped, but things like gaols, penguins, lighthouses and blowholes were becoming a bit mundane. And we had certainly seen our fair share of historic towns in six weeks of travel. Our complacency may have caused us to miss some good sights, but it's a risk we were prepared to take.

So on to the wineries. We decided to visit Best's and Seppelt's. Best's is a highly-regarded winery with a good selection of quality wines. Neither of the people who served us could have been described as talkative, but I suppose the wine did the talking. In fact, it told us to buy a Chardonnay and a Cab Sav. Back in Tassie, we had resolved to buy no more than two bottles from any one winery if we wanted the Beast and our budgets to survive. But you gotta live, right?

On to the large and impressive Seppelt's, best known for its sparkling wines. We spent about half an hour tasting some good whites before embarking on a great one-hour tour of the winery and its three kilometres of underground tunnels known as 'drives'. The drives are narrow and dark, and filled with thousands of bottles of ageing wines, some over 20 years old. Throughout the arched tunnels, eerie cobweb-like bits of mould accidentally imported from France hung from the walls and ceiling as though they were put there by a movie prop crew. Well down the drives, a small underground room stores wines for Australian Prime Ministers. Malcolm Fraser was the last PM to take advantage of this service and apparently still visits to raid his locked cellar. It sure beats keeping wine in the closet or under the bed in cardboard boxes. The room is shrouded in the mould and has an old chandelier hanging from the ceiling. It looks like a great room for a small party, but you wouldn't want anyone to get too sloshed on the product or you might lose a few of the thousands of bottles carefully stacked along the walls.

Straight after the tour we continued tasting some of the premium quality reds, which were indeed premium and well rewarded as such. We lashed out on a few expensive bottles, including the surprisingly good sparkling Shiraz, a wine style of gradually increasing popularity in Australia. So much for our resolution.

Glen couldn't be bothered driving back to the National Park and I was not sober enough to drive or care, so we stopped for the night at the Town Hall Hotel in Stawell, famous for the annual Stawell Gift running race (the town, not the hotel). Not only is it the best known professional running race in the country, but it's the oldest, having been run since 1878. Thrill seekers preferring to work out their eyes rather than their legs can get their rocks off at *Casper's World in Miniature Tourist Park*.

Stawell is an old gold mining town - as are most communities around here - but now benefits from wine and ecotourism. The town grew from the 1850s gold rush and used to be called The Reef. Then the golden reef started running dry and the name was changed to Pleasant Creek. When the reef was altogether gone, the name was again changed. It was called Stawell, after the attorney-general who had shot to stardom when he led the prosecution against the Eureka Stockade gold mining rebels who reckoned that self government was the way to go.

The pub was a local hangout for those who liked a bet. The walls were stacked with television screens showing various forms of racing (other than by human foot) and all eyes were glued to the screens, except ours and a couple of old diggers playing darts. The barman was a big bald bloke who looked as though he was not to be messed with. He presided over the bar with a big cigar poking out of his mouth as he served up endless pots of draught beer.

Over dinner at the hotel's bistro, Glen and I discussed the various methods of cooking a steak, prompted by a story in the newspaper and by our overcooked meat. I'm of the two-turns-only school. Glen is not. We didn't reach a resolution on the matter, but we could have both done better than the hotel chef did. We decided against bringing this to the attention of the barman, however.

There was a TV room for the hotel guests and some bloke who should have known better was watching some teenybopper crap. It prompted a quiet night with a book, so I guess we should have thanked him. At least there were no loud-mouthed brats keeping us up all night; just the loud-mouthed locals downstairs yelling at their chosen hound to bring home the bacon at the Dapto dogs.

Despite heavily overcast conditions, we headed back to the Grampians and did about six hours of walking. The first was a rough scamper through the *Grand Canyon*, a fraction of the size of its namesake in the States, but a nice rock-hopping walk through a sandstone gorge.

The next stop was the *Balconies* walk, which features in just about every poster, postcard or brochure about the Grampians. The rock formation at the end of the short walk looks like a big open bird's beak protruding from a clifftop, with spectacular sweeping views over the rocky valley shaded by the greens and reds of the leaves and rocks, out to distant hazy mountain ranges. We each stood in the 'beak' for the obligatory photo.

We marched over to nearby *Broken Falls* and a lookout with a distant overview of the much written about and photographed *Mackenzie Falls*. The Falls were quite pretty – a big expanse of water cascading down layers of rock like champagne down a tower of glasses.

The final stop was an Aboriginal art site called *Manja Shelter*, a.k.a. the *Cave of Hands*. It was a long drive down heavily corrugated dirt tracks but at the end of the walk, we were rewarded with several hand stencils and a few other rock paintings. It was my first closeup look at authentic Aboriginal rock art, an exciting experience. There was a real feeling of wonder and amazement as we sat there and thought back to the time when the ochre was spat over small and large hands to leave the tribe's mark. Little did they know there would be strange-looking people in strange-looking clothes peering through strange-looking contraptions at their simple artistic expression. I suspect the environment around here is little changed from that time, except of course for camera-toting tourists traipsing through the tall grass. Unfortunately for the tourist, the artwork is fenced off, keeping us back a few metres from the cave surface. I suppose there are too many thoughtless graffitists out there who couldn't resist the temptation to add their own 'art'.

Our plan to check out another Aboriginal site was dashed by a sudden downpour. It probably wouldn't have worried the original inhabitants, but we're a bit more sensitive. So back to the Beast and we were en route to Little Desert National Park.

We had planned to stay at a hostel near Horsham, not far from the park, which had among other things an indoor rock-climbing wall. We had seen it advertised in a few hostels and thought we'd better check it out. When we got the Horsham, Glen decided that he didn't want to go to the hostel. Glen wanted to go to Nhill and didn't know why. In fact, I also wanted to go to Nhill, and for the same reason. I suspected that Glen also wanted to be in a pub for the opening State of Origin rugby league game between NSW and Queensland. The problem was that I wanted to go to the Horsham hostel before the park and Nhill after because I thought we'd get better information on the park there. The disagreement was our biggest of the entire trip, and made for a tense evening and somewhat awkward morning, but soon faded away. After living in each other's pockets for 48 days with only our tents (which we hadn't used as much as we expected) for solitude, I figure we did pretty well not to have had more confrontations than we did.

Horsham sits at the junction of the Western, Henty and Wimmera Highways, and it is the largest town of the Wimmera region of Victoria. Not far from Horsham is Natimuk.
Natimuk is, of course, the gateway to 'Victoria's Ayres Rock', Mt Arapiles ('The Piles'?). Explorer extraordinaire Thomas Mitchell climbed the rock back in 1836 and Bridgette Muir, the first Australian woman to climb Mt Everest, used it to train for her somewhat more challenging climb in the Himalayas. We read that people come from all over the

world to use its 2,000 different climbing routes (and one sealed road) to the top. If we had known that at the time, we might have bothered to go and see it, and possibly climb or drive up.

Nhill is certainly an interestingly named place, but on the way there we passed or drove down Asses Ears Road, That Road and Rifle Butts Road. Nhill is far from boring; it is home to the world's largest single-bin wheat silo, and was the first country town in Victoria to have electric light. It was named from the Aboriginal word *nyell*, meaning *'white mist on water'* by its first white settlers in 1844. The pub we had chosen to stay in was full so we tried out the one across the road where we scored single rooms for $15 each. The guests' lounge featured a giant TV just made for watching footie. It was complemented with a talkative guest who couldn't string two words together without one of them being 'fuck' or 'shit' or their derivatives. Friendly chap though, and quite keen on his footie.

I tried questioning the barman about the very Australian movie *Road to Nhill*, a story about life in this isolated town. He didn't think it was filmed there, but I was obviously a lot more interested than him in getting to the bottom of it so I let it go through to the keeper.

The downside to the lodging was that it was on the main highway to Adelaide, which carried hundreds of barrelling semi-trailers past my window. I was also beginning to pick up a suspect odour in the room. Otherwise, it was a decent enough place to watch the game over a few drinks and crash for the night. For $15, I couldn't complain. Actually, I could. After trying to sleep in one of the worst beds on which I have ever laid my head, with the smell and the noise playing at my nerves, we got going at the usual time – mid morning.

Glen wasn't interested in walking around beautiful downtown Nhill (we were still a little edgy with one another) so I took a quick stroll myself. I got a photo of the toys, guns, ammo and sports store sign (toys and guns?) before we headed off in search of information about Little Desert National Park. The National Parks office at Nhill was closed. Our next stop and entrance point to the park was Dimboola, where the information centre was also closed. The bookish library assistant tried to help, as did another local, but we still didn't really have any solid information on the park so we backtracked further to the town of Wail and the Little Desert National Parks office. They were open and friendly enough but not exactly loaded with information. All we wanted was a bit of background on the area and a map, but it was proving to be pretty challenging. We noticed on our way out of the office that the ranger's four-wheel drive had a lorikeet splattered on its front grille.

We headed off into the park and started with a short walk through the low vegetation and sand. We spent the next few hours driving through the park. The roads were narrow and sandy, which made it a slow journey. The colours ranged from white beach-like sand to a rich red sunburnt grain.

Despite its name, Little Desert is not, in fact, a desert; neither is it little. I have read all I could and am still in the dark as to why it was called Little Desert. It does, however, have a certain desert-like quality in the sand and low scrub, but it gets a few metres of annual rainfall. Much of the vegetation is chest-high desert banksia and the occasional stringy bark eucalypt amongst the ti-trees and she-oaks. In fact, over 650 species of plants have been recorded in the park. As usual, we saw several kangaroos, some emu tracks and those of a dog, presumably wild, as pets are banned from the park. The park's mallee fowl eluded us, despite the fact that they build nests of sand that are a couple of metres tall.

We drove past a couple of dry salt lakes, on which the local hoons appeared to like doing doughnuts, and the surface of which sticks to one's boots like cement. The eastern edge of the park is a flood plain bounded by the Wimmera River. The western side is bounded by the South Australia-Victoria border.

We had to turn back on a couple of the tracks, as they were too much for the heavily laden Beast, despite its formidable low-range four-wheel drive capabilities. The map we were given by the ranger bore little resemblance to the park's geography or its roads. The tracks that were supposed to be 'surfaced' were no different to the 'vehicular tracks (4WD)' and the sealed roads were at best on par with a mediocre unsealed road.

By the time we'd traversed the park from top to bottom a couple of times, Glen was stuffed and I did the remaining couple of hours driving to the creatively-named South Australian town of Bordertown, unsurprisingly near the border of Victoria and South Australia. Our journey was a little delayed by a flock of sheep being herded across the road. We were content to sit and wait but a local barely slowed down to avoid hitting them and dispersed them into fences on both sides of the road allowing us to pass. Spot the tourists!

Bordertown's single claim to fame is as the birthplace of former Australian Prime Minister Bob Hawke. There's a bronze bust of him in town, and his childhood home is now a museum. The town is located in the *Tatiara* district, meaning *'good country'* in the native tongue. It was an important goldfields centre but now survives on agriculture and overpriced tourist accommodation.

The caravan park's one cabin was occupied, the weather still looked ominous and camping in the rain again didn't appeal. We couldn't find anything else in terms of budget accommodation. Not with our definition of budget anyway, so we settled on The Woolshed pub/motel. The television situation was interesting. Being on the border of two states, we could tune into the Victorian and South Australian versions of each station, except of course the one we wanted to watch. And because SA is half an hour behind Victoria, if you miss something on Vic TV, you can switch over to SA TV and watch it half an hour later.

How cool is that?

That evening, we also roughly planned our route for the next month. We would head north though South Australia, Victoria, NSW and Queensland to Birdsville and then back down to Adelaide via the famous Birdsville Track. Four states in four weeks.

Before forking out $5 on a pasta dinner at the Woolshed we took the Beast for a spin to try to locate the incessant noise which we hadn't been able to isolate. It was to no avail, so we completely repacked the car the next morning but the infuriating noise persisted.

Along the highway, we passed the remains of the old vermin proof fence. It was built in 1885 along the 36th parallel to confine rabbits and wild dogs to Victoria's north-west, away from fertile farmland. It was maintained until the late 1950s and has since been replaced. This was also the start of the Ngarkat Conservation Park, which had been burnt out and didn't seem to have much left to conserve. The contrast between the surprisingly white sand and the blackened scrub was fascinating and stretched as far as we could see. With the cloud overhead and the endless bitumen road, we felt like we were in a black and white movie. All through the Wimmera and more northerly Mallee country were roads signposted 'dry weather road only'. Some of them looked very rough and uncomfortable.

We were amazed at how many national parks and reserves there are in this country. In the next section of road, we passed through or near the Big Desert Wilderness Park (presumably larger than Little Desert), Ngarkat Conservation Park, Mount Shaugh Conservation Park, Red Bluff Flora and Fauna Reserve, Mount Rescue conservation Park and Scorpion Springs Conservation Park. If only we had time to visit each one.

After 133 kilometres of driving along virtually dead straight and barren road, we reached the town of Pinnaroo (*'big man'*), six kilometres inside South Australia, where we were to hang a right and head back east into Victoria and then north again into New South Wales. Pinnaroo's minor claims to fame are being home to South Australia's first community library and the Pinnaroo Institute, which houses the country's largest cereal collection (1,300 varieties). Gosh.

We drove into this standard medium sized country town – two or three pubs, butcher, newsagent, bakery, thrift shop, a few other small businesses and a few vacant shells all straddling a wide main road. One of the pubs was called the Golden Grain Hotel, highlighting the major output of this area, wheat. Wheat fields stretched as far as the eye could see, in various stages of growth. The newly planted paddocks had impressive rich red soil that would have contrasted well with a blue sky if so many grey clouds weren't covering it up.

Every town is built close to the highway, which itself is built along the train line. And every town has a train siding with massive grain silos. Several of the smaller towns (Cowangie, Galah and Boinka) seem to have a pub and a general store (which no doubt sells ammo) and that's about it. Several of them have two roads, one on either side of the highway, one with the town name followed by 'North' and the other with 'South'. There were many dry dams, so the rain must be welcome when it comes, and it looked like it was on its way.

On our way out of Pinnaroo, we stopped at a petrol station/roadhouse for lunch. It was obviously the coach stop as well. Weary travellers were scattered around the place, staring into the nothingness and looking very glum. No one looked interested (or interesting) and everyone was ignoring everyone else. It was a strange scene after getting used to friendly outback hospitality.

The sign said it was only 1,250 kilometres to Sydney. Not even tempting.

The drive along the Mallee Highway was a little monotonous, the road straight, and the environment unchanging, giving the impression that you're not actually getting anywhere. There were even tumbleweeds blowing across the road. We didn't see any mallee fowls on the road though, despite the warning signs.

At Ouyen (home to the Big Mallee Root), in the heart of the aptly named Sunset Country, we turned left and headed north. We were getting park withdrawal symptoms and drove the short distance to Hattah-Kulkyne National Park, which is linked to the Murray-Kulkyne Park. We pitched camp in the Murray-Kulkyne Park along the bank of the Murray under the swaying river red gums. We were bush camping (not in a formal campground) so we chose a designated urinal bush and kept the trowel handy in case of number twos.

Diary entry: 'We're in the middle of nowhere, only a few metres from the big brown Murray River, which divides NSW and Victoria. No fear of loutish school kids showing up here to spoil the atmosphere. The tents are up, dinner is simmering and a cleansing ale is going down a treat. This is still the life!'

The Murray River is part of one of the largest river systems in the world. It starts in the Snowy Mountains and meanders for 2,560 kilometres. The Murray basin stretches over four states and drains an area of more than one million square kilometres. That's about one seventh of the whole country. A few years after Hume and Hovell's visit in 1824, Sturt came along and named it the Murray after Sir George Murray, thinking it was a different river, and that's the name that stuck.

As we enjoyed the serenity under a spectacular display of stars, a small well-camouflaged scorpion crawled over my boot. I was vaguely excited to see a scorpion for the first time, until thinking about these and hundreds of other creepy crawlies, including ants the size of small Korean cars, scurrying around the place. I didn't envy Glen, whose tent zipper was stuffed.

The next morning, hundreds of parrots laughed at us as we packed up our equipment in the rain.

The riverside track through the park was badly corrugated so we headed back to the main road to resume our northerly trail. We drove through Red Cliffs, which is home to 'Big Lizzy', a very big tractor, and Mildura, a large country town producing lots of wine grapes and lots of oranges. 'Orange World' is there, along with the largest vineyard in the Southern Hemisphere (Lindemans) which proudly displayed a giant wine cask out front. Obviously hooked on 'bigs', Mildura is also home to the country's largest deck chair, providing a massive tourist drawcard for the motel that displays the chair in a heavily competitive accommodation market along the main road. Yet another claim to fame is the Workingmen's Club, which professes to have the longest bar in the world (92 metres). Unfortunately, we missed this amazing example of human ingenuity and thirst, a casualty of sloppy research. I'm sure the 27 beer taps would have drawn Glen in if we had known about it before we got there and I had to admit to being a little interested myself.

Mildura is in the heart of '*Sunraysia*' country and is brimming with 20,000 people, a lot of them Italian immigrants. Its name is thought to come from the Aboriginal word for 'red earth', although 'sore eyes caused by flies' is another possibility. You've got to admit that the natives have a certain knack for describing a place. Mildura's grapes and fruit are sold around the world, thanks to good soil and irrigation from the Murray. In fact, this was the place where Murray River irrigation was born. Its production of wine is tinged with irony because liquor was prohibited in the town's earlier days.

We gave in to temptation and visited the Mildara Blass winery. We only tried a couple of the locally grown products, a Chardonnay and Cab Shiraz/Cab Franc blend, both quite reasonable drops. We bought one of each and hit the trail north to Broken Hill, ready for the real outback experience.

10. Back of Bourke

From Mildura, we were travelling north on the Silver City Highway. Our excellent *Lonely Planet Outback Australia* travel guide described the road as 'one of the best introductions to the vastness and uniqueness of the Australian outback'. I couldn't agree more. The road was in quite good nick between Mildura and Broken Hill, but enjoy it while you can – it was a different story further north. This part of Australia is rich in history, thanks largely to the likes of explorers Charles Sturt and Burke and Wills, and at its heart is the big mining town of Broken Hill – the Silver City.

According to our map, it was exactly 300 kilometres from Mildura to Broken Hill. Early on, we drove through the town of Wentworth at the point where the Darling River, Australia's longest, meets the Murray and brushes the Vic/NSW border, snaking along the Murray. In 24 hours, we'd been in three different states.

There's a sameness to the drive up to Broken Hill, yet for me it's an interesting sameness. The soil is parched red, sporadically vegetated by low greeny-brown shrubs and the occasional gum tree, usually dead. This flat desert landscape stretches in all directions to a primary colour convergence of red land and blue sky. This is the view I've been waiting a long time to see. We were now positively girt by dirt.

The region's pastoral properties are gigantic, almost barren, tracts of land with little livestock to be seen, save for a few lonely sheep and a few dead sheep. A handful of very scrawny kangaroos was grazing by the side of the road where the vegetation was least sparse. Occasionally we'd see a flock of gangly emus looking into space with that confused look of theirs or running into the distance or straight towards a car. What really amazed and distressed us was the number of dead kangaroos by the side of the road. The first kangaroo sign we saw (riddled with bullet holes, of course) warned us of their presence for the next 240 kilometres. And boy, were there a lot of them, the majority dead by the side (or in the middle) of the road, which was also littered with dead sheep and skeletons of various other animals. I'm not kidding when I say that every few seconds we passed one in some stage of decay. The road smelt of decaying carcasses, and there was nothing we could do to avoid the stench. The crows were having a feast and seemed to be smarter than most other birds, flying clear of the road well before cars flatten them. Parrots and various other of your more stupid birds were often lucky not to become hood ornaments. Plenty must. Keeping watch for potentially hazardous wandering kangaroos certainly keeps one alert in this desolate and occasionally monotonous environment. Thankfully we collected nothing larger than bugs.

The weather for the drive was pretty average, with a few scattered light showers and a bit of sun. The rain was particularly annoying – just enough that the slowest wiper speed is that little bit too fast.

The land along the road was generally flat, but undulated a bit like a moderate ocean swell. Atop one of the waves, the Silver City finally appeared in front of us.

Broken Hill remains indubitably an industrial town, pumping out smoke from the scattering of tall chimneys. As the guidebooks say, Broken Hill is an oasis in the desert. It was the first time we'd seen anything really green in days. After checking in at the huge information centre and driving through the large and well pubbed main drag, we went to the local caravan park and lined up behind numerous other four-wheel drives for a spot. We were worried about getting a van or cabin but as it happened, most of the other travellers were camping. We couldn't get motivated enough to pitch our wet tents and wanted to give them a good clean and airing anyway.

The $35 cabin we got was decked out in relative luxury. We refrigerated the Esky contents, froze the ice blocks and cooked up a storm for dinner. We had spent a considerable amount of time before the trip deciding whether to go with an esky or battery-powered fridge and decided on the Esky, largely due to cost and space considerations. For the space both took up in the car, you could fit a lot more in the Esky. It was a bit of an inconvenience having to keep the esky cold enough, but we managed to always find ice when we needed it, often at an outback premium.

The air was very dry; nothing like the humidity we were used to back in Sydney. We took the opportunity to hang our tents on the washing line to dry off, which they did in minutes in the warm dry wind. We heard that the odd spots of rain over the previous days were the first they'd had in about two years. At least we could wander around in t-shirts at dusk, unlike the previous night, which was a chilly six degrees. No complaints from us!

Broken Hill is a surprisingly interesting place for a mining town in the middle of nowhere. Maybe that's part of the attraction. The tourist brochure called it 'The Accessible Outback'. It was also referred to as 'The Artback' and 'The Living Museum'. The 22,000 residents of the Silver City live about 1,200 kilometres by road from Sydney, 850 kilometres from Melbourne, 500 kilometres from Adelaide, and 50 kilometres from the South Australian Border. It's not like the rest of New South Wales, and isn't even in the same time zone.

Charles Sturt blazed a trail to the area, naming the hump-backed range, 'the Broken Hill'. In 1844 he nearly died of thirst there, and came back for more a year later. 40 years on, stockman Charles Rasp discovered silver nearby and staked out a claim of 16 hectares.

Not long after, he formed a syndicate with some of his mates and pegged out more land. With £15,000 and 6 mates, Rasp started up a mining company. That company, Broken Hill Proprietary Company, was to become the country's largest, and one of the world's great mining and steel-making companies.

Rasp became a very wealthy entrepreneur, eventually living in style in Adelaide until he died suddenly of a heart attack in 1907. Today his company lives on, as does his town, which still possesses the world's richest deposits of silver, lead and zinc.

Twenty-five kilometres from Broken Hill is the virtual ghost town of Silverton, which must come close to being the ultimate outback community. Silverton was settled in the late 19th century, with the population believed to have peaked at around 3,000 when the lead, silver and zinc mining was most prosperous. The population fell to 600 by the turn of the century and is now less than 100.

Silverton is in the middle of a visibly harsh desert environment. There's a house here and there, some stone ruins, a cemetery and a few art galleries. We visited two of the galleries, the old gaol which is now a very interesting museum and the famous Silverton Hotel. The Hotel has been used in numerous films and has gone by all sorts of names. The 'town' and its surrounds have attracted dozens of filmmakers and have featured in several films from Mad Max II to Priscilla, Queen of the Desert. A great XXXX beer ad was also shot here - the ute is loaded with several cartons of beer, a bottle of sherry is added for the wife, and the axle snaps. Obviously it's the wife's fault for ordering the sherry. Our guidebooks suggested that we take 'The Test' at the pub, which we did with an immense amount of curiosity and apprehension. Assorted celebrities have taken 'The Test' so we decided we had nothing to lose. Well, we both passed but I am unable to record what 'The Test' actually involved; suffice to say it's worth the challenge, but don't wear your Sunday best.

At the pub, we also had one of the tastiest and biggest hot dogs I've ever eaten, and washed it down with a middy of VB. It would have been a crime to come to such an outback pub and not have a beer, although being on the tourist trail detracts slightly from the authenticity. The pub's walls were lined with photos from the films shot in town, and were stacked with empty cans of every different beer ever produced in Australia. From the ceiling hung banners with adages such as 'If arseholes could fly this place would be an international airport' and 'Please don't ask for credit as a slap in the face often offends'. Bookshelves with second hand books for sale were almost out of place, but seemed to work with the decor. I bought an Isaac Asimov novel for $2 to go with my meal. Silverton Hotel stubby holders and cans of Aeroguard personal insect repellent also seemed to be big sellers.

The topic of conversation and level of excitement among the locals who were propped up at the bar in their rugged clothes was the few drops of rain starting to hit the iron roof like bullets, and the prospect of more decent falls. That's the way of life in the bush.

On the way out of town we checked out the cemetery, sparsely populated with some very well-preserved headstones and some that had been cracked and lay strewn over their residents. It was quite a chilling place; quiet, desolate and dead. Literally.

An early start (for us) to the next day was required to get to the School of the Air by 8:30. We just made it. For the grand sum of $2, it was a very interesting hour with the School, starting with an introduction by the principal, a video rundown of the school, roll call and assembly. The school was established in 1956 and at its peak in the 80s covered 1.3 million square kilometres and about 150 children from kindergarten to year six. Ten teachers and 70 students are now scattered around the region. The roll call had the dual purpose of checking who was present and to find out how well, if at all, the various individual VHF radios and relay towers were working. If a group from one area didn't respond, a technician had to be sent out to fix the area's tower. Telephones substitute for the radio in the meantime, but that's only if the phones are working.

The school was trying out a computer video link while we were there, enabling the teacher and students to see each other on their computer screens rather than using the ancient-looking scratchy radios, which reminded me of the old Skippy the Bush Kangaroo TV series. Communication will no doubt be greatly enhanced as satellites and internet are used rather than the traditional expensive and unreliable radio network.

The roll call was also time for a regional weather check to find out if the drought was being broken anywhere, and it seemed there were a few glimmers of hope around the place with some moderate falls overnight. I couldn't help but feel a sense of relief for the kids and their families.

The second half-hour of our visit contained the assembly, where two families prepared a brief programme to follow the singing of the national anthem and school song. Our special event was country music aerobics. I wonder if anyone actually jumped around with their radios in their hands. The singing of the national anthem was enchanting in a funny kind of way, thanks to the one-way radios used. When the kids pressed their radio transmitter buttons, they couldn't hear the music being played by the school so there were 70 kids singing in different keys and in different times and taking about 15 seconds to taper off at the end.

The isolation of these kids is broken with several events during the year, including education week, an athletics carnival and a music festival. At least once a year each student is visited by one of the teachers and when the kids are in Broken Hill they can sit in on regular school classes and not have to worry about unreliable and scratchy radio reception.

The visit was a great insight into outback life and what these kids and families go through to live on the land.

Driving through Broken Hill on our way north, we noticed that the road names reflected its mining heritage: Bromide St, Iodide St, Oxide St, Chloride St, Sulphide St, Crystal St, Cobalt St and many more criss-crossing the town. Another that caught our attention was Lane Lane. Very very funny funny.

There was plenty more to do in Broken Hill, including a multitude of small galleries, but we were anxious to delve further into the outback, away from civilization. After enquiring about road conditions at the information centre for our northward journey, we departed the Silver City. All relevant roads were open and in relatively good condition. Relative to what was the question.

11. Corner Country

The Silver City Highway north of Broken Hill is only intermittently sealed. Often the unsealed bits were in better condition than the sealed ones, with some rough exceptions. The road kill wasn't as bad but still occasionally grossed us out with the smell. We tried shutting the air vents if we spotted a dead roo in the distance but the stench usually permeated the car anyway. We saw plenty of living animals too. Most of the farms weren't fenced, so livestock was an additional obstacle on the roads.

We passed through yet another time zone because Broken Hill is on central Australian time but surrounding areas of New South Wales are on eastern standard or summer time.

Most of the environment we drove through was very arid, evidenced by an arid zone research centre to study the ecosystems of this unforgiving environment. Not one river or creek we drove past had a skerrick of water. This was good for us as there were no bridges along the highway – just dips, potholes and cattle grids. I guess the locals would have liked a good drenching though.

I understand that this sort of landscape bores some people to sobs and that there is a definite monotony about driving for hundreds of kilometres without much of a change of scenery, but I really love it. It is truly the outback and there's plenty of it. I love the road stretching off to the horizon and blending in with the surrounding land, barely different in colour and texture to the red dirt road. I love the hardy vegetation, often sparse and rarely green except for some pastel shades around some watercourses that must have an underground flow. I love the mirage effect that makes the distant land look like water. I love the way you can see the heat radiate from the ground, making the horizon shimmer. I love the colour of the wispy clouds that don't even threaten to bless the farmers with desperately needed moisture. The clouds are bright white but with lavender undersides. As far as I was concerned, this was utopia.

Further north and not far short of the NSW/Queensland border, Tibooburra seems to have more pubs than people but is a very welcoming outback town. As much as we would have liked to sit a spell in one of the hotels for the night and down a few cold ones on the veranda with the locals, our plan was to camp in the Sturt National Park.

Tibooburra is a longer way from anywhere than even Broken Hill. Its name means something like 'heaps of rocks'. The town's information brochure was very informative and witty but reproduction was discouraged so you'll have to take my word for it. The town looked old, homely and relaxed, and in hindsight, an overnight stop probably would have been worthwhile.

After topping up the petrol tank and checking in with the National Parks office, we took a photo of the infrequently used ramshackle but very photogenic Tobooburra outdoor cinema and drove into the park, which is essentially Tibooburra's back yard.

Charles Sturt was the first European to visit what is now Sturt National Park. The discovery of gold in 1880 brought thousands to the area and forced the Aborigines out, but the lode wasn't as prosperous as the optimistic prospectors had hoped. This, combined with a rough life and disease, resulted in the self-destruction of the gold rush within ten years. Pastoralists reclaimed some of the land until 1972 when the 344,000hectare national park was established.

Not wanting to get stuck with other campers, we chose Olive Downs, the most remote campsite, and deposited our $5 into the collection box. My tent was set up on the hard sandy ground between the skull of some previously cute furry animal and a few medium-sized trees that were handy as snoring and wind buffers.

The campsite dunnies here were top class commodes. We're talking lavatorial luxury for the outback, cleaner than several of the pubs and hostels we'd been to and for holes in the ground, they didn't smell one bit. I relieved myself in total comfort and style. Ahhhh.

Glen cooked up the leftover mince from last night's spag bol into a couple of tasty rissoles for dinner after we ambled up a nearby hill for some sunset pics. This was one of the most memorable moments of the trip for me. We traipsed up the 'jump-up' mesa with tripod and camera and just sat and soaked up the atmosphere. Though not far above the campsite, we were treated to awesome and endless views over the national park. All around us were barren gibber (red rock) plains blanketed with tufts of tall grass. From our rocky moonscape perch, we just sat and watched the sun sink slowly in the west, as old documentaries are wont to say. It would have been romantic for anyone but a couple of dusty sweating blokes, but we were undoubtedly appreciative of the occasion. As the sky advanced through its spectrum of pinks and oranges, the contrast with the rising pale bluish moon became more spectacular. Just after the sun fell below the horizon, the narrow strip of sky beneath the pink sphere covering the sky was a shade of brilliant blue I've never seen before. As the sun left us, so did the warm weather, so Glen returned to the campsite. I couldn't resist sitting there and taking in more of this wondrous outback experience until I got too cold to sit still; then I scurried down to Glen's hearty dinner.

There aren't many radio stations to listen to in these parts, but the radio still played an important role in our trip. Eating soup at the card table, shivering from the desert winter's chill, warming up with a soothing bottle of red, and listening to the ubiquitous ABC local radio will be one of my fondest memories of the trip. At Sturt National Park we found 3WM – Radio Wimmera Mallee which kept us going through Little Desert and Murray country. It played some decent music and kept us up to date with local weather forecasts. Not that weather reports were necessary - it was hot and dry by day and cold and dry at night.

After dinner and visit to the pee tree, I snuggled into my cosy sleeping bag and drifted off to the music of the desert.

Our first bit of excitement for the next day was driving briefly along the famed dingo fence, the longest fence in the world. It was originally built to keep the rabbits out but by the time it was finished there were equal numbers of rabbits on each side, so it is now used to keep dingoes out of the southern sheep country. The fence creeps along the NSW-Queensland border over the undulating desert landscape and begs for a photo or two. The twisted and patched rusty wire is juxtaposed beautifully against the brilliant blue sky and orange-red earth.

The unsealed road we took from the campsite, the Middle Road, was in better condition than many of the highways we had travelled. Two words together are of prime importance when driving through the outback: 'just' and 'graded'. According to the ranger in Tibooburra the Middle Road was just graded and in good condition.

Sturt National Park is known for its mixture of red and grey kangaroos. We saw both, and plenty of them. I mean, we've seen a lot of roos on this trip, but I think on our first day in Sturt, we saw at least as many as I've ever seen in my life, and they were all alive too, grazing peacefully as Australian symbols are supposed to do.

We also saw numerous emus, a particularly gangly, clumsy, and let's face it, stupid looking bird when it runs, if not at all times. If only it had arms it would look a lot less awkward. It's the second largest bird on the planet and perhaps the daftest, but as the John Williamson song says, it can run the pants off a kangaroo. Its scientific name means 'swift-footed bird of New Holland'. And they can really make a mess of your windscreen. So here we have our coat of arms: the emu and the kangaroo. Both will run in front of an oncoming vehicle rather than the opposite direction and you can often find one of each lying dead on either side of the road. Don't we have more intelligent animals to stick on the coat of arms? I'd like the suave-looking and perennially mirthful kookaburra. Maybe even a koala. At least koalas have the excuse of being stoned on eucalyptus leaves.

Other bird life was restricted (from what we saw) to flocks of small birds which zipped in front of the car so fast we couldn't see what they looked like, large flocks of Major Mitchell cockatoos, and the occasional wedge-tailed eagle. The eagles were massive, with wingspans of at least a couple of metres and they have to be the most graceful animals on the planet. It's a real pleasure watching them wheel and soar above the road searching for some unsuspecting live victim or fresh road kill.

There weren't many trees more than about two metres tall, but those which were – dead or alive – had at least one bird's nest wedged in their branches. I was amazed at the number of nests. It was certainly high density living in the outback.

The end of Glen's driving stint was at Cameron Corner, the point at which the borders of South Australia, New South Wales and Queensland meet. Scottish surveyor John Cameron surveyed the spot in 1880. It seems he was spot on, even back then, so they named it after him. It is the home to the Corner Store, which sells petrol, a ripper of a meat pie, soft drinks and 'icy cold beer'. It also has flushing toilets - for us a welcome novelty at that point in the journey.

Before leaving, I had to get a photo of Glen running around the border post, covering three states in five seconds.

From there it was my turn to take the wheel as we returned to South Australia and continued heading north. The road started well, but gradually deteriorated to a bone jarring mess. As far as we could see, there was just red sand, some gangly trees and a patchwork of grasses perched along or between the long parallel dunes over which we were driving. It was like a roller coaster ride. The road was badly corrugated in most places, with potholes and soft spots of bulldust hidden by the deceptive red sand. You can't see what is coming over the other side of the dunes except an occasional rising plume of dust. We passed one car travelling in the opposite direction (a Britz Australia rental van) and overtook a four-wheel drive labouring with a caravan over the dunes. They were the only signs of life apart from an abandoned roadwork outpost complete with satellite dish.

When we finally got to the Strzelecki Track, we needed a break, some water and a headache pill. Glen took over the driving and the road was substantially better, except for being a road train route. We quickly learnt that you just have to pull over and the massive triple-trailer trucks roar past because the dust they whip up drops visibility to a couple of metres. Also, the road shoulders are too soft to drive on and there are white posts about a metre into the road which you can't see in a dust cloud. The road is wide though, and driving down the middle avoids the corrugations near the shoulder and is obviously the most common practice in driving the Track. Part of the road was being graded, so a growing stretch of it was in excellent condition.

On his search for the inland sea, our old friend Charles Sturt came along here in 1845 and 'discovered' and named the Strzelecki Creek after Count Paul Edmond de Strzelecki, a polish-born geologist and explorer. For most Australians these days, Strzelecki's claim to fame was climbing and naming our highest mountain, Mt Kosciuszko in 1840. It doesn't appear that he came this far inland. I'm not sure if I'd want this nightmare of a track named after me, but the Strzelecki Track it is. It runs 460 kilometres up from Lyndhurst on the northern rim of the Flinders ranges (560 kilometres north of Adelaide) to Innamincka, still in South Australia.

The track was used in 1870 by the infamous Captain Starlight to drive his 1,000 stolen cattle 1,300 kilometres through the desert from Queensland to South Australia. When he arrived, he sold them for 5,000 guineas hoping that the cattle brand would not be recognised. But pastoralists in Queensland discovered the tracks and realised they were missing a few cattle. He was found out when an imported bull he had sold was returned to Queensland and recognised. Starlight was captured and tried but despite a strong case, he somehow managed to persuade the jury of his innocence and was set free.

We drove past Moomba in SA, which is easily the largest onshore petroleum producer in the country. Natural gas is piped from there to Sydney, Canberra and Adelaide. It's an odd outpost in the middle of the Strzelecki Desert, which outsiders are not permitted to enter.

When we finally arrived in the tiny settlement of Innamincka in South Australia's northeast late in the day (getting all the way to Birdsville in a day was excessively ambitious), we were turned away from the pub and the hotel next door. The tourist coach which was just pulling up outside had booked out all the beds in 'town'. Rather than fork out $60 for a park camping pass we drove a short distance away to the Town Common where for $5 you could camp by Cooper Creek amongst river red gums and coolabah trees and hundreds of screeching cockatoos.

The prominent coolabah, or river ghost gum was an important part of the Aboriginal way of life, as well as of 'Waltzing Matilda'. Its leaves were used to poison fish, the roots were used for water and the bark used as a cure for snakebites. We found ourselves a pleasant spot on the edge of the river and set up camp. As we began getting our cooked dinner under way, our hitherto trusty gas stove fell apart and burst into flames. So after a cold dinner, we sat by the Creek enjoying the mild weather as the waning moon rose on the eastern horizon and the magnificent pink sunset faded for another day.

Innamincka (population approx. 13) is about as small as a country community gets, but it sits in the massive 13,800 square kilometre Innamincka Regional Reserve. To the resident Aborigines Innamincka was 'my shelter'. To the famously misguided explorers Burke and Wills it is a permanent shelter – it's where they both came to grief. From 1929 to 1951, a nursing home at Innamincka served the surrounding 12,000 square kilometres and was one of the few buildings on the site, along with a pub and police station. In 1994, the nursing home was restored by the Australian Geographic Society and is now a tourist attraction.

The long day's drive allowed us both a solid night's sleep. That is until hundreds of parrots saw to it that we both woke up before the alarm went off at seven with their chalk-on-blackboard screeching. That gave us a head start and we were under way shortly after eight after watching a spectacular sunrise. And that was early for us.

From town, we drove about 75 kilometres to the famous 'Dig Tree', where explorers Burke and Wills were beaten by the outback. Robert O'Hara Burke was an Irishman who came to Australia in 1853. He started out in Tasmania and then moved up to the Victorian goldfields where he became a police inspector. In 1860, he was chosen to lead an expedition from Melbourne through the guts of Australia to the Gulf of Carpentaria on the northern coast of the continent. His second in command was William John Wills, a Brit who came to Australia in 1852 and became a surveyor and meteorologist. Sixteen other men and 25 camels took off from Melbourne on the treacherous and controversial journey. In February 1861 Burke, Wills, Charles Gray and John King made it to the Gulf. On their way up, they had strategically hidden supplies for the return journey. When the party arrived at the Cooper Creek site, Gray had already perished and it looked as if the other three would suffer the same fate: the depot party had abandoned the site, supposedly only hours before the explorers arrived. A small amount of supplies had been left at the tree and the party didn't waste time continuing southwards. Friendly Aborigines helped them survive, but not long enough. Burke and Wills died in July 1861 and King was later found alive by a search party. A Royal Commission into the deaths was highly critical of the party's leadership, judgement, poor planning and general conduct. As it happened, the search parties gathered more valuable scientific information on the desert country than did the expedition.

A couple of the old coolabahs still have some writing and a likeness of one of the explorers clearly carved into their trunks. A local let us in on a secret to wet the carvings to enhance the results of our photos. The

Dig Tree has the characters 'DIG 3FT NW APR 21 1861' carved in its trunk. It's in a very peaceful location on the riverbank, now within a large cattle station. While there, I snapped some great photos of a huge brown wedge-tailed eagle keeping watch over its turf from a bone-white dead tree. My approach and shooting didn't seem to bother it.

Before we left, a bloke drove up in a ute with a little dachshund on the back. This struck us as a very un-outback dog and we wondered if his neighbours ribbed him about his poor excuse for a dog. It couldn't even jump into the back of the ute by itself. He asked if we had seen three white Toyota Landcruisers, one with a green canopy, in our travels from Innamincka as someone was trying to get a message to them. At first, we thought he was joking because most cars in the outback are white Landcruisers, but he was serious and we hadn't noticed them, but said we'd keep a lookout. Not even this bloke's mate, who went out in his aeroplane looking for them, could spot the small convoy.

Before leaving, we asked the chatty bloke if we could bypass Innamincka on the way to Birdsville to avoid backtracking. He showed us how to get to the recently graded track via Arrabury, which involved a short section through Queensland, back into South Australia and then finishing off in Queensland again. We took his advice and it was an enjoyable drive through a sparse landscape down a generally sandy but relatively easy road through several burnt-out areas offering a spectacular contrast between the deep red sand, blackened trees and rich blue sky. We were quite impressed and took a couple of photos to prove it. The latter part of the road hadn't seen a grader in a long time, but was still in quite good nick. In fact, it didn't look to carry much traffic at all - it narrowed to one lane in some places due to trees growing on the edges, and in some cases in the middle of the track.

From Arrabury we had the choice of two tracks north. The longer road was supposed to be in quite good condition, but added 110 kilometres to the trip and was not direct. We decided on the shorter Cordillo Downs road, which the bloke we met at the Dig Tree described as 'a dog's breakfast,' but that we would be able to get through. He'd heard that even caravans were coming down it, but he wasn't sure how.

'Dog's breakfast' was an appropriate description. 'Completely shithouse' would be another apt portrayal. And it was my turn to drive too.

We wasted an hour (and some very expensive fuel) by missing the turnoff to the Cordillo Downs Road because the inconspicuous sign faced the opposite direction. Luckily, further up the very sandy road we were on, a sign confirmed our suspicions that we were heading back down to Innamincka. We decided that it pays to look at your compass while driving.

The Cordillo Downs Road is so called because it traverses Cordillo Downs station, once the largest sheep station in Australia but now a Hereford cattle stud. Our *Explore Australia by 4WD* book rates the track 'difficult'. The station is in the thick of the Sturt Stony Desert, named after the explorer and the fact that it is made up of stones and not much else except desert. Most of the stones are *gibber*, a word descending from the Aboriginal word for stone. They're smooth red rocks, which, when broken by heavy trucks or graders, make small shards as sharp as glass that completely stuff your suspension, tyres and sanity. The desert is bordered by the Diamantina and Warburton Rivers and Cooper Creek and sits baking in the harsh sun between the Simpson and Strzelecki deserts. It is big, red, rocky and according to Sturt, had 'no parallel on the earth's surface'. It reminded me of the images sent back to Earth by the Mars rovers. Except for a few spots around dried creek beds, there was no plant - or other - life. A couple of small reflective billabongs were welcome sights.

Much of the trail was particularly rough, littered with gibber and carved by very bad erosion. Most of the bad spots could be seen in advance, but a few soft spots and hidden ditches in the middle of a good stretch of road caught us unawares. You soon learn to take it easy. The river crossings were the roughest but thankfully for us were dry. The Beast and our emotional health were getting a good workout.

Eventually my jarred bones and throbbing head told me to take a break from driving so after a short leg stretch, Glen took over until we reached the good quality Birdsville Development Road. Even before that, as soon as we crossed the border into Queensland (for the second time that day) the road was infinitely better and we could drive safely at about 90kph. This seemed to be a recurring experience – cross the border into SA and the roads instantly deteriorated.

We drove past a place called Durrie. Glen got out to have a smoke.

We were both getting frustrated with a longer than expected drive. Back on the road, we hoped that every turn (not that there were many) would present a view of the famed outback town of Birdsville. Finally, civilisation was in sight, and thankfully a civilisation known for its pub with good food and great beer.

12. Down By the Billabong

Weary and gritty from the enveloping dust, we drove into Birdsville at dusk. Unfortunately, we were travelling west into the blinding sunset and there was nothing to block the view until the sun hit the distant dusty horizon. It had been a very long and thirsty day and we were wondering if we were ever going to make it, but it was a fantastically rugged experience and a memorable day. We just kept going and going. We had driven further than the last Birdsville sign told us we needed to and the fuel light was getting on my nerves, along with everything else.

Finally, after the sun fell below the horizon and yet another wonderful sunset had faded, we passed the famous Birdsville Race Track and made it to the outskirts of town with equally low fuel and energy. We'd been driving over some horrible roads for about ten hours, with regular short stops, and were more than ready for a cold beer, warm shower and real bed. Ergo, we headed straight to the Birdsville Hotel.

There are two parking lots outside the Hotel - one for cars and the other for planes. Seriously. We kept with tradition, parked in the car park and stumbled into the welcoming bar.

I tried a thirst-quenching West End Draught, which I quite enjoyed, although I think even a XXXX would have hit the mark. A beer has honestly never tasted as good, and probably never will again. There was a lot of dust to wash down. How we were still talking to each other at the end of this day I don't know, but we were still managing bloke jokes as we rolled into town and settled in at the bar.

While speedily downing a couple of brews, we chatted to a bohemian drifter who had been travelling around the country for several months and showed no signs of stopping. He did sketches along the way to earn a few bob and was obviously a fan of the outback, a part of the attraction of the outback and fun to meet - a little weird but some great insights on life and fascinating stories. If we'd been thinking straight, we would have asked him to sketch us with the Beast.

Soon after we arrived, the amiable barman asked us for the time, and both of our watches were wrong. And covered in dirt. It's hard keeping track of what time it is when you hop from one state to another several times in a day.

We briefly checked out our pleasant but expensive motel-style twin room, unpacked a few things, charged some batteries, put the freezer blocks in the freezer and proceeded back to the bar for dinner. No matter how tightly you seal containers, the dust gets in. There was fine bulldust on and in everything, including us.

Glen, in his never-ending search for the country's best mixed grill, ordered the Birdsville version and I had an excellent marinated T-bone. Both of us were very impressed with our eleven-buck outlay. I ranked it as one of the best steaks I've ever eaten. All up, Birdsville had treated us well so far. I topped the steak off with a pretty good tiramisu, but Glen was sated by his MG.

As with most country pubs, watching the patrons is part of the experience and fun, especially the locals, who usually stand out. I've never seen so many sweat-stained and worn out Akubra hats in one place in my life. Everyone wore them, new and old. Naturally, mine stays on at all times, partly because it was covered in Aeroguard to keep the ubiquitous flies away. In addition to those being worn, there was an impressive collection of old hats on the walls, as well as a mass of paraphernalia hanging from the ceiling. One sign proclaimed that

'This is Australia. Wearing a baseball cap backwards incurs a $2 fine to the Royal Flying Doctor Service'.

The Royal Flying Doctor Service of Australia is a not-for-profit charitable service that flies around providing medical services, communication and education support to people who live, work and travel in regional and remote Australia. It's a great cause that relies heavily on donations. Most outback pubs encourage visitors to make a contribution, a request with which we were happy to comply on several occasions.

Hardly able to move after dinner, we sauntered back to our room and I collapsed within seconds of hitting the pillow. It was a long and exhausting day, but one of the most memorable of the journey.

Birdsville has to be the ultimate outback town. It is a whole 48 metres above sea level and gets about a metre of rain each year. That's why they have to get their boiling town water from an artesian bore well over one kilometre deep. Not too much has changed since it was founded as a village in 1873. The original settlers had travelled a couple of thousand kilometres from Brisbane and wanted to name the settlement Burtsville after its first settler, J. Burt. He wasn't too keen on the idea so they compromised on Birdsville.

Birdsville is still Queensland's most isolated town and home to about 100 people. Before the turn of the century, Birdsville had three pubs, three stores, a cordial factory, a border customs post, and almost three times as many people as it now has. Men carried guns for protection and cattle duffing was commonplace, as was illegal transportation of various commodities. Federation in 1901 was a difficult time for Birdsville as the toll on cattle crossing the border was abolished. But the town survived that, in addition to drought, flood and wind storms, not to mention the annual Birdsville Races.

The Birdsville Races are held in September each year and expand the town's population to about 5,000. From what we heard, more than a few of the locals leave town, and much prefer the less populated race meetings of other towns in the region.

There's not too much in the way of accommodation in Birdsville. During the races, people who fly in just throw a tarpaulin over the aircraft wing or pitch a tent on the tarmac across the road from the pub. The alternative accommodation to the pub is the campground just down the road. Everything in Birdsville is just down the road. It's not a big place.

One of our guidebooks listed at the top of the 'Things to do' list, 'getting drunk'. We saw plenty of people having a refreshing beer or two, but no one too inebriated.

The locals are friendly as are the other travellers passing through. The Aborigines and others seemed to get on well and while we were in town there was a fair bit of work being done by the townsfolk in the Aboriginal community.

The shower at the hotel was a welcome treat, although the hot and cold water were the same temperature – lukewarm. After three days without a decent soaking, we each had a conglomerate of dust and sweat forming a glue over our bodies. And the car wasn't smelling all that good either.

Freshly cleansed, we visited the Birdsville Working Museum (just down the road, of course). This was a fascinating place, and indeed a *working* museum. The owner, John Menzies, gave a few of us a tour of the place. The insightful tour included demos of much of the antique farm equipment, including a small cardboard record player, a working horse wheel, used to turn bails of hay into chaff (using a Clydesdale named Prince), an ingenious water pump from England, a vigorous butter churn from the turn of the century and several other unique and innovative inventions from times long past.

The museum owner specialised in restoring old horse drawn coaches and had several on display. There were several old signs on the walls, and old Kellogg's Cornflakes and Rice Bubbles packets that looked like they should have disintegrated decades ago. One of my favourites was a rare *Bushell's Tea* billy can. There was a collection of tobacco boxes, including a couple with the following advice: 'Does not affect heart or throat. No bite – no cough'. Truth in advertising obviously wasn't a big deal back then, or else tobacco research wasn't what you could call advanced. We saw early fridges, phones, hospital equipment, farm equipment, irons and manual washing machines and dryers. We saw a moustache mug which had a small guard across the top so as to avoid one's moustache becoming moistened by one's tea, and a milk jug shaped in the likeness of Don Bradman. The handle was shaped like a cricket bat. Of course. We saw an original May Gibbs Gum Blossom Babies painting, and a bit of Melbourne Olympics memorabilia.

Another highlight was the antique Furphy water tank. During World War I, solders would gather around the Furphy water tank telling yarns, many of them apocryphal, and so came the phrase, 'to tell a furphy'. You've probably heard Furphy's old motto: 'Good, better, best; never let it rest until your good is better and your better best'. Originally made by John Furphy's fledgling but diverse manufacturing operation in Victoria in the late eighteen hundreds, the company *J. Furphy and Sons* continues to produce water carts, storage tanks and large industrial products.

You can only go to so many historical museums in one period, but this one was a corker. Afterwards we drove around the corner to the spacious campground and pitched our tents under a few small eucalypts near the billabong. There wasn't a cloud in the sky and the heat was strong enough, but thankfully nothing like the literally scorching summer temperatures. We strolled up to the service station for a loaf of 'sun baked bread' which really tasted and felt sun baked. It was, however, frozen so we had to sun bake it a little more to thaw it out. That took all of a minute, and then we made a couple of sandwiches for a peaceful lunch by the billabong. Glen thought I looked like a real fashion victim in my hiking boots and socks, shorts, t-shirt, fly veil and wide-brimmed hat but I felt like I fit right in.

After lunch, a read, updating the journal and just sitting around soaking in the serenity, we went for a stroll through town. As usual, the bar was lined with several interesting locals. We chatted to an old bloke for a while. I would love to have snapped a photo of this classic outback character; he was a big old country type with big red nose, chiselled brown face and a typically well-worn hat. Unfortunately, he was also deaf as a post, so the conversation didn't get very far.

Two doubtful blokes with matching track suits and sheepskin boots were back from the previous night, and one young guy we had picked for either a pilot or doctor turned out to be an electrician. We were told by the barman that the planes parked across the road often belonged to people travelling the country by air – Australia in six days. Some people fork out $7,000 for the experience, much to the amusement of the locals. There was another mob coming in that evening. Another of the planes belonged to a council member whom I was told flew around like most of us drive. I guess it's a bit tricky if your constituents live so far apart.

We went back to the campsite for the sunset. Under the pink sky, the opposite side of the billabong was lined with tall trees blanketed with thousands of ear piercing Cockatoos and galahs. The general noise was bad enough, but when one of the several eagles circling overhead came down for a rest (or a meal) in one of the trees, the sky turned white with shit-scared birds and the noise was deafening. Something told me we were in for another early start.

As predicted, the birds were up early the next day, including the crow that crapped on my tent and tried drinking beer out of the empties outside our tents. Glen swears he saw one falling about, drunk.

After packing the car, we enjoyed a hearty breakfast cooked by the owner of the campground and were intrigued by some of the local gossip we heard over brekkie. Our confusion about the distances on signs was laid to rest when she confirmed that none of them was terribly accurate. You've got to be prepared for just about anything and expect nothing in the outback.

13. Back Tracking

Time for one of the most enthusiastically anticipated parts of our trip – the Birdsville Track. The Track follows an old stock route from Queensland's channel country to the Adelaide cattle market. The Track now begins at Birdsville and stretches 517 kilometres south to Marree in South Australia. For our journey it was in good repair, allowing for a smooth and swift trip. It was almost too smooth. We weren't roughing it quite as much as we had expected, but the Cordillo Downs road and Strzelecki Track made up for it, and made us appreciate the easy Birdsville run.

While the road may have been relatively easy on the car, our bones and our temperament, the environment was harsh. The land surrounding us in all directions was truly desolate - flat, red, and covered with little other than rocks and the occasional tuft of resilient grass. We were surprised to spot a dingo prowling along the roadside in such an environment. The gangly dog just stood there staring at us while we stopped and snapped a couple of photos. How he survived in such a barren place is a mystery. There wasn't a tree in sight – where did he pee?

We were lucky – the Track is not always in such good repair, but there were still some patches of bulldust to catch out the unwary driver. We passed the Clifton Hills cattle station, once one of the largest in the world at more than 23,000 square kilometres. Now it's a mere half that size, but still bloody big (New York City is 20,000 square kilometres and houses over 20 million people). The section of road from Birdsville to the station is known as the outer track. It was built in the 1960s to bypass the massive Goyder Lagoon, mainly for the sake of the leviathan road trains that hurtle down the track. Along this section is *Dead Man's Sandhill*, named for five stockmen from Innamincka who didn't make it to the Birdsville Races in 1912. It was also the final resting-place of a tourist family whose car didn't survive the trip. No one knew to expect them, they had insufficient water supplies, and they made the big mistake of leaving their car when it conked out – an absolute no-no in outback survival. Unfortunately for them, traffic was much less frequent back then.

Which brings us to our next adventure. As we drove along the trail, a couple of blokes flagged us down in the middle of nowhere. It turned out that they had two punctures simultaneously and had run out of spares. We had no room in the car for passengers, so after some negotiation, we decided to try our spare on their larger car, meaning there would be no spares for the two cars until the next road house 150 kilometres away. They agreed to give it back if we lost a tyre on the way. The wheel fit but the tyre was slightly smaller. Not a problem for the short trip and not much in the way of alternatives anyway.

Before we got on our way from the dry creek bed in which our new friends had come to grief, one of them ducked into the scattering of trees by the road. We assumed he was taking a quick leak, but he emerged seconds later with a shotgun in his hand. After nearly taking a leak ourselves (in our pants), he assured us he was just passing time by taking pot shots at an old plastic container until help arrived. We laughed it off and jumped in the car for a slow ride south to Mungeranie Roadhouse.

Time passed quickly with jokes going both ways over the radio, and with the others being in front, we had warnings about bad patches of road, bad cattle grids or oncoming traffic.
It felt good that the CB was actually in operation for some useful communication for once.

As we approached the Mungerannie Roadhouse we were greeted by signs every few hundred metres proclaiming 'cold beer', 'burgers', 'cold beer', 'tyres', 'cold beer', and 'hot dogs'. The roadhouse was run by a friendly couple who whipped up a mean hot dog and their beer was indeed cold; just right to wash down the dust as we waited to get our wheel and tyre back. While we were in the roadhouse, one of our new friends came around to tell us that our spare that they were using was now flat as well. They had just made it to the roadhouse, but now all the tyres were patched and we got on our way to Marree. They promised to buy us a thankyou beer if we met them in the Marree pub.

Before leaving the roadhouse, we called the caravan park at Marree from a solar powered public phone to book an on-site van, which suited our needs. We were warned to stay away from town and particularly the pub as there was to be a big Aboriginal funeral the next day with people coming from all over the place to mourn. It was going to be a heavy night in Marree.

From Mungerannie the Birdsville Track slices between the Strzelecki Desert to the east and the Tirari Desert to the west. Then, next door to the Tirari Desert, is Lake Eyre. It's worth mentioning some of the features of the Tirari, just for the challenge of pronouncing them: Lake Kittakittaooloo, Lake Ngapakaldi, Lake Puntawolona, Lake Killalpaninna and Lake Palankarinna. Then there was the Cannuwaukaninna Bore, one of the foul-smelling sulphurous bores beside the road.

Lake Eyre is one of the most fascinating features of the country. It's a mostly dry salt lake that sits 15.2 metres below sea level, the lowest point in Australia. It's the country's largest salt lake, the largest saltpan in the world and permanently holds about 500 million tonnes of salt. That's a hell of a lot of salt. The crusted surface covers over 9,000 square kilometres, and the lake is served by one of the world's biggest internal drainage systems at 1.2 million square kilometres or about 15 per cent of the whole country. Unfortunately, we just missed out on the fourth time it was filled with water in 150 years – apparently it's quite a spectacle with an active ecosystem under the water encouraging huge numbers of birds.

Lake Eyre South was discovered by Edward John Eyre in 1840. The larger Lake Eyre wasn't discovered until 18 years later. It's a pity Eyre didn't keep going; this was the inland sea he was looking for. Another one of Lake Eyre's claims to fame is as the site for Englishman Donald Campbell's land speed record, set in 1964.

After lengthy deliberations, we decided not to take the significant detour to see the dry lake and all its salt because our good Samaritan act had put back our schedule a bit, not that we had much of a schedule. So, on we went to Marree, known at the time to most Australians because of the 'Marree Man', an outline of a man cut into pasture that stretched several kilometres, only distinguishable from the air. I'm not sure if they ever discovered who made it, but I'm reasonably sure it wasn't aliens in flying saucers as many people speculated.

We were now 645 kilometres from Adelaide. We were closing in on civilisation but weren't there yet. Marree is where the Birdsville and Oodnadatta tracks meet and in its heyday was truly a frontier town. It was settled in 1883 and in no time had a population of 600. Stockmen brought cattle from throughout the outback to load onto the Great Northern Railway to Port Augusta. The area was also a stop for dozens of Afghani cameleers. The camel trains delivered supplies to outlying areas and many of the camel drivers lived at Marree. The town became known as 'Ghantown' and the Adelaide to Darwin train as the Ghan, short for Afghan. Ironically, the Ghan train, recently extended from

Alice Springs to Darwin, finished off most of the camel driving business long ago.

One of the town's main points of interest is a large sundial in the shape of a camel and made from old railway sleepers. The Marree Camel Cup, which is held in June of odd-numbered years, draws big crowds. The Outback Ball is held on the even numbered years at nearby Curdimurka (basically just a railway siding) and brings in revellers from all around to raise money for the Gahn Railway Preservation Society. It's a big social gathering that draws all sorts of people from all over the place. They dress up in tuxedos and evening gowns and afterwards walk, stumble or crawl to their car, tent or plane. There's no hotel or motel, but there is a landing strip and free campground. In the meantime, you can check out the old truck used by local legend Tom Kruse for mail deliveries up the Birdsville Track.

In the outback, one of the aspects advertised by caravan parks is 'shade'. It's a key enticement and there's not much of it around. But the trouble with camping under eucalypts is that they are notorious for dropping huge branches onto unsuspecting campers sheltering from the scorching outback sun. We opted for a van in Marree so we didn't have to worry on this occasion.

We pulled into town late in the day and as we unpacked the car, we noticed a deflating rear tyre. Another close call.

The problem was, Glen needed some smokes and for that we needed to go into town. So we sprayed some tyre repair spray into the sick-looking tyre and nursed the car into town. The only place open was the pub, we immediately bumped into our friends from the Birdsville Track and they bought us a drink for our troubles. There were several Aboriginal men in the bar, and a couple of cheerful and friendly

Afghans. We chatted for a while but became increasingly concerned by an increasingly rowdy mob outside. Tempers appeared to be getting frayed and the activity was right next to our car. Unfortunately, the warnings we'd received earlier were coming to fruition. We bade farewell to our friends and went back to the van for some of Glen's home cooked dinner while listening to the cricket on the radio. Glen chatted to our friendly neighbour while venturing outside for a smoke. He was a Maori lay preacher who was in town to conduct the Aboriginal funeral on the following day.

We started the next day with a tyre repair. Luckily the caravan park owner had a good supply of tyres, tubes and patches. The whole process was completed under the watchful gaze of the park dog and a handsome red-headed grey stork-like brolga. The bird and dog seemed to get on well most of the time until we were about to leave when the chest height brolga started jumping up and down and flapping its big wings at us. Brolgas are famed for their mating dances. Maybe it took a fancy to one of us. Then the dog started snatching at it. They liked to compete for photos. Being so close to such a large bird was a rare opportunity and I snapped a great photo of Glen staring out the bird.

On the way through town we filled up the tank and checked out the unique camel sundial. Unfortunately, the clouds that had dropped a light rain overnight precluded us from confirming the time from the sundial, but our watches told us we were running late. Well, we thought we were, but we still weren't sure what time zone we were in and what day or date it was. In other words, we were settling nicely into the outback lifestyle.

Despite our guidebooks proclaiming that this was the real Aussie outback, we hit a sealed road not far away at Lyndhurst and for us that was effectively civilisation.

Other drivers this far south were reactive rather than proactive wavers, if they even bothered to wave at all. Further inland everyone waves. Down here, traffic isn't a novelty and they don't make the effort.

Before getting to Lyndhurst we stopped at an ochre pit, a naturally multicoloured formation mined by local Aborigines for painting and trading. It was a big hole in the ground several dozen metres across and a few metres down. The white, red, yellow and brown ochre was traded by tribes from the southern to the northern coast.

South of Lyndhurst, we caught a great view of the spectacular, vast and jagged Flinders Ranges, shaded hazy pastel purple with cloud stretched over their length almost to the horizon, as though they were a watercolour backdrop on a giant stage.

Watercourses in the area had some great names that seemed more creative than the standard Eight Mile Creek or the ubiquitous Stony Creek: Deception Ck, Trebilcock Ck, Bitter Springs, Manners Ck, Weetowie Ck, Lame Horse Ck, Screech Owl Ck, Deadman Ck, Blackfellow Ck, Loch Ness Well, Breakfast Time Ck, No Name Ck, Eating House Ck, and Black Swamp Ck. Not one of them was crossed by a bridge - the roads just dipped, presumably making them virtually impassable after heavy rain.

Well into Flinders territory in southeast South Australia, we checked into the Flinders Caravan Park in Hawker ('gateway to the Flinders Ranges') where a very enthusiastic lady gave us heaps of material on the area and showed us to our caravan with TV and private adjoining shower/bathroom. The weather didn't look promising so we were still not interested in camping, not that it took much to influence our decision. The caravan park was a bit out of town and had the feeling of being out in the middle of nowhere, which suited us down to the red ground. Some might have said that we were, indeed, still in the middle of nowhere.

After settling in, we headed into town to find some dinner. While planning to just drop in briefly at the pub, our stop off ended up dragging on for two or three hours while we chatted to the publican about Hawker life, bush driving and outback pubs. Another insightful visit. It seemed to be customary in outback pubs that if you hang around for a while and chat to the staff, the bar shouts you a drink. However, since we had lost a beer in the Hawker bar challenge we were even. The publican reckoned he would have bought us one anyway. He was a friendly bloke with a couple of pleasant barmaids taking all sorts of crap from the increasingly inebriated and intermittently jocular locals.

I realise that it sounds like we were obsessed with drinking at pubs, but often they were the only place in town to get food (or the only place that looked safe to eat at) and they are almost always the best place in town to mingle with the locals and learn about their lives and the ways of the outback. I'd be lying if I didn't also say that a beer at the end of a long day's drive or walking was pretty darn tasty.

On the next day, we headed straight into the National Park. The 95,000-hectare park takes in some of the 430-kilometre-long range and an array of animals including more than 100 bird species. Its diverse environments include everything from flat sandy plains to pastel coloured rolling mountain ranges with barren desert and thick forest. Some parts of the Flinders Ranges have been dated at 1.6 billion years old, making them among the oldest places on the planet. I'm not quite sure what that means though – how can one part of the planet be older than another?

The southern part of the park contains the much-photographed Wilpena Pound, a large crater of solid rock covering 83 square kilometres with a lush and unique environment nestled in its centre. The first European to visit the area was William Chance in 1850. Within a year, the bowl was used as pasture for sheep and horses. A small homestead built in 1889 still sits at the bottom. Well before Bill got there, Matthew Flinders spotted the ranges from his ship *Investigator* in 1802 when he sailed into Spencer Gulf. There's also plenty of rock art in the area by its original inhabitants.

We drove through a couple of dry high-walled gorges that put The Beast through its paces. The ancient mountains, in common with the Grampians, are huge extrusions pushed up at angles all pointing in the same direction like waves of rock. The Flinders though, have more of a desert feel - redder and sparser. With the morning sun on the mountains, they were a spectacular palette of colour through a light haze. Eucalypts with massive bulging bases are all over the place, but native pines are also plentiful. There is wildlife galore: eagles, big mobs of kangaroos, yellow-footed rock wallabies, euros (not the European currency, but a common stocky little grey wallaby) and emus.

After driving slowly through the park (Glen was understandably paranoid about getting another flat tyre – he was the one who did all of the tyre changes), we headed to its visitors' centre for a quick bite of lunch and to take a walking tour with Sharpy, a local Aborigine. We were the only ones on the two-and-a-half-hour walk, which was a real privilege. We kept to a standard trail into the famous Wilpena Pound formation. The massive circular mountain range covers 83 square kilometres and resembles a meteor crater, but isn't. The white fellah version of its formation is that it was once a huge mountain weathered away over millions of years, leaving only the rim. The native version comes from a story of two huge serpents lying in a ring formation.

Along the way, Sharpy (nicknamed from his youth as a slingshot sharpshooter) explained his own and his tribe's heritage and showed us some bush medicines and bush tucker. The turnaround point was a lookout with sweeping views of the Pound, named by early settlers because of its shape resembling a pound or enclosure. As we sat on a rock at the top of the mountain, Sharpy told us the Dreamtime story of how the Pound came to existence with the two serpents, and other interesting stories and folklore about the native fauna. A fascinating experience. The sky was blue, the weather mild and we were away from our world with views of natural grandeur, listening to intriguing stories from a time we too rarely ponder. Why didn't we learn more about this at school? On the way back, Sharpy showed us a few more bush remedies. I asked him if he played the didgeridoo, to which he replied that he only played the harmonica – a bit of Beatles and Creedence.

After farewells and thanks, we went back to the pub for dinner of meat and vegies and delved deeper into the outback way of life. It was an interesting contrast to our native history lesson, but in many ways similar. Outback Australians are a special breed. Adversity is never far away, but most take it in their stride and battle on with rock-hard determination, a wicked sense of humour and a wry smile across their sun-scarred faces. A beer or two with their mates at the local pub helps, too.

14. A Winery Somewhere

As we headed south past the Flinders Ranges, the outback faded away and relative urbanity loomed. We drove through the towns of Quorn, Wilmington (once called Beautiful Valley), and Laura, eventually arriving at Clare and the famous wine region of Clare Valley.

Naturally, we visited a few wineries; call it research. The region's dominant produce is riesling. Neither of us is a great fan of riesling but there were plenty of other varieties to try, and we tried a few rieslings that had some appeal. The first visit was Seven Hill, a Jesuit winery that still produced communion wine for export. Then we went to the family-owned Paulettes and tasted some of their impressive collection. Finally, we visited the large and family owned Taylor's Winery, tasted several very agreeable wines and hung around for quite a while talking with the friendly young attendant at the cellar door who had recently finished studying wine marketing. He told us that wine was Australia's second biggest export earner behind wheat and was expected to hit number one soon. Our wine exports have increased from about $150 million in 1990 to over $2.5 billion now, as quality and price provide an increasingly competitive edge in foreign markets. Two thirds goes to the UK and US.

The Clare is only about an hour and a half from Adelaide so we headed straight down to the 'burbs to stay with Sean, an old friend from Sydney. We were warned that we'd have to entertain ourselves the first night of our stay because Sean and his housemate had a test the next day for their wine marketing degree so they were going to be studying all night. At midnight we were all still eating, drinking and talking so while we felt a bit guilty, I'm glad it wasn't me in the exam room on the next day.

In common with our other capital cities, Adelaide has a rich history. Flinders sailed by in 1802 but it wasn't until 1836 that William Light came along and established a settlement. While in England, he scored a generous inheritance and resigned his army job. Travelling in Egypt, Light met Captain John Hindmarsh who was to become the first South Australian governor after Light was appointed surveyor general of a new colony at what is now Adelaide. He named it after Queen Adelaide, wife of William IV. There was plenty of controversy surrounding Light's work, and when Hindmarsh arrived at the settlement, he didn't like Light's choice and tried to move it. The conflict didn't last long – Hindmarsh was soon recalled to London and before long Light died of tuberculosis.

Today, Light's well-planned city spreads out from Victoria Square, ten kilometres inland from the Gulf of St Vincent on the River Torrens. The downtown area, surrounded by a greenbelt of parkland, is split down the middle by King William Street. For some reason, all the east-west running streets change their names when they intersect King William Street. It adds to the challenge of navigating an unfamiliar city. The East End district around Rundle Street has become the city's cosmopolitan café and restaurant precinct and we enjoyed a meal or two there with some nice South Australian wine to wash down the food. This area helps give Adelaide its place as having the largest number of restaurants per capita of any city in the country. And it's a great place to sit back and watch the beautiful people parade by. We didn't feel that we fit in too well with our unshaven faces, dusty jeans and ragged flannel shirts, but neither of us could get unduly concerned after our recent experiences.

Adelaide is a pleasant city, relaxed and pretty, with its river and old cricket ground and excellent central market. It's a city that really feels like it has come a long way yet retains strong links to its early history.

We didn't see many of the famed churches in the 'City of Churches', but there are a lot of pubs and licensed cafes and restaurants. 'City of Pubs' I'd call it.

Not far from downtown Adelaide is Penfolds' McGill Estate Winery. The winery is neighboured by lots of huge, mostly very ugly houses, proving once more that wealth and taste do not necessarily go hand in hand. But the handsome Penfolds buildings are heritage listed and surrounded by rows of mature grapevines. This is where Penfolds was established by Dr Christopher Rawson in 1844. The vineyard is now only about five hectares compared to 100 hectares a century ago but the wine is still excellent. We tried several quality offerings. Unfortunately, Penfolds' most famous creation, Grange, was not available for tasting but could be bought by the glass in the restaurant. It was tempting, but would have wiped out a week's food budget in a few quick sips.

As tempting as it was to visit the McLaren Vale Wine Festival next, we opted to wait until post-festival to avoid the weekend crowds and to ensure some serious tasting. So we headed south-east to the Coonawarra region. The coastal drive down the Princes Highway was pleasant, with sweeping views over a narrow channel and Coorong, which must be the narrowest national park in the country. The park stretches 145 kilometres down the coast from the mouth of the River Murray and is less than three kilometres wide. Its system of lagoons sustains about 90 bird species and is the world's largest breeding colony of the Australian Pelican. Apart from flora and fauna, the area includes significant Aboriginal heritage sites.

The route we took to Coonawarra was about 430 kilometres and we anxiously anticipated tasting some of the region's renowned reds. As we left Adelaide, we tried in vain to find accommodation somewhere near the wineries. Even campsites were sparse. We finally found a place in our dated issue of *Lonely Planet* that the book told us was cheap, big and in an old woolshed. We called and they had room so we headed down to Whisker's Woolshed near Penola, just outside Coonawarra.

The drive was a bit longer than we had expected. Coonawarra isn't really near anything or on the way to anywhere unless you're driving between Melbourne and Adelaide. As usual, our destination was planned on the morning of our departure so our preparation was typically wanting, but that was how we liked it. The drive was scenic and comfortable by our standards, mostly along the coast. On the way, we passed (and photographed) the big Lobster at Kingston, drove through a town called Murray Bridge which boasts the first bridge built over the mighty Murray River and briefly visited Tailem Bend, a small town with a long straight road through its centre. We assumed the bend was in the river.

It was after five o'clock by the time we reached Whisker's Woolshed in the chilly South Australian twilight. We found Whisker (aka Andy) at his house and he showed us down to his Woolshed, where we were the only guests. There was no mistaking it as an old woolshed, complete with a few old shearing motors attached to the ceiling near the kitchen. There were several rooms off the main area, presumably formerly sheep holding pens but now substantially more comfortable and thankfully, heated.

The heaters and open fire tried their hardest, but the weather remained cold and a woolshed just isn't built with good insulation. Apart from the winter chill, the gale-force winds outside made the woolshed's corrugated iron shell shake, well, like a big corrugated woolshed in strong wind. It's all part of the atmosphere. When I opened the door to go to the outdoor dunny it blew open and nearly knocked me down. Camping would not have been fun. The common room was huge with a big log fire next to the old wool press. Strangely, the out-of-place Coke machine accepted only nickels, dimes or quarters. I can't believe our luck firstly finding this unique place (and unique owner) and then having it all to ourselves over the long weekend. All for the bargain price of only $7 each.

We were about 12 kilometres south of Historic (here we go again) Penola which claims to be the oldest town in the south east of South Australia. Interestingly (for us), the town was founded by Alexander Cameron after whom Cameron Corner was named. More than 125 years ago, Mother Mary MacKillop together with Father Julian Woods founded a religious order there. Some 'world famous poets' were born there, but I've never heard of them. Fame, apparently, is relative, or selective.

Whisker was an interesting chap; a country bloke with a generously proportioned belly, bushy beard and beanie full of long since dead vegetation. He already had the fire going for us and after giving the grand tour hung around for a chat. He asked what we'd be having for dinner so we told him that it would probably just be some soup with extra vegies thrown in. That's our freezing cold weather easy to prepare standard. He couldn't believe that we could survive on such a meagre meal so he kindly left us enough bacon to provide a large Sunday brunch to a medium-sized country town. 'I'll eat what you don't', says Whisker. We would have been lucky to get through half. He offered to help bring in some stuff and then before leaving asked what time we'd be up so he didn't wake us when he came down for a morning chat over a hot life-giving cuppa.

Cyclonic winds and a year's worth of rainfall made for a challenging night's sleep, but the genuinely special place and great host made up for it. As promised, Whisker came in for a chat and a cuppa the next morning, before seeing us off for some wine tasting up the road in Coonawarra.

It was a moment I'd been waiting a long time for: this is the ultimate destination for those of us who enjoy quality red wine. Until the second half of the twentieth century, Coonawarra grapes weren't much chop and most were distilled to make brandy, but now the regional name is jealously guarded and encompasses its rich red terra rossa soil. Times have sure changed.

Most of the wineries are conveniently clustered together along the highway. Our first stop was Lindemans. They had a cosy cellar door area complete with potbelly stove and big fluffy cat. I wanted the cat's job, sitting in front of the fire and looking disdainfully at tourists swilling down dram after dram of fine wine. On second thought, the wine appealed to me more. They had some excellent wines available for tasting and we happily sampled their fare with some cheese palate cleansers in between.

Wynns is synonymous with Coonawarra and produces some excellent wines. At both Lindemans and Wynns, we were able to taste and compare different vintages of the same high quality wines, some with remarkable differences. It was a rare opportunity, enhanced by a limited number of other tasters, with the McLaren Vale festival drawing in the vinaceous crowds. We were beginning to enjoy taking our time, gradually savouring the wine and chatting with the staff, rather than rushing a tasting and heading to the next place.

After tasting the impressive but small range of Redman reds, we stopped for a late lunch break at the Hermitage Café and Restaurant. I enjoyed a yabby chowder, complete with whole yabby. Glen also had soup and we each had cheese for desert. Glen opted for the Black Label cheddar with semidried olives and tomatoes and I went for the King Island Black Label Brie with Quince sauce. Both were excellent and neither of us could walk by the time we had finished. Perhaps having wine with lunch wasn't the best decision of the day. We probably could have done without desert too.

We decided to check out one more winery before heading back to the shed and stopped at the small Bowens winery. Again, only a few wines were on offer, all of them quite good. Before we left, a couple of guys walked in, one with the sort of moustache you'd expect to see on the Red Baron, and a thick German accent. He commented that there was no spittoon, but swallowing the wine didn't seem to bother him too much. Then he loudly proclaimed in his very heavy accent that during a recent illness, 'my doctor told me to shpit more often. He said I should shpit instead of swallow!'

'Get a new doctor' was the suggestion from the vintner. Good advice.

On that note we headed back to the woolshed to collapse in front of the fire and wait to digest all the wine and cheese. The rain pounded against the iron walls and roof of the woolshed to the point that we could hardly hear the World Cup cricket commentary on the TV.

We finally got away from Penola when the weather broke and after our morning visit from Whisker. We headed north back through Coonawarra to Naracoorte. *Let's Go* accurately described Naracoorte as 'utterly forgettable...' It had a few caves, but we'd done the cave thing, thanks.

We kept driving until we reached the wine region of Padthaway. There was only one cellar door outlet, which offered wines of many of the local wineries. It was in a magnificent old homestead (or at least its historic horse stables). Alas, after making the effort to go there, no one was at the cellar door or homestead and after waiting a while, we gave up. Luckily, we had tried a few Padthaway wines in Coonawarra, not to mention back home in Sydney. The area itself is alluring, with kilometres of massive photogenic vineyards covering the undulating landscape and stretching to the horizon under the chilly overcast sky.

With the festival over, we set out for our next destination, McLaren Vale, just south of Adelaide. The drive again was enjoyable, passing smoothly through numerous vineyards and farms blanketing some very hilly terrain. We chose to take a free car ferry across the Murray River instead of returning over the bridge at Murray Bridge. Being the end of the long weekend, we had to wait 40 minutes for several other crossings before we made it across the muddy river.

Thanks to the continued crappy weather, we settled on an on-site caravan in a pleasant caravan park. Unfortunately, it was unheated but the electric stove provided some respite from the bitter evening chill. We settled in to rest up before another tough day of tasting.

On the next day, we visited a total of seven wineries and only overlapped with other tasters once briefly the entire day. Seven may not sound like much (or maybe it does), but we usually spent about an hour in a winery, firstly so we didn't get too sloshed, and secondly to appreciate the wine and talk to the cellar door people. I had too many wines to remember everything about each winery, but took copious notes at each one to recall the standouts. Reviewing these notes, I seem to have commented more on the cellar door girls rather than the wine. There was something for all of the senses.

It was another happy and enjoyable day and we were very glad to have waited until after the long weekend festival to visit. We heard one story of a drunken partygoer who wanted all the whites mixed in one glass. At another winery, a bloke asked for beer at the cellar door. We were still in awe at the extent of vineyards in the region and the vast quantity and quality of wines. The amiability and knowledge of cellar door staff was also impressive.

With the Beast heavily laden with wine, we left McLaren Vale for the trip northeast to the famous and some say overrated Barossa Valley. We drove up the coast rather than taking a direct route so that we could visit the beachside Adelaide suburb of Glenelg. We drove through some attractive seaside suburbs with tasteful houses and others with ugly monstrosities, but all with views out to Gulf St Vincent. Glenelg was one of the most pleasant.

Settled in 1836 when South Australia's first colonists touched down, it was named after Lord Glenelg, Secretary of State for the Colonies. The gum tree under which Governor Hindmarsh read the first proclamation in 1836 still stands. Glenelg now attracts its residents and visitors with sun, surf, bars, cafes and restaurants. It's also the convenient beachside terminus of Adelaide's only remaining tram, which rattles down the tracks from Victoria Square in the centre of downtown Adelaide.

After a pleasant lunch on the promenade under the first real sunshine since Birdsville, we took off for the two-hour drive to the Barossa. We decided that on the way through we would visit some wineries, as one does.

There are about 40 wineries in the Barossa and it and produces about half of Australia's quality wines. Southcorp is the king with a huge and opulent compound not far from the hostel we chose. The Barossa's winegrowing history began in 1847 when Johann Gramp planted the first grapes at Jacob's Creek, now a famous Barossa brand. Germans contributed extensively to the Barossa's growth and there is still a strong German influence. Local *wurst*, bread and German mustard are a happy combination.

We visited a range of small to massive wineries, all with some appealing offerings. The small family-run Bethany was a favourite of ours.

The Bunkhaus Hostel was between two of the larger towns of the Barossa, Nuriootpa and Tanunda. The hostel had a couple of small dorms and was right in the middle of a vineyard with vines only metres from the front door. We were greeted by a welcoming wood fire and very welcoming host (the longest running hostel proprietor in South Australia), and immediately felt at home. If only this could be home.

Water was in short supply at the time and the hostel had a sign on the wall reading 'save water – drink wine'.

A young reclusive Japanese girl who didn't seem to speak English was staying at the Bunkhaus. Being a seasoned hosteller, I struggled through a conversation with her, only to find that she didn't drink wine. I hope she got her money back from her travel agent when she returned home.

Another day of tastings took us far and wide. We had trouble finding an open door at one winery, but we had driven a long way so we persevered; in hindsight, probably unnecessary. Eventually someone saw us and opened up for us to have a tasting. The wine was very ordinary, and the girl behind the counter broke the cork while opening one of the bottles, proclaiming, 'I always do that'. It was the first winery we left without making a purchase.

Our award for the best wine label goes to the very impressive Rockford winery. Their light semillon was described on the bottle thus: 'In time will massage into a slippery yellow wine that just invites itself to lunch'. Priceless.

Indulgence complete and further weighed down with wine, it was time to get back on the road proper and head west again.

15. Back Outback

As we drove north along Highway 1 alongside Spencer Gulf, the land on our left was flat as a pancake but on the other side the continuous flowing Flinders Ranges snaked along with smooth undulations.

The road took us past some pink lakes. It's an interesting effect and a lovely contrast between the colour of the water, trees, pasture and sky. Alongside one of the lakes, someone had cleverly rigged together a series of tyres and a stick to look like the Loch Ness Monster. It is one of those moments I wish we could have stopped for a photo but we had a monster road train on our tail and didn't fancy being a hood ornament ourselves.

About three quarters of the way between Adelaide and Port Augusta is the small town of Port Germein. When built, its spectacular 1.6-kilometre wooden jetty was the longest in the Southern Hemisphere. Port Germein's other point of interest is the annual *Festival of the Crab* in January. Wrong end of the year for us unfortunately.

As we approached Port Augusta at the head of Spencer Gulf we could see tall smokestacks reaching out of the flatness and belching a steady stream of smoke into the atmosphere. It was quite eerie really. The traditional owners of the area called it Kurdnatta, meaning 'place of shifting sands'. Matthew Flinders was the first foreigner to visit the area when he anchored there 200 years ago. Two blokes named Elder and Grainger entered the harbour in 1852 and named the settlement after the wife of the Governor of South Australia. These days, Port Augusta is significant for most forms of transport. Both the north-south running Ghan and the east-west running Indian Pacific railways pass through the town, and the port has provided shipping services for a diverse area and a wide range of imports and exports. The city also generates about one third of the state's electricity. And of course, it's a convenient stop off point for weary travellers.

As we drove north from Port Augusta, we were accompanied for about 90 kilometres by Port Augusta local radio's Saturday morning blues program, hosted by a very enthusiastic but barely understandable DJ. The music was very much to our liking and we had the radio blaring until it finally and disappointingly faded out on a Blues Brothers classic. We were back on that old lonesome road, long past the crossroads, with the key to the highway.

A couple of kilometres out of town we passed over a railway line which was carrying an enormous train stretching further than we could see, snaking slowly beneath us like a caterpillar on Valium emitting a loud and monotonously repetitive clickity-clack clickity-clack. Things tend to be big out here: along the road north we saw our first four-trailer road train. King of the road indeed!

It didn't take long to see the signs of being back in the desert: the red soil, the unfenced paddocks and cattle grids, straight roads stretching to the horizon without a kink, dead kangaroos, and eagles soaring above the desolate landscape or fighting ravenous crows for a tasty feast of road kill.

Along the way, we stumbled across Lake Hart, a huge body of water in the middle of the red desert. It was surprising to see so much water out there, but we got close enough to ensure that it wasn't a mirage. The contrast of sparkling water with red soil surrounds was captivating. Judging by the whitened shoreline, it was yet another salt lake. The railway track, presumably for the Adelaide to Darwin Ghan Railway, ran along the shoreline offering excellent views for those travelling north.

There were several large signs along the highway warning of livestock grazing, most accompanied by a translation in some sort of mystery language, perhaps Afghan in memory of the cameleers. Another peculiarity of outback highways is the straight stretches of road doubling as landing strips for the Royal Flying Doctor Service, complete with those zebra crossings you see at each end of runways.

We stopped for petrol at the Glendambo roadhouse, the last service station for the 257kilometre journey back inland to Coober Pedy. The welcome sign proclaimed a population of 30 humans, 22,500 sheep and 2,000,000 (approx) flies. From our brief visit it appeared to be accurate.

The approach to Coober Pedy was signposted with warnings about the thousands of open opal mineshafts in the area. The signs warned not to walk backwards or to run. We later found out that both mistakes have taken a toll on unwary tourists. Stretching out to the horizon from the road, thousands of mounds of extracted dirt cover the landscape like a bad case of acne. Next to every mound is a deep hole stripped of any trace of opal. It's not only tourists who come to grief out here; several miners who should have known better and some who were just plain unlucky have lost their lives below the crusty sunburnt surface.

As everyone says, Coober Pedy is an 'interesting' town. Its unique oddity made it one of the most fascinating places I've been. The streets were being resurfaced during our visit because electricity cables had just been laid underground. We were told that mining trucks kept driving through town and knocking over the power lines, blacking out the town for days at a time. Having said that, we were told numerous stories of suspect accuracy by an eclectic mix of enthusiastic and proud locals.

John McDouall Stuart (not to be confused with Charles Sturt) passed through what is now Coober Pedy in 1858 but it wasn't until 1911 that opals were first discovered and mined in a small venture. A larger mining operation kicked off four years later and the town was settled and eventually turned into a big flat block of Swiss cheese. To this day, opals are still the main industry, along with tourism and the occasional film production.

About 1,000 kilometres from Adelaide towards the red centre of Australia, Coober Pedy is a hot town. In summer, the temperature hits the mid 50s and night time desert winter temperatures get close to zero. Consequently, most residents live underground to avoid outrageous electricity bills from air conditioning. This is reputed to be how the town got its name, which means something like 'white man in a hole' in the local Aboriginal dialect.

We arrived in town in the late afternoon and checked in at Radeka's, an underground hostel. It wasn't the quietest hostel I've stayed at, but it was certainly the first subterranean one and a welcome respite from the outside heat. The temperature inside hovers at around 23 degrees year-round, regardless of the outside temperature. The walls were solid rock but strangely smooth and light coloured with maroon veins criss-crossing at right angles.

After checking in, we took a stroll down the main road and had a drink at the Desert Cave Hotel, which had an underground upmarket bar claiming to have the world's only underground poker machines. The barman was very friendly and very keen to espouse the virtues (seemingly regardless of fact) of his chosen hometown. We had a couple of very refreshing beers and talked with him about opal mining, and the unique (dare I say odd) Coober Pedy lifestyle and community.

On the barman's recommendation, we had dinner at one of the (not very) Greek restaurants and talked away the night with some fellow travellers back at the hostel bar.

We kicked off the next day with an eye-opening wander around town. We started by walking past a van with a bumper sticker advising that the 'driver is on drugs and has a gun'. Nothing would surprise me in Coober Pedy. How many bars do you go into where they have to tell you that explosives are not permitted?

A multitude of shops selling didgeridoos, Aboriginal art and of course, opals lined the main street. Some of the shopkeepers were too pushy for my liking but I was careful to be polite – this is a town with a short fuse. Several of the buildings have been bombed, including the police station which is now bomb proof, so we were told. We heard one story of when footpaths were first constructed along the main road. Because someone couldn't park in his usual spot, he took to the footpath with a jackhammer one night. No more footpath, although it was being rebuilt, along with the road, during our visit.

That afternoon, we took a four-hour tour around Coober Pedy and surrounds. They like their sport in Coober Pedy; first stop was the *gravel* football field. Ouch. That's next to a large area of land where they tried to establish a grass sports surface with drought resistant grass. Unfortunately, shortly after the grass was planted the area flooded and the grass died. No further attempt had been made, so they settled for gravel.

Golf is another popular sport in Coober Pedy, although the course also has a lack of natural greenery (despite the sarcastic 'please keep off the grass' sign). The tees are on a square metre of synthetic grass and you have to carry a small patch of it with you so you don't leave divots in the fairway dirt. The greens are in fact blacks (sand blended with left over sump oil from the diesel power station) and need to be raked before putting. The balls must not be white because the local lizards take white balls thinking that they are eggs. During the summer, it's too hot to play during the day so evening golf is played with fluorescent balls. If your ball lands by a dangerous snake (several of the world's most deadly snakes live around Coober Pedy) it may be moved for a one stroke penalty. Mining is banned from the course and cars may be used in lieu of buggies. Rather than bunkers they have 'grass traps'. Actually I made that last one up. The president of the golf club was the colourful Father Tony of the Catholic Church. More about him later.

The cemetery, not far from town, is on Boot Hill, marked by a sign reading 'Hill' with an old boot stuck to the top of it. The most interesting story we heard about the cemetery (and there were plenty) was the story of a bloke named Karl, who had himself buried in a corrugated iron coffin, and whose headstone is a beer keg with the epitaph, 'have a drink on me'. The presiding minister's job was not only to conduct the funeral service, but also to pump beer for the thirsty mourners.

Other than opals, Coober Pedy is most famous for its underground houses. Hundreds of homes are hidden in the ranges near town. The area would just look like barren hills except for all the cars parked outside. There are few street signs, and no letterboxes (or mail deliveries). If you want mail you get a post office box. They're harder to blow up with mining explosives. Coober Pedy has 'good' and 'bad' parts of town and areas dominated by particular nationalities. A few have indoor pools and most have numerous bedrooms deep inside the mountains.

The land is very cheap ($5,000 to $15,000) and then it doesn't cost much to get your place drilled out. A space of four metres is required between houses to allow for errors in digging directions, just to make sure you don't drill into your neighbour's bedroom. Some of the dugouts are particularly large. This is because opal mining is not permitted within the town limit so people build dugouts and keep applying for extensions and not surprisingly find thousands of dollars worth of opal in the process. We heard of one bachelor who recently applied for a 100-square-foot lounge room with thirty bedrooms attached. Must have a lot of friends. You can usually tell how big the house is by the size of the pile of rock and dirt outside. The structure of the dugouts is generally kitchen at front with panoramic views of nothing but soil and rock. The bedroom is usually the deepest room to keep it cool in the heat of summer.

There are several community halls in town, reflecting the various nationalities, including Greek, Italian, Serbian and Croatian. One of the people on our tour asked if there is an Australian club, to which our guide replied, 'there aren't enough of us'. We were told that the school had children of 48 nationalities, speaking 58 languages. The population of 3,500 is about 60 per cent European, most of whom migrated after World War II.

Coober Pedy is primarily known for its vast opal reserves. A massive 80 per cent of the world's opal production comes from around here, with one and a half million holes in the ground to prove it. They can reach down 25m (10 storeys) and are rarely covered over when abandoned. It is illegal to fill them up in case someone else drills into one and gets tonnes of rubble falling on them. The open holes also aid the release of toxic chemicals from blasting. An American tourist is said to have been killed not long before our visit when she walked backwards into an open hole while taking a photo of her family in an off-limits mine field (but again, you never know which stories to take seriously in Coober Pedy). After driving through an obstacle course of holes and mounds we went to the Radeka mining lease, a small open cut mine where we were given half an hour to see what we could find. I dug through the rubble to unearth a couple of low value opals, probably not quite sufficient to give up my day job, but a bit of excitement nonetheless.

Also on the tour we visited the underground home of Crocodile Harry, an old Latvian upon whom Crocodile Dundee is reputedly based. His dugout, painted white over the orange rock walls, was a bizarre collection of photos, statues of naked women with big boobs and the names of hundreds of women whom he claims were virgins when they came in, but not when they left. There was a collection of lingerie hanging from the ceiling, including Tina Turner's bra from when she was there filming Mad Max III. His toilet was outside the house and has been dubbed 'The Shitatorium'. Harry had obviously been enjoying a few beverages on the morning of our visit and was having a little trouble standing up when we were there, but he still managed to chase the girls in our group. We were told that Harry divorced his wife (or vice versa) after only weeks of marriage and that was years ago, but she still lives in a dugout across the road. Nothing is too bizarre for Coober Pedy.

Finally, we went out to the nearby mesas known as the breakaways. Just below the surface of the tabletop mountains were several small caves dug by kangaroos to escape the summer heat. Maybe they're not so dumb after all. The mountaintops offered spectacular views into the desert void. It is no wonder films set in deserts or on other planets are shot there so frequently, Mad Max and Pricilla among them. Most of the area is known as the Moon Plain for obvious reasons.

Two small twin hills caught my eye; one bright white and the other peppery brown from erosion of dark rock at its peak. They're known, logically enough, as Salt and Pepper. Other mountains in view from our vantage point looked like islands rising from an ocean of shimmering heat. Millions of years ago, they were real islands surrounded by a real ocean.

After the tour, Glen and I went back to have an early dinner and chat at the underground bar. It was the night of the World Cup Cricket final between Australia and Pakistan, so Glen changed his mind about the star tour we had planned to do. I was still keen and Martin the guide was happy to take just me up the mountain to gaze at the glittering night sky: 'Ten bucks is ten bucks' was his logic. I was quite impressed with Martin's self-taught knowledge of astronomy, but it was clear that the cricket was on his mind too.

When we got back to the bar at Radeka's the cricket was in full swing and Australia was knocking the Pakies around very early. One of the hostel proprietors, Doug, was a keen cricket fan so the bar was kept open until the last ball was bowled. Also watching the game with us was Father Tony. He had been the Catholic minister at Coober Pedy for several years and had a parish covering what I think he said was about 5 per cent of the country. This was one hip preacher – he was knocking back the beers throughout the match and after every big hit or wicket taken, he would loudly proclaim, 'Shit o'day!' The classic was at the end of the match when commentator Bill Laury was babbling on about the spectators and Father Tony shouted 'Shut up Bill, we don't give a shit about the spectators', and hobbled home. I think I'd go to church if I lived here.

Australia whipped the Pakistanis to take out the trophy.

A late and boozy night resulted in a late and lethargic start the next day so we only drove the 370 kilometres to Woomera. Back home 370 kilometres would be a big deal. In the outback, it's just up the road.

Woomera was established in 1947 to launch British experimental rockets in the Empire's attempt to be a dominant nuclear power. After thousands of launches the Poms abandoned the project at its prime and bought American bombs. Until 1982 the town was off limits to tourists, and is still administered by the Defence Department. There are rarely launches these days although the local high school had a successful launch a week before our visit, perhaps on a slightly smaller scale. Unfortunately, when London pulled the pin the government razed most of the facility. There are still some American aerospace based companies in the area and consequently the biggest day of the year is the Fourth of July, although a local told us they're slowly leaving.

While these days Woomera is better known for detaining illegal immigrants, there is now hope for a revival of the town's aerospace industry. I have read that a US aerospace company is constructing the world's first fully operational commercial spaceport at Woomera to launch reusable vehicles for low earth orbit satellites. Who knows whether it will ever happen, but it would be nice to be a key player in the world of space exploration or now more likely, space tourism.

Most of the town looks like it was purpose built (as it was). Rows of 70s style apartment blocks line the streets with drab monotony. There's an interesting heritage centre full of historical photos and information, which we spent time exploring, but not much else.

Before leaving the next day, we stopped at the servo to top up the fuel tank before returning south towards the South Australian coast. Several US soldiers were doing the same, no doubt bound for their nearby base, Nurrungar, which we briefly glimpsed from the highway. It looks like a couple of huge golf balls stuck in the middle of the desert. As we drove past (at quite a distance), Glen gave them the message, 'Hey Yanks, get a big black dingo up ya!' just in case they were listening in to our conversation.

16. Treeless Plain (But Mind The Trees)

As we headed back towards the southern coast, the friendly outback waving between vehicles was abundant, ranging from a nonchalant raising of the index finger from the steering wheel to an all-out two-handed wave. We were trying to get a motorcyclist to wave but without success. The closer we got to Port Augusta the fewer people waved. Glen was driving that leg and gave up waving in disgust at the unfriendliness of our fellow travellers (although the retirees towing their shiny (or dusty) new caravans always came through with a wave and smile).

Our destination for the day (chosen en route) was Tumby Bay on the Eyre Peninsula. After arriving in town and checking in, we did the usual drive/walk around town. We had arrived in yet another fishing town where it was nigh on impossible to find fresh seafood. Is it just me or is that weird? When we got back to the caravan park, I wandered down to the pristine white-sand beach (just metres from our van) and took some photos of pelicans waddling around the jetty, with a soft pink and purple sunset in the background. Yet another 'unknown' but spectacular part of the country.

When we eventually got moving the next morning, we stopped at Port Lincoln to cash up and gas up. At the petrol station was a notice pleading for passers through to keep an eye out for a lost galah: 'Good talker. Says 'shut up', 'good-bye' and waves its foot'. Alas, we saw no galah.

Next stop was a brief detour to the small fishing town of Coffin Bay, famous for its oysters. All we did there was purchase a dozen opened oysters for $7 for my dinner. Yum. This curiously named town (not surprisingly described as 'picturesque seaside town' – aren't they all?)

was visited by Matthew Flinders on his great journey of the early nineteenth century. He named it Coffin Bay after his friend Sir Isaac Coffin. Not the exciting story of treachery I was hoping for.

The landscape continued to change on a daily basis. Well, it didn't really change, we were just driving through different environments. The landscape around the western shore of the Eyre Peninsula is less mountainous than the east, but is similarly blanketed by endless kilometres of wheat fields. It's a rocky region and farmers had piled the rocks into small mounds around their paddocks and just ploughed around them. I guess there's nowhere else to put them. One industrious farmer had built a wall out of his rocks, but most didn't bother. Several of the farms backed onto the ocean, offering the sheep and a few select people million dollar views south over the Great Australian Bight.

Further on up the road we stumbled upon 'Murphy's Haystacks', a bunch of large naturally formed wave-like rocks scattered around someone's farm. Some of them really do bear a striking resemblance to haystacks, hence the name. Although on private property, tourists were permitted to wander around the rocky area for the grand sum of $1. Apparently tour guides used to tell their passengers as they whizzed by that the formations were actually haystacks, a deception which continued for years. Who Murphy was remains a mystery.

At the junction of the Flinders and Eyre Highways in the north-western corner of the peninsula and about mid way between the eastern and western borders of South Australia, lies Ceduna, 'eastern gateway to the Nullarbor', the vast open plain across which we were soon to traverse. The town's name comes from the Aboriginal word for 'place to sit and rest'. I suspect many people coming the other way out of the Nullarbor do just that. The settlement was originally at nearby Denial

Bay, so named by Flinders because from a distance he thought the bay would penetrate further inland. It didn't.

We had a quick shop for dinner and noticed that the supermarket sold kangaroo tails. We weren't tempted, but there were plenty of Aboriginal shoppers with them sticking out of their trolleys. My indigenous cookbook comments on cooking up various bits of a roo (and other native fauna), but has this to say about tails:

'The tail is traditionally the best meat and can also be skinned and boiled up in a camp oven with a few vegetables. The cartilage is sticky to the touch and the meat rather elusive but the overall taste is excellent. The tail cooked in the ashes, as described above, is a more challenging proposition'.

In what was becoming an all too common habit, we decided against camping and opted for an on-site van at Ceduna. Our indulgence was due to the New South Wales vs. Queensland State of Origin football being played that night. We needn't have bothered – it was a boring game.

Just as we were bedding down before the big drive across the Nullarbor, a large mob of locals went rampaging past the caravan park. There was a lot of screaming and swearing but they didn't appear to cause any trouble within the park. We learnt the next day that this is an almost daily occurrence at closing time at the pub.

The Aboriginal story is not a happy one. Throughout the trip, we didn't run into any trouble, but we heard dozens of stories about the Aboriginal way of life and difficulty fitting in with the imposing and sometimes hostile white outback society. We saw examples in so many of the towns we went to. It's a shame that the locals and we tourists often see and hear more of the bad side than the good. Life in the Aboriginal communities, most of which ban alcohol and foster a reasonably traditional upbringing for their children, is no doubt more healthy and conventional but still suffering from poor housing and health standards. Unfortunately, the bad seeds seem to gravitate towards the towns where they are more visible and troublesome. We heard stories of violence and poor relations throughout the trip. Even accounting for local bias and exaggeration, there were some disquieting stories. Unfortunately, we were asked to buy alcohol by Aborigines in a couple of towns. They have so much to offer in terms of their rich and fascinating culture; it is sad to see opportunities for education and integration wasted. What better way to help the reconciliation process than teach people from an early age what a rich culture the people of our country have. Thankfully, these days Aboriginal culture gets a considerably more prominent place in the school syllabus than in my school days. Hundreds or thousands of people marching through capital cities for reconciliation, in my view, means very little to the Aborigines who live in the outback. It's the 'grass roots' problems that need to be addressed. Whose fault is it that these problems even exist? I don't know, but trying to solve the problem by throwing money at it isn't working. It's going to take a lot more effort than that. It is a very perplexing situation for all, and sadly, I don't see a satisfactory solution in the offing.

Before we left Ceduna, we both got a haircut from one of the four hairdressers in town. With my increasing interest in the indigenous issue, I asked if the hairdresser had ever had any trouble from the local Aborigines. She replied 'Not really. I got hit once but that was probably my fault, and I got my car smashed up and my bike stolen, but that's it'. She wanted to move away, despite having growing up in Ceduna. This is the part of Australia that the guidebooks mostly avoid telling us about. It's a sad situation, but true.

Just 75 kilometres from Ceduna is Penong, a town covered by windmills. Our Nullarbor brochure told us it is known as 'the town of 100 windmills', but it looked like more as we drove through. Its name derives from the Aboriginal for 'waterhole'. I guess that was a while ago, before they needed to tap underground flows. At Penong, we hooked a left and headed south for the coast and the spectacular Point Sinclair and Cactus Beach. The drive over a good gravel road led to huge sand dunes shadowing pink pools and crystal clear aqua-coloured water. The sky was beautifully clear. Everything looked perfect. Surfers like it there for more practical reasons though.

Back on the Eyre Highway for a while, we took another diversion to the coast. Fowlers Bay is the westernmost coastal settlement in South Australia. Flinders named it after his first Lieutenant and later Eyre and Giles used it as a base camp. It's now almost a ghost town but there's a shop and small caravan park there. And that's where we decided to stop for the night. Crossing the Nullarbor would have to wait another day.

Before setting up the tents, we took a memorable journey along the coast of nearby Scotts Beach. There wasn't really a road to take us over the huge, undulating empty expanse of sand atop the cliffs overlooking the Bight, just rough tracks and dunes. We had a feeling of such awesome good fortune to be in such a spectacular place without another soul in sight.

The view out to the Bight was sensational, the massive undulating and constantly shifting dunes fascinating. As we drove to the shoreline there were white dunes to our left and orange to our right. We drove along the sandy coastal cliff face for quite a while on a track that was only intermittently visible.

Naturally, for our first camp since Birdsville, it rained. The girl at the kiosk/caravan park check-in laughed when I asked about a weather forecast, as if to say, 'It just doesn't rain here. Ever. Why would you ask such a silly question'? Not only did it rain but also it sounded and felt like a blizzard. Again, we half-heartedly packed the wet equipment into The Beast (after wiping paw prints off the table and chairs) the next morning and prepared to cross the Nullarbor Plain, with Western Australia in our sights.

We stopped about 40 kilometres up the road to check out yet another crossing of the dingo fence. I would like to have taken the track to where the fence meets the coast but the road was very rough and we'd been through enough tyres already. We met three blokes who had been fishing at the point where the fence and coast converge, and they had gone through four tyres and enough other mechanical trouble to turn us off.

We next passed through Yalata, an Aboriginal community that includes a roadhouse, souvenir shop and caravan park. The community was settled in the early 1950s when the people were displaced from their inland traditional land for nuclear weapons testing. We'd heard that the locals hang out by and even on the road, selling souvenirs but we didn't see any. We didn't need food, drink or petrol and had seen enough Aboriginal souvenirs and artefacts and would no doubt see plenty more, so on we drove.

Just past Yalata we found the sign I've most wanted to see and photograph: 'Camels, wombats and kangaroos, next 96 kilometres'. 96 kilometres later there was another one. As Tim Bowden says in his entertaining book, Penelope Goes West, there's probably some truck which has scored the trifecta, but thankfully all we collected was bugs. Thankfully for us that is, not for the bugs.

Shortly after Yalata we got to the Nullarbor proper, evidenced by the sign, 'Nullarbor Plain – Eastern End of Treeless Plain'. Yee ha! Treeless plain is a misnomer though. 'Nullarbor' isn't, as I thought, an Aboriginal word, but in fact poor Latin for 'no tree', despite the fact that in places there are plenty of smallish and weather-worn trees. The more appropriate Aboriginal name for the area was 'bunda bunda', meaning 'high cliffs', upon which the plain is perched. Passengers aboard the trans-continental Indian Pacific railway would have a better idea of the Nullarbor's treeless side. It darts through the desert about 100 kilometres further inland than the highway. The railway line has the honour of containing the longest straight stretch of railway track in the world – 478 kilometres without a bend.

In my ignorance, I thought the Nullarbor was not only more desert-like, but more deserted. I wasn't expecting roadhouses every 100 kilometres or so, almost all with accommodation, campsites, showers & toilets and, of course, expensive petrol.

The Nullarbor Plain is the largest slab of limestone in the world, covering 250,000 square kilometres of southern Australia, stretching from the Great Australian Bight inland about 400 kilometres. Below the surface, the limestone has been eroded to form one of the world's largest underwater cave systems. Our informative tourist brochure told us that the Plain would cover the area of England, The Netherlands, Belgium and Switzerland with a chunk left over. The guide also tells us that 'The Nullarbor Plain is one of the most unique tracts of unspoilt wilderness on the face of this planet'. *Most unique?* It gets worse: 'more than just a drive – it is a fair dinkum outback experience'. Supposedly, the azure blue sky 'seems to reach down and grab you'. I could go on, but I won't.

The road is now sealed all the way so it's not quite the great Australian rugged road trip that it used to be, but still a great journey. The highway is named after Edward John Eyre, the first explorer to make the east-west journey. He thought the area was 'a hideous anomaly, a blot on the face of nature, the sort of place one gets into in bad dreams'. I guess that means he didn't like it. We didn't agree.

Edward John Eyre migrated to New South Wales in 1833 aged only 18. After farming for a while he decided to take an overland trip to Adelaide in 1838 and liked it so much that he did it again the next year but this time didn't return. His first expedition from his new home was to the Flinders Ranges and the second was to what is now the Eyre Peninsula. The next one took him further inland in 1840. It doesn't sound like he was too impressed, naming Mt Hopeless and Mt Deception along the way. Giving up on the inland idea, he took some of his team west along the Bight. After a couple of months of travelling (about the same as us) two of his Aboriginal guides killed his cohort John Baxter and pilfered all the supplies they could carry. Eyre carried on with his remaining Aboriginal companion. They chanced upon a French whaling boat on the shore and were able to score some supplies to keep them going to Albany at the south west tip of the continent. The expedition wasn't one of the better ones. It merely proved that the trip could be done (just) and confirmed the observations that Flinders had already made from his ship. Back in Adelaide, Eyre was appointed magistrate and protector of Aborigines. He wrote favourably of Aborigines in his journals, but was later tried three times in England for permitting the hanging of a rebellious Negro politician when he was Governor of Jamaica.

About 80 kilometres from Yalata is the Head of Bight lookout, known as an excellent vantage point for whale spotting. Our brochure told us that it was 'truly unique'. We took a free ride past the abandoned ranger station to the coast. A few Southern Right Whales were frolicking out to sea and one lonely one floated nearer to the shore like a big blob. There wasn't too much activity. I guess it wasn't mating season or there'd be some more action. Sadly, we missed out on the transmission of 'messages of benevolence and tranquillity' promised by the brochure. According to the radio there were nine whales hanging around the coast. Apparently the number gets closer to 100 later in the season. I'll bet a ranger is there to collect the park fee then.

A surfeit of caravans crowd the Eyre Highway. Most are shiny new numbers being towed by shiny new four-wheel drives, both bought with the retirement package by a rambling community on wheels that has become widely known as 'Grey Nomads', thanks to an ABC television documentary. Some of the caravans look like mansions, and they probably are in caravan terms. It's a very friendly mobile community, never shying away from a chat and always happy to help with a car problem or lack of sugar. You tend to bump into the same ones throughout the day, week, month and entire journey. It's one of the pleasures of this sort of travel. Usually.

Just after a roadhouse at which we stopped for food and petrol was another of the camel/wombat/kangaroo signs, this time with far fewer trees around, so we stopped for another photo. From then on it became open flat land with occasional outcrops of thinly spread trees over tall grasses, mallee scrub and heath.

Every 20 kilometres along the highway were rest stops, all with a caravan or two stopped for a cuppa. The stops also all had garbage bins. The Nullarbor garbage men must have the best (or worst?) and longest run in the country.

We stopped at a few of the lookouts along the highway to view the spectacular coastline over the Bunda Cliffs. These amazing cliffs looked to us like a half-eaten carrot cake stretching up the coast.

We drove through the state border village of Border Village which is a road house, caravan park and quarantine checkpoint on the border between South Australia and Western Australia. We handed over our onions and honey at the quarantine station as requested and continued on - dodging tumbleweed - to Eucla, a short distance up the road from the border.

Somehow, a century ago Eucla had a population of 100. Back then, it was the main telegraph station outside of the capital cities. We checked out the old sandstone telegraph station built in 1877, now all but covered by the drifting sand dunes. The contrast of pale sandstone against the white sand and rich cobalt sky was spectacular. Accordingly, I went snap-happy with the camera.

Back in 1841, Eyre found a water hole near where the current township now sits. It saved his life. Not surprising though, he didn't hang around. Neither did the telegraph line. It moved further inland 70 years ago, and now runs along the railway line.

Back at the campground, we forked over $4 to camp under a couple of semi-shady gum trees. As soon as the sun fell past the horizon, the winter chill set in. Perfect weather for a soup and shiraz dinner.

Since Eucla sits in the narrow central western time zone 45 minutes behind South Australia, we were both up at dawn to watch the impressive sunrise. The sky was pitch black and a beautiful sight with all the stars shimmering brightly in the outback stillness. I was up again an hour later for a coin-operated shower as the first of our fellow travellers was setting off.

Not far out of town the police had busted a four-wheel drive for speeding. We had heard the cops were out in force around the border and they certainly were. We were then entertained for a while by all the truckies warning each other to slow down on the CB radio.

We filled up the tank at Madura roadhouse with the most expensive petrol thus far. Madura is half way between Perth and Adelaide, which I believe is its attraction/claim to fame. A large farm was settled there in 1876 and bred horses for the British Imperial Army in India.

Most of the journey west from Eucla was through thickly treed terrain with the Hampton Tablelands stretching along the northern side of the highway for much of the 710kilometre journey to Norseman. The road varies from excellent to needs-to-be-resurfacedvery-soon. Avoiding road trains wasn't as hard as we thought. I gather it's worse in summer when the dust clouds churned up by the trucks are so thick you just need to stop and have a break to let them hurtle past.

No sightings of any living kangaroos along the highway (many dead ones though) or camels, but we saw a few emus, hundreds of crows and several huge wedge tailed eagles chowing down on road kill or soaring majestically over the Nullarbor. Eagles are such cool animals.

The percentage of hand wavers along the highway was very high. Occasionally someone couldn't be bothered with at least a raising of the index finger from the steering wheel, let alone a full-blown wave, but they were in a small minority. We got a couple of very enthusiastic wavers on this stretch or road, and after days of trying we finally got a motorcyclist to wave back. You have to find something to amuse yourself out here and Glen refused to play *I spy*.

After Eucla the road becomes less straight, perhaps on purpose, just to make sure drivers are paying attention. That is, until you get to the famous 90 mile (or 146.6 kilometres) stretch, which claimed to be

Australia's longest straight stretch of road. We were very disappointed not to find the 'Next bend 146.6 kilometres' sign we'd seen in a TV ad, but there was a big brown sign with similar wording at each end of the stretch. A few Royal Flying Doctor Service emergency landing strips were painted on the bitumen along the way. I hoped they didn't tangle with any road trains. Getting here was yet another milestone for the trip.

Further on up the highway is Cocklebiddy, which houses the Eyre Bird Observatory, operated by the Royal Ornithological Society, and some spectacular caves, one of which has one of the longest underwater passages in the world.

Shortly after Cocklebiddy we hit a plague of grasshoppers. A roadhouse waitress told us that it was a quiet day for the suicidal bugs, in which case I'd hate to drive through on a bad day. It was like driving through a blizzard of black snowflakes. The windscreen was covered in glue-like bug guts, as was every bit of the car facing forward, including the CB aerial. The sound was like rain on an iron roof. I felt like I was in the Millennium Falcon going into hyper drive. We were both amazed by the almost comical onslaught. Then the smell set in.

At the end of the 90-mile stretch, we stopped at Caiguna for lunch. I had the biggest hot dog I've ever seen and Glen had the 'Truckie Burger'. He did well to get through the multi-layered monster work of culinary art.

Our final stop of the Nullarbor trek was at Balladonia roadhouse for a chocolate fix and some drinks and to scrape more bug guts off the windscreen. We had initially planned to overnight there, but were ahead of schedule so we decided to continue to the end of the Eyre Highway. The bloke behind the counter was amazingly unfriendly which made us glad we weren't staying at his caravan park, described by *Lonely Planet* as exorbitantly priced at $10 for a campsite. They are obviously good at getting people off side, not the norm on the roadhouse circuit.

Balladonia is notable for being the 'landing' site of debris from Skylab, the space station that crashed to Earth in 1979, so any bits were long gone when we drove through to Noreseman, the town that sits at the other end of the Eyre Highway. We, too, were ready to crash.

17. The Other Side

We finally made it to Norseman as the sun reached the horizon and the CD player fittingly belted out 'Break on through to the other side', by the Doors. We collapsed in a tiny $25 cabin in a caravan park, with our bodies still on SA time, one and a half hours ahead. And seven hours of driving the Nullarbor had taken its toll. It was going to be an early night. Not even Glen's snoring reverberating through the flimsy cabin could keep me from sleeping through to morning.

Norseman was supposedly named for 1890s prospector Laurie Sinclair, who travelled the area with his horse, Hardy Norseman. He tied the horse to a tree one night and by morning its hooves had uncovered a gold reef. Mining in and around the town continues to this day. For most people, it's just the end or beginning of the ultimate Aussie road trip. For those of us travelling west the road ends, with the choice of going north to inland Kalgoorlie and Coolgardie or South to coastal Esperance, both along the creatively named Coolgardie-Esperance Highway.

Thanks to the change in time zones we were both up to enjoy another spectacular sunrise. We decided on the northern route and drove the 210 kilometres to the goldmining town of Kalgoorlie. On the way (while I was driving) an emu sprinted in its awkward fashion right in front of the car and with some frantic manoeuvring we barely missed it. Emus are not good to hit; the bulky body will take out your windscreen. We hoped that it would be our closest encounter between beast and The Beast.

The twin cities of Kalgoorlie and Boulder straddle the Golden Mile, reputedly the richest square mile on Earth. Kalgoorlie was built and still survives on its seemingly endless supply of gold. It has so far produced more than 1,300 tonnes of the stuff. A middle-aged Irish prospector named Paddy Hannan came to what is now Kalgoorlie in 1893 after prospecting around the country, and found himself a good supply of surface gold. The area had been visited by some ambitious pastoralists some 30 years earlier, but the lack of water either killed them or drove them away.

Word got around about Paddy's find and by 1905, 200,000 miners found their way to Kalgoorlie, enough to service nearly 100 hotels. The rapid population growth necessitated one of the country's greatest engineering feats – piping water 550 kilometres from a reservoir near Perth at a cost of £3 million.

Kalgoorlie was first proclaimed Hannan after old Paddy, but was soon changed to its current Aboriginal name meaning 'silky pear'. The town's prosperity has fluctuated over the century as gold prices and mining techniques have changed. It was helped along by a nickel boom in the 1970s, when it became one of the world's leading nickel producers.

These days the alluvial gold is long gone, as are small-time prospectors. The population of Kalgoorlie-Boulder is now closer to 30,000. The gold is still there, but it's a long way down and you need a lot of money to get it out.

Before exploring Kalgoorlie proper, we went for a drive around the quiet next-door city of Boulder, which looked like it had been deserted; there's not much activity in an outback town on a Sunday. Back towards Kalgoorlie, we checked out the 'Superpit' open cut mine, the biggest hole in the Southern Hemisphere. It was an awesome spectacle. Over the years, it has slowly expanded down and out as blasts extend its reach. Massive trucks slowly traverse the terraces to the top of the massive mine and back down for a new load of rock. Watching them was surprisingly mesmerising.

Afterwards we headed back to our chosen hostel and watched some TV with the other guests, most of whom were rather strange, some possibly less than stable. I later found out that a lot of people in mining town hostels are there to do mining work and are about as friendly as they look. When one of the more talkative guests told us that some rooms had been broken into the night before, we decided to move on the next day.

On our second day, we visited the local Royal Flying Doctor Service headquarters. The very friendly staff showed us around an historical display and gave us a personal tour of one of the planes. They provide such a great service to the people of the outback and it was a pleasure to be able to tell them so in person and make a modest financial contribution.

Not far down the road is the Bureau of Meteorology and we'd heard that visitors were welcome so we dropped in. The meteorologists spent a couple of hours chatting to us and giving us a surprisingly interesting informal tour. We talked not only about the weather, but also about life in Kalgoorlie and in Antarctica, where two of the staff had worked. What little faith I had in weather forecasts was now completely shot to hell. The Kalgoorlie people only recorded data rather than forecast. Their data was sent to a central forecasting centre and fed into computer simulators. It seemed that the central forecasters would rather believe their whiz bang hi tech equipment than the people out in the field, regardless of what the weather was actually doing.

Next stop was the bush two-up arena for some good old Aussie gambling. A game of chance particularly popular with Australian and

New Zealand soldiers throughout the decades, the player's luck rests with the fall of two flipped coins. Kalgoorlie's is the only year-round legal two-up place other than the city casinos.

We struggled to find the out of the way place a little bit out of town and battled a rough driveway in dense bushland to get to there. The circular pit was surrounded by narrow wooden benches that were partially sheltered from the elements by a patchwork of corrugated iron walls and roof. The punters perched on and behind the benches throwing their money away were the main attraction for me, being a mix of Aboriginal and several nationalities clutching and exchanging bundles of money. Repeatedly the spinner flipped the pair of coins off the wooden kip, people yelled, others remained pokerfaced, and hundreds of dollars changed grimy and hard-worn hands. I wagered $10 on heads, came out with $20 after a favourable toss and quit while, for once, I was ahead.

The next morning, we retraced our steps to Norseman and continued south to the coastal town of Esperance. The only thing of note between Norseman and Esperance was the small curiously named township of Grass Patch, home, presumably, to a patch of grass.

It became increasingly evident that we had struck an extraordinarily cold period in WA's weather pattern. It was forecast to be zero over night in Kalgoorlie and wasn't far off in Esperance. Perth had just recorded its coldest day in 30 years. Lucky us.

Esperance takes its name from the ship L'Espérance in which Huon de Kermadec surveyed the coastline in 1792. It's a pity they didn't use the much more interesting Aboriginal name, *Gabba-Kyle*, meaning 'the place where the water lies down like a boomerang'. I like it. A pastoralist family settled Esperance in the 1860s, and it later became an important port for the gold mining centres up north. Its fortunes tended to fluctuate with the gold industry but it got a boost from its pioneering agricultural research in the 1950s, and it seemed to be doing pretty well these days, thanks largely to the tourist trade.

After checking into a caravan park, we took advantage of the narrow window of opportunity at the municipal museum that was only open between 1:30 and 4:30. The main drawcard was the fragments of the big Skylab space station, which crashed (or as NASA says, 'returned') in the area. It turned out to be a significant if only vaguely interesting collection of chunks of charred and twisted metal.

A particularly attractive feature of Esperance is nearby Pink Lake, which sits beside the 38-kilometre tourist Loop Road. Unfortunately, in the cold and overcast gloom, the lake wasn't pink. The road meanders along the coast past Australia's first commercial wind generation farm, which then supplied 12% of the town's electricity and is likely to be expanded. The bay is littered with small islands which accounts for its name, the Bay of Isles. Amazingly ice-coloured water rolled up onto the pristine beach. The picturesque road twists and turns over rough mountains like a knotted black ribbon, almost as though it were a Roadrunner cartoon background. The eleven-mile beach road takes the driver to Nine Mile Beach.

Esperance hosts the Festival of the Wind over the Christmas period. It's a pity we missed it - Glen could have been on a winner there.

After the tourist drive, we headed 60 kilometres east to Cape Le Grand National Park. The cape is named after an officer aboard L'Espérance. On the way, we passed the long tanker jetty that I gathered was no longer used for tankers, or any other vessel for that matter; just fishing. Strolling to the end of the jetty, we spotted a few dolphins jumping out of the water not far away, but of course the cameras were back in the car so we enjoyed watching without being concerned with framing or f-stop.

Once inside the national park, we headed to Rossiter Bay, where Eyre and his Aboriginal companion Wylie were given supplies by a passing French whaling boat commanded by Captain Rossiter. Eyre was so relieved (and running out of names after which to name things) that he named the bay after his rescuer. Sated, he and Wylie then continued west to Albany.

Not far away is the unspoiled Lucky Bay. The lagoon-like bay is fringed by a deserted bright white sandy beach with amazingly fine sand. The small rolling waves were a spectacular sparkling aqua, forming marvellous tree-like patterns in the sand as if they had been etched. Together with the kangaroo footprints, the beach looked like a giant work of art.

I was very keen to climb Frenchman Peak, a 260m tall granite rock with a big beret on its top. Glen lacked enthusiasm for the climb, but I managed to talk him into climbing some of the way up the steep mountain. There was not really a trail so we had to trudge up the dark rocky surface. Glen was happy to stop and rest for a while at a cave and slowly make his way down, and I pushed on to the summit. My fitness wasn't quite what I thought it was. The final steep climb to the top nearly killed me, but the view was awesome over the green park and out to where islands clustered around the coast, as beams of sun shone through gaps in the low silver-lined clouds. The only other climbers were on their way down as I reached the top so I was able to enjoy the moment in solitude. After taking a 360-degree panorama with my camera and settling my wobbly legs I began my descent. By the time I had scurried down Glen was still on his post-walk smoke so he hadn't been waiting too long.

On the way back to Esperance, we stopped at the tanker jetty again and wet the fishing lines for a while. As usual, we were struggling to get even a nibble and left empty handed, frustrated by the local kids running up the jetty with buckets full of decent sized fish. It's an annoyingly recurring theme.

As we departed Esperance the next day, the weather was much improved so we took the Loop Road again. The coastal drive was spectacular in fine, bright conditions. The water was icy blue and the beaches bright white. Pink Lake was indeed pink, made so by an alga that thrives in bright salty conditions and produces beta carotene, the pigment in carrots. I would have thought that would make an orange lake, but who am I to argue with Mother Nature.

Much of the 500-kilometre drive to Albany was through fairly dense forest. It was an easy and pleasing drive with very little traffic. We stopped for lunch at Ravensthorpe, a quaint one-pub town and made another stop later at a roadhouse that was being refuelled by a tanker brightly painted with huge insects. Not something you expect to see in the middle of nowhere, but then not much is.

Albany has a lot of people and a lot of traffic. It's the regional centre for south-west Western Australia and was the state's first white settlement. It is pronounced al-bany rather than all-bany as was brusquely pointed out to us by a local. After visiting the crowded town in peak hour, we checked in at an over-priced caravan park. From our early investigations, caravan parks in WA appeared to be much more expensive than anywhere else in the country, with the possible exception of the Northern Territory.

Albany was first charted by Captain George Vancouver, a contemporary of Captain Cook, in 1791 but wasn't settled until 1826. Throughout the nineteenth century, it was Western Australia's major port until Fremantle took over in 1900. During World War I, many of the AIF troop ships gathered at Albany harbour before sailing to Egypt, en route to Gallipoli. Whaling aided the town's survival until the late 1970s. I couldn't believe we were still whaling so recently. While the town didn't really do much for us, the coastal scenery around Albany was attractive.

The main attraction for us was the *Whaleworld* museum, built at the site of a relatively recent whaling station at Frenchman Bay, not far from town. There were several signs warning that it was not built for the purpose for which it is now used, so enter at your own risk. The smell of whale oil still lingered 20 years after the end of hunting. Plenty of photos of whales being slaughtered with massive exploding harpoons and then being sliced up were on display. Every bit of the mammoth whales was used. They were carved up on a deck and chunks tossed down holes in the floor into boilers. There was a good tour and movie, and typical of our luck, the whaling ship that had been undergoing renovations for the previous five years was being opened to the public on the day after our stopover.

Not far away we visited yet another blowhole that, despite the gusty winds, wasn't blowing. We hurried back up the steepish 400-metre path to see if the Beast and its contents remained, because signs at the car park entrance advised that it was a high-risk theft area. It always upsets me to see this. I guess people know you'll be gone for about 20 minutes, ample time to stick a screwdriver into your lock and swipe a laptop or whatever else they can get their hands on. We shouldn't have to worry about things like that, but we do.

Rock formations known as the Gap and Natural Bridge were a short distance up the road.

The Gap is a big gap and the Natural Bridge is a big natural bridge.

We stopped in town to pick up some film and grab lunch before continuing our journey westward. Western Australia has 63 National Parks and along the southern Coast Highway you drive past a large portion of them. The area of Western Australia south of Perth out to the South Australian border, has more than 60 national parks, reserves and state forests, all presided over by the Department of Conservation and Land Management, peacefully known as CALM. It's pleasing that the loggers' chainsaws won't be wreaking havoc in so many valuable and fragile places. Unfortunately, there's a lot of beautiful land around the national parks still being destroyed.

We considered taking a short drive north to the wine region of Mt Barker for the night, but decided that if we went we would just spend more money on supplies of which we already had ample quantity in the car.

Through the herbal town of Denmark, we soon came to the Valley of the Giants, named for the massive trees inhabiting the area. Having been born of the timber industry, the citizens of Denmark are a remarkably tree friendly lot. The Valley of the Giants sits in the Walpole-Nornalup National Park and the short treetop walk is the big drawcard. We forked over the $5 entry fee and loitered in the canopy for half an hour. The path is a 600m steel walkway suspended near the canopy of the karri and red tingle forest, about 40 metres off the ground. The treetop walk is a bouncy stroll but very pleasant. A few people didn't make it far before turning back after looking down. The walkway is almost as much of a spectacle (certainly more of a novelty) as the actual trees, especially after walking amongst the massive trees at Russell Falls in Tasmania. But the daddy of them all is an ancient giant tingle tree, which has a circumference of 24m at its burnt-out base. As a result, it's the largest known living Eucalypt in the world. My Corolla would fit comfortably inside the base. And despite being hollow at ground level, it still appeared to be thriving.

It was getting late in the afternoon and, being Friday, we weren't sure how easy it would be to find accommodation in nearby Walpole. The volunteer-run tourist information centre told us that the pub would be $60 for a night and while we were both ready for another pub stay, the price was out of our league, so we settled on the painfully named but recently renovated *Tingle All Over* backpackers' lodge. It was run by a very friendly couple, Geoff and Kerri, and turned out to be a little ripper. The cosy lounge room was warmed by an open fire, and tall travel tales flew from couch to couch.

Before we departed the hostel the next day, Kerri insisted on giving us some herbs from her small garden, booked our accommodation in Augusta and Geoff took a photo of us for their guest album. We were touched.

The drive west from Walpole through kilometres of old growth forest was spectacular. The huge and majestic trees variously shaded white, grey, brown and orange stood tall above the bright green undergrowth. The weather was ordinary, with constant and often heavy rain, but a picturesque eerie mist loitering in the forest made up for the rain.

Peace and tranquillity were shattered when we arrived at a logging site. An army of protesters from around the country was chaining themselves to trees, trucks and their environmentally unfriendly cars and cementing themselves to the ground. It had been a particularly major issue in Western Australia while we were there, splitting the conservative state government, resulting in the formation of a splinter (no pun intended) party being formed. Public support for them seemed to be very high and the premier was being very quiet on the whole issue. How they could get away with this senseless destruction for the sake of making newspapers from old growth trees, I don't know. The protesters' astute slogan appealed to me: 'wood-chipping costs the earth'.

We stopped for lunch at the Nannup bakery and had the best pies (chicken for me and steak and kidney and a sausage roll for Glen) of the entire trip. And we should know – we've tried a few. So we bought a couple more for dinner.

Our weather conditions were summed up rather ironically by two songs on the radio as we drove through pine and jarrah forests after lunch: *Have You Ever Seen the Rain?* (You'd better believe it!) by CCR and *I Wish it Would Rain Down* (Not!) by Phil Collins.

We drove past no fewer than ten national parks in one day. Along with WA's 63 national parks, there are two and a half million hectares of State Forest and six marine parks. All up, more than five million hectares of the state are protected. I was impressed.

On the recommendation of Kerri and Geoff at Walpole, we stayed in the small town of Augusta rather than the touristy and more populous winemaking town of Margaret River, but we drove straight to Margaret River to taste some wine before checking in. We stopped first at the tourist centre. The only way we could get a decent map of the area was to pay for it, which we declined to do on principle. This seemed a rather odd PR strategy and not one I have seen at any other wine region in Australia.

There were a couple of nice wineries but generally we were disappointed. Unfortunately, our time was limited and we stuck to the major (and expensive) wineries. A return trip to try some of the smaller places would be warranted.

The hostel, twice voted best hostel in Australia in its four years of operation, was indeed impressive. It was purpose built, had a warm fire, comfortable TV room, soap and hand towels in the bathrooms and a large clean kitchen. The hosts were friendly and helpful and the lodging was in a quiet location. There was almost no one else there and those that were there seemed to hide in their rooms all evening.

Augusta is one of WA's oldest settlements and has lived off the timber industry since its early days. It started its European life as part of New South Wales, despite being on the other side of the continent. It is perched at the south-west tip of Australia and has an imposing old lighthouse overlooking the junction of the Indian and Southern Oceans. I had the obligatory photo taken at the two oceans sign.

The next day we returned to Margaret River for some wine and cheese tasting. A highlight was visiting the Margaret River Cheese Company where we tasted some fine fromages and bought some dip and smoked cheese. Yummy.

In keeping with the precipitous weather patterns following our journey, the road north from Augusta and Margaret River was flooded. The river had broken its banks and water was lapping at peoples' front doors. The fates were kinder from there, with the weather improving as we journeyed north. To our great relief, that was just about the last rain we would see for the next two months.

We passed through the large town of Bunbury, which offered dolphin viewing and little else from what we could see, although I'm sure the holidaymakers from Perth held onto some secrets. Next up, attractive

Mandurah is a popular beach resort for Perthites looking for a break from capital city life, with its waterfront setting and close proximity to Perth (74 kilometres). Long ago it was also a hive of activity for the Aboriginal people, reflected in its name, from the Aboriginal word for 'watering place' or 'trading place'. Different books tell me different meanings.

We were hoping to stop at the deceptively quaint town for lunch, but being the beginning of school holidays it was chock-a-block so we kept going and settled on Hungry Jacks, the only place where we could park. It had been a long time since we last subjected our bodies to fast food (excluding the odd pie), so the guilt factor was low, not that it ever reached dizzying heights.

While munching on my Whopper, I noticed that most licence plates had no corny phrase like the other states, although there were a few with 'home of the Americas Cup' (it's time to move on people!) or 'WA – The Golden State'. I've heard that WA has also been branded as 'The state of excitement.' Another peculiar thing about vehicular transport was that hardly anyone was speeding. Everyone drifts up the highway at the speed limit or below, which is a refreshing change from some of the rev-head states we had travelled through.

We chose to enter Perth through Fremantle, *former* home of the Americas Cup, and then continued on through some of the suburbs where the other half live (or lived before they were thrown in gaol).

Our lodging in Perth was a hostel named the Witch's Hat, a very attractive building with a tall spire protruding from its Tudor frame, housing predominantly friendly and boisterous English backpackers.

After checking in, we took the free tourist bus into town. It drove past a place called the Lucky Shag, but didn't stop. From then on, we did a pub crawl of sorts back to the hostel. In fact, it was more of a pub stroll. Unfortunately Monday is not the happening night in Perth. We started at Bobbie Dazzlers in town and then went to Northbridge and the posh Brass Monkey, the Deen (at which hung a sign saying about their security guards, 'cab service, escort to your vehicle and harassment protection'. What sort of place were we in?), and finally Rosie O'Grady's. We settled in there for some draught beers from around the world, dinner and some live music. The staff weren't very friendly, but the beer and music made it worthwhile. The singer had a strong Irish accent despite his 29 years in Australia and sang a mixture of traditional Irish songs, along with some tunes from those classic Irish singers Eric Clapton, Paul Kelly and Simon & Garfunkel.

We ran the gauntlet of the park between the pub and hostel but made it back without being harassed by the hooligans hanging out in the park, about whom we had been warned. Then we just had drunken backpackers to contend with.

We spent the next relaxed day wandering around Perth. It's a fairly compact, laid back city with the obligatory street mall which all Aussie capital cities seem to have. Perth, in fact, has two: Hay St and Forrest Place. The city's CBD sits along the shore of the Swan River and nestles against the four square kilometre Kings Park over which the remaining millionaire entrepreneurs (those still alive, in the country and not in gaol) look. Perth is the sunniest of our capital cities, a fact not lost on the water loving locals who flock to one of its 19 metropolitan beaches for a dip before diving back into the rat race.

Back in 1827, a Scottish chap named Captain James Stirling came to the western coast of Australia in the knowledge that if the English Empire claimed a patch of land on the other side of the continent from Sydney, they could claim the whole place. He also knew he was racing against the French for southern real estate. When James surveyed the

Swan River region, he wrote that the conditions were perfect for a settlement, thanks to favourable climate, fertile soil and plentiful water. This turned out not to be one of his better judgements. He returned from England two years later to oversee establishment of the settlement. People came to settle in the convict-free area and soon realised that his enthusiasm was somewhat misguided. They weren't very happy but struggled for years to build up their new home town. Stirling was recalled to London in 1832 and somehow scored a knighthood for his troubles. Perth flirted with being a penal colony, but that too ended in failure. Thirty years after its establishment, Perth could only boast a population of 15,000. It wasn't until the 1890s gold rush that the town really took off. Ninety years later Perth thrived in the Australian economic boom, only to crash and take some of the country's highest profile entrepreneurs with it. But life goes on.

Of the many historic buildings dotted around town, we visited the century old Perth Mint. Among the highlights were watching a gold bar being poured, and (through holes in a thick cabinet) being able to feel and pick up a bar. It was very heavy with a silky-smooth texture and quite remarkable in that it almost felt soft. The Mint also had a set of scales where we were told our weight in terms of the current gold price. I was worth nearly $900,000 but Glen hit the jackpot at $1.4 million.

After our wanderings, we headed back to Northbridge, the social hub of the town. We settled on a quick Thai dinner after an agonising procrastination over what Glen felt like. Glen is a man who likes to carefully consider his culinary options to ensure optimal satisfaction. In the end, he was most impressed with his cheap four meats Thai feast. I was a little less enthusiastic about my choice but we were both stuffed by the end.

Barely able to move, we jumped in a cab to the Charles Hotel in North Perth to catch a triple-header blues concert. That was right up our alley. It was a great gig with local acts and the famous Hippos, all the way from Sydney. All were very good and we sat with an eccentric, nigh on weird, but pleasant local couple of blues heads who gave us some good tips for the trip north.

We pulled out of Perth the next day to continue heading up the western coast of Australia. On the way to Sorrento, a pleasant coastal suburb north of Perth, we passed delightful waterfront scenery and houses of a vast array of tastefulness. We also clicked over 20,000 kilometres since leaving Sydney. We lunched at a good restaurant at the large Sorrento marina. Kerri at the Walpole hostel had raved about Jetties restaurant so much we thought we'd better try their $19 buffet. And try we did, to resolute excess. Neither of us could recall being as full, as we painfully waddled back to the car. At least we wouldn't have to worry about dinner. Or breakfast and possibly lunch the next day.

18. Pinnacles, Pirates and Porpoises

Travelling north along the Brand Highway, we waved a fond farewell to urbanity. Much of the land through which we drove had been flooded in previous days. The rain had been so heavy and persistent at a place called Regans Ford that the river had broken its banks and the water was up to the tops of the riverside picnic tables.

We eventually made it to Cervantes, 'Gateway to the Pinnacles', and set up camp. I was surprised it was only 250 kilometres from Perth. I always thought of the strange looking rocks known as the Pinnacles to be further into nowhere, but long distances to others were becoming less significant to us. You don't expect to find such a Spanish-sounding place name as Cervantes out here after all the English and Aboriginal names dotting the country, but it was named after an American whaling boat that was wrecked on a nearby reef. On the way, we passed up driving through Yanchep, a small coastal town with a nearby waterway named Loch McNess, surely a marketing opportunity for a fast food chain.

We were in a small grassy area of a caravan park, metres from a beach. Alas, it was not exactly beach weather. In fact, it was decidedly wintry and the post-dusk dew was settling on everything. There were a few other campers with dogs and kids, a nightmarish combination when camping in close proximity. One of the dogs was little but loud, resembling a vociferous rat. At least they all went to bed early. The catch, of course, is that they were also early to rise.

After more indoor accommodation in the wintry conditions than we had budgeted for, we used our tents more frequently, I became quite attached to my little home away from home. Despite being only a couple of thin layers of material, it offered an escape from the hustle and bustle of a caravan park full of people. Mine was a small sturdy Macpac two-person dome - very cosy. It took me literally a couple of minutes to set up and take down and it was furnished with a self-inflating mattress and a hanging light. It wasn't too spacious but it was home. It was my only little space with no mozzies, spiders, scorpions or other tourists and I could set things out as I pleased.

The moon was almost new and the sky was fantastically clear and smothered with bright and surprisingly colourful twinkling stars. I zipped up the tent after admiring the cosmos and brushing my teeth, snuggled into my sleeping bag and drifted off to the sound of waves washing up on the nearby beach. What a life.

The next day we went straight to the nearby Nambung National Park, home to the spectacular Pinnacles Desert. It's a big park and the Pinnacles formations take up only a relatively small patch of it. Within about 150 kilometres there are no fewer than five other national parks, but this one is a doozy.

On the way in, we spotted an emu with two really cute striped small chicks. They look nothing like their gangly parents when they're young. Male emus are real SNAGs, looking after the big dark green eggs – up to 18 of them – until they hatch. It's a pity the cute little buggers have to grow up.

The Pinnacles Desert is made up of hundreds of sandy-coloured pointy anthill-like limestone formations varying from a few centimetres in height to three or four metres, protruding from the sandy and barren coastal plain. They are formed from seashell fragments blown up from the nearby coast and compacted over thousands of years. Surrounding sand has blown away to expose the prominent pillars. The multitude of shapes covers an expansive area almost stretching to the Indian Ocean to the west. Early and imaginative Dutch sailors thought that the Pinnacles were ruins of an ancient city.

The road snaking through the formations allows up-close views, and it's easy to pull over and explore them more closely on foot. We drove over the road twice, partly because my camera was on the wrong exposure setting on the first loop, but also to take in the great scene properly. We also took a diversion on the second loop, which took us to the most interesting of the formations we had seen, and where we think Billy Connolly did his naked romp in his around Australia TV show. Neither of us was tempted to emulate his bare-bottomed show.

On our way out of the park, we stopped at the beautiful and curiously named Hangover Bay. We walked up the beach for some time to what we thought was a shipwreck but it turned out to be a large rock several metres from the water's edge. It was jam-packed with large sea birds and large sea bird poo. The walk up the beach was particularly enjoyable in the beautiful weather we were finally encountering.

Back on the road, we drove through country claimed to be home to some of the world's greatest wildflower regions. The season is supposed to start in August, but the amount of sneezing and sniffling I did warned us that the bright yellow wattle in abundance by the side of the road was well and truly in full bloom. There are seventy different types of mucus-generating wattles in this part of the country. And speaking of seasons, we were a couple of weeks on the wrong side of the lobster season in what was known as the 'lobster coast'. Damn.

We were also back in eagle country. Several of the huge birds sailed majestically over the Beast, knowing a good car when they see one, and then crapping on it. The road was pleasant enough, traversing

214

some coastal areas but mainly inland through low scrub as far as the eye could see.

We stopped for petrol in Geraldton, a large country town that didn't entice us to stay. It's the main centre of the mid-west and has adopted for itself the name 'Sun City', but lacks the golf courses, casinos and exotic animals of its more famous namesake in South Africa. According to our tourist booklet, when people think of Geraldton, they think of rock lobster. Could have fooled me. While the town didn't enthral us, the area's history did. Geraldton sits right in the middle of a stretch of coastline called the Batavia Coast, named after a Dutch ship that ran aground in the area...

The luxury Dutch trading ship *Batavia* was wrecked in 1629 in an island group called *Houtman Abrolhos*, which means 'open your eyes' in Portuguese. The hint seemed to have escaped many a seafarer since, judging by the number of shipwrecks in the islands. It seems that Captain Pelsaert of the wrecked *Batavia* took a small party to the coast in search of fresh water and help. He left behind about 270 people on the wreck and on two waterless islands.

Pelsaert managed to make copious observations of the environment through which he travelled, and these were of great value to his superiors back in Holland. His was the first recorded description of a wallaby (other than the hundreds of invaluable Aboriginal rock paintings scattered throughout the country).

While he was busy touring the coast, a group of the sailors he left behind formed a pirate group to rule their new home. The group massacred 125 of the remaining passengers, men, women and children who they perceived as non-followers. Some though, managed to escape into the Australian outback and were thought to have married into Aboriginal communities. Their half-caste offspring were found and described generations later by inquisitive explorers.

Pelsaert didn't have much luck finding any help along the Aussie coast so he continued on to Batavia (now Jakarta), arriving 33 days after his departure from Houtman Abrolhos. When they arrived, Pelsaert ordered the execution of the high boatswain (who had gone with him) for 'outrageous behaviour' prior to the shipwreck. After exerting his authority, the Captain procured another larger ship to rescue the remaining passengers and crew back down south. Unfortunately, he got lost and it took him twice as long to get back as it took him to get to Batavia. When he returned to find that most of the people he came back to rescue had been slaughtered he executed the mutiny leaders and rescued the remaining survivors. He left two of the pirates on land, supposedly to make further observations of the environment. Not surprisingly, they were never seen again. The mutineers Pelsaert had 'spared' were flogged, keelhauled and pushed from the yardarm.

When the ship returned to Batavia, he had them executed. All in all, the trip was a financial and political disaster, and became known at the time as 'the unlucky voyage of the ship Batavia'. After all his effort, the unforgiving Pelsaert dropped dead one year later. In 1995 Queen Beatrix launched a replica of the ship and in September 1999 it set sail from the Netherlands for Australia, where it stayed on show for a year before returning home.

Tourists can undertake a tour of the ship at the Batavia Yard in Lelystad, the Netherlands, where it is now moored, or there's an excellent virtual tour available on the yard's website (www.bataviawerf.nl). Mike Dash gives a brilliantly descriptive and riveting account of the original ship's saga in Batavia's Graveyard (published in Australia by Orion Publishing Co, 2003).

Years after *Batavia* came to grief, another Dutch East India Company ship was lost in the area. The *Zuytdorp* vanished in 1712 while sailing from Holland to Batavia. It's the only one of the seven East India Company shipwrecks off the Western Australian coast whose survivors, if there were any, didn't reach Batavia to tell their story. In 1927 a small group of pastoralists was fencing and dingo trapping on the coast and spotted the wreck that was later proven to be the *Zuytdorp*. They also found bottles, coins (dated 1711), pots and gun pieces on the cliff top overlooking the wreck. If the passengers and crew did make it to shore, no one knows how they survived the violent ocean crashing against the rugged coast (which has also made salvage and research difficult) or what became of them. Perhaps a mast was used as a bridge to land or perhaps they were assisted in some way by the local Aborigines. Their fate remains a mystery.

There must be scores of similarly colourful stories sitting in our history books that have gone unnoticed by most of us. The richness of this country's history is remarkably deep for the relatively short period since discovery and European occupation.

North of Geraldton the Brand Highway becomes the North West Coastal Highway. There are some wonderful places along the Western Australian coast, but most are a fair distance from the highway. Our own next diversion was Kalbarri. On the way, we passed through Historic Northampton. 'If there is one word to describe the essence of Northampton, it is history'. We didn't stop at Historic Northampton but we would have if it were October, when Historic Northampton plays host to the 'Airing of the Quilts' festival which 'promises to be an event highlight of the region'. Reading the tourist brochure is entertainment in itself.

We were now nearly 600 kilometres north of Perth but didn't really seem to be getting anywhere along the endless coastline. It just keeps going and going, as did the trusty Beast.

During school holiday time, finding an uncrowded patch of real estate to pitch camp was challenging. We settled on a large park abutting the Murchison River. It was a late arrival and fast set-up. Establishing a campsite in the dark is not easy or pleasant, but it's quite entertaining watching others make the attempt.

At least we had the modern camper's luxuries, unlike Wouter Loos and Jan Pelgrom, the two souls cut loose by Captain Pelsaert of the good ship *Batavia*. They set up shop here back in 1629 with little more than the clothes they wore, and as such, were probably our first permanent European settlers, if not voluntarily.

'The part of the Batavia Coast known as Kalbarri is as old as the hills yet as new as its modern lobster-fishing industry'. Need I say more? Yes: 'The climate is mild and sunny for most of the year. Indeed, it's hard to find a resident who owns an umbrella'. Well it was bloody freezing the night we were there.

After dinner, we got chatting to a bloke camping next to us. He had been in a motorbike accident some time before and walked with a cane as a result. The accident and flirtation with death seemed to have changed his life. He had been reading the works of some eminent economists and politicians and had developed an interesting, and as Sir Humphrey would say, 'courageous', theory on how Australia should be governed. The foundation of his grand plan was that the land belongs to everyone and that rather than paying income tax, people should pay taxes based on the value of the land that they use. And that was just the beginning. We found several flaws in the plan relayed to us; some, as Glen said later, were large enough to drive a road train through. I started questioning some of his logic but got bored, gave up and went to bed. He'd have to do some more thinking before getting the publishing deal he was looking for.

To get to Kalbarri from the south, you drive through the Kalbarri National Park. The 1,000-square-kilometre park is real red rock Aussie outback stuff, famous for its gorges. Fast flowing rivers race through the red rock canyons punctuated with pale green eucalypt leaves on ghostly white trunks that cling perilously to the sun scorched rock in search of a foothold and nutrients. The Murchison River carves a winding path through the park, creating the 80-kilometre-long Murchison Gorge. We clambered, strolled and drove through the park, stopping at some spectacular lookouts. One, appropriately named 'Natures Window' at the Loop lookout, is atop a high rocky ridge formed by thin layers of red rock that have the appearance of being stacked on top of each other. The window is a large hole in the middle through which is a view of the vast expanse of red and pale green shades on the other side.

The last and least populated lookout we visited, Hawks Head, was definitely the most spectacular, and even more appealing with an uncrowded atmosphere. The lookout is a small rock overhang that hooks around at its tip like a Hawk's beak. It's not for those wary of heights, but the views over dusty scrub plains and the winding, striking red gorges cut into them are wondrous.

Out of the park and back to the highway, we continued north. I would like to have visited the town called Sandstone, mainly to see what the houses were made of, but the diversion was significant. It actually looked quite interesting in the travel brochure, but what place doesn't? Instead, we settled for the roadhouse settlement of Billabong for lunch.

One hundred and eighty kilometres further up the road, we reached the turnoff to Shark Bay and dolphin and tourist mecca, Monkey Mia. Our intended destination for the night was Denham, not far from Monkey Mia, 130 kilometres from the highway and the country's westernmost town. Instead, we stopped at Hamelin Pool, a windblown old telegraph station outpost, and decided it was the place to stay.

We were now in the region known as the Gascoyne - the 'Outback Coast' - that stretches 600 kilometres beside the Indian Ocean to Exmouth. It was around here in 1616 that Dirk Hartog became the first recorded white man to set foot on Australian soil (long before the Batavia's tumultuous arrival), and the one with the weirdest name. The region is named after the Gascoyne River, at the mouth of which sits Carnarvon.

Hamelin Pool consists of a small patch of dirt for caravans, some grass for tents, a teahouse and an old telegraph station. The station was established in 1884 and is now a surprisingly interesting little museum.

Just over a sand dune from the settlement is a 60-kilometre long beach consisting entirely of millions of tiny cockleshells so tightly packed that they are cemented together but still distinguishable as individual shells. Before times of environmental consciousness large blocks of the stuff were quarried and used to construct buildings. These days such use is limited to repair work on existing heritage buildings, but a couple of quarries remain a blot on the otherwise pristine and unique beach.

Hamelin Pool's 'fame' comes from being one of only two places on earth which supports ancient marine stromatolites that sit in the water just off the shell beach. Stromatolites are the oldest form of life on Earth, with a family tree dating back 3.5 billion years. They survive there because the water is twice as saline as normal seawater and sea grasses can't survive. Tiny organisms too small to see build the half metre tall rock-like structures in the water. The final product can be several million times larger than the organism that built it, so understandably they take hundreds of millions of years to build. And that's without unions.

There's a boardwalk over the stromatolites so you can enjoy them close up. From a distance, they just look like clumps of rock in the water. Closer up, they still look like clumps of rock in the water. If not for their age, I don't think they'd be much of a drawcard. Again, when environmental sensitivities were less of an issue, boats would anchor off the coast of Hamelin Pool and camel trains would wade out to deliver produce. The camel hooves and wagon wheels have left scars on the stromatolite community that will probably be there as near to forever as we need to know. Even if they look boring, I'm sure they're worth preserving. We humans have caused enough extinction.

We pitched our tents on a small patch of grass beneath the large dune flanking the tiny Hamelin Pool settlement. There were only a few caravans parked for the night and only one other group of campers: a mother and two daughters from Denmark in southern WA. We were all cooking dinner in the old camel shed next to the camping area and had a good chat. Their lifestyle probably fit into the 'alternative' category and was unashamedly government funded. Neither of us was in the mood to argue the point. As with our economist friend in Kalbarri, we found it easier and more interesting just to let these people reveal all rather than jump on them for what they are doing with their lives at the taxpayers' expense. They seemed surprisingly interested in the world of investment banking, but maybe they were just being friendly too.

Our little patch of turf was so appealing that we decided to stay for another night and make Monkey Mia a day trip. After doing a load of washing and hanging out the clothes to dry we feasted on scones with jam and cream in the teahouse. We then requested and got the $4 half-hour tour of the telegraph station. The ad hoc tour covered the stromatolites, shell beach and history of the telegraph station and Hamelin settlement.

The station has an interesting background, although that part of the two-room tour was a little rushed. I'm sure there were many more stories of interest emanating from the old wooden building. On one of the walls of the station was a large photo of a linesman up a telegraph pole fixing the line. Nothing unusual about that, except that he was fully naked. As the story goes, he had to cross a river to get to the inoperative line and rather than having wet clothes on the journey back to the station, he dropped his daks. Luckily, there was someone waiting on the other side of the swollen river to capture the priceless sight on film.

We also heard the story of a lady telephone operator at the station who had to relay an emergency discussion between Exmouth and Woomera when the usual telecommunications line was disabled. The two towns had to communicate in order to continue tracking a satellite. The operator admirably acted as a conduit, using terminology that may as well have been a foreign language, and the satellite continued to be tracked.

These days the settlement is served by a radiophone linked to the nearby Billabong roadhouse, which is in turn linked to the national optical fibre network. An optical fibre the thickness of a human hair can carry 30,000 conversations simultaneously. Try telling that to the telephone operators of yesteryear.

After a quick bite of early lunch at the tearoom, we hit the road for the hour-long drive to Monkey Mia. It appears that Monkey Mia is named after a ship, *The Monkey*, which moored at the area, combined with the Aboriginal word *mia mia*, meaning either house or view. Every source says something different. Monkey Mia is known for its dolphins, which swim up to the beach every day for a feed and a pat from ogling tourists in knee-deep water. Shark Bay, on which Monkey Mia sits, is one of 11 World Heritage Areas that satisfies all four criteria for listing. It is therefore no surprise that people have questioned the appropriateness of letting people mingle with dolphins and feed them fish. Shark Bay got its name from William Dampier who probably mistook the dolphins' dorsal fins for those of sharks.

In keeping with our record of poor luck, no dolphins came up to the shallows. According to the ranger, they had been and gone for the day. I was even going to brave the freezing water to be with them, but we could barely see any of them through binoculars. After about an hour and a half of waiting in the sun as the dolphinless water lapped the beach, we gave up and went back to Hamelin. Monkey Mia was a surprisingly pleasant place, and not nearly as crowded as I had expected. It resembled a small beach resort with crystal clear water, an attractive beach and tasteful restaurant and other businesses nearby. The rangers were very friendly and I don't know how they cope with being constantly asked by tourists (including me) if there were any dolphins around. My consolation prize was a great opportunity for pelican photos.

Back at the park, we witnessed – along with several excited grey nomads sipping on cask wine – one of the most spectacular sunsets I have ever seen. There was an amazing array of colours: pinks, oranges, purples and reds. We snapped several shots to try to capture its excellence as it set over the stromatolites for the 1.3 trillionth time.

We bade farewell to Hamelin Pool after downing a few more scones the next morning, and continued northward to Carnarvon, 'hub of the Gascoyne'. Every town in the west, as well as the south, is either a hub or gateway, and most are historic to varying degrees. I suppose anything can be called historic if it's been around for a few dozen years.

The drive was through lonely, desolate country. It was flat with low scrub and small trees sparsely scattered, similar to parts of the Nullarbor. There was no sign of much wildlife – dead or alive – unlike Hamelin Pool, which was home to hundreds of birds. Also along the way to Carnarvon, we crossed the 26th parallel, thereby officially entering the northwest of WA. Golly.

After arriving in tropical Carnarvon, we checked out a couple of caravan parks and settled on one abutting a banana plantation. We joined a national chain of caravan parks, bringing the cost of camping to a few bucks each at most places. Our patch of turf/dirt was right on the border of the plantation, which made for a pleasant tropical setting. If I'd really thought about it, I guess I would have worked out what the weather would be like at this latitude (hot and humid), but I hadn't. I felt like I was in tropical north Queensland, rather than the coast of dusty Western Australia, which I guess I had naively envisaged as one big desert.

Our chosen park was home to numerous retirees living in permanent residences (caravans and cabins) on the grounds. Many had quaint hand-painted signs out the front like 'Horrie and Merle's place' often brightened by a jungle of colourful flowers, gnomes and ornaments.

The residents were all super-friendly and always on for a chat about the weather, gardening or their current ailment.

After setting up camp, we explored the town and its two jetties. The prawn jetty was packed with kids and adults fishing. Several were hauling up decent sized crabs and bucket loads of fish. One kid wandered up to us, dropped his shorts, took a dump right in front of us and looked quite proud as he ran back to the water. Not the visitor greeting you expect, really. The mile-long jetty for which Carnarvon is known doesn't look anywhere near a mile, but we didn't walk it as Glen refused to pay $2 simply to walk up a jetty when we'd seen almost as many jetties as lighthouses. It was in a dilapidated condition, having been built in 1897, and the money was supposed to help a restoration project. It looked as though not nearly enough people had taken the walk.

We also visited Pelican Point and Oyster Creek. No sign of any pelicans or oysters. Both were sadly unscenic and unproductive for us.

There was a large indigenous population in Carnarvon and we saw the bad side when we stopped for supplies. An old drunken Aborigine asked us to buy some booze for him after the bottle shop staff had rejected him. Glen handled the tricky situation very well. As we were driving through town, I noticed an Aboriginal kid playing with a boomerang in one of the local parks. It gave me a good feeling. I hoped that he would learn with interest his culture from his elders. Unfortunately, we were to hear later that some members of the Aboriginal community had caused significant damage in town – all the shops had bars and grilles over their windows – and on one evening 80 windscreens were smashed at one of the caravan parks in town. I don't wish to be negative but this is a problem that needs more meaningful attention. I have since been heartened to hear that closer ties between native Australians and native Americans are being developed so that our indigenous people might learn from the successes of America's early inhabitants in the modern world.

On the way back to the caravan park we passed a big banana, obviously in competition with the Coffs Harbour, New South Wales version, but not to be outdone by the Queensland country town named 'Banana'. There are several plantations in Carnarvon and visitors can do tours at a couple of them. The park shop even sold chocolate-coated bananas.

Carnarvon is also built on commercial fishing, as evidenced by several large wholesale seafood businesses near the wharves. An additional, but now departed, industry was the nearby NASA satellite tracking station that still overlooks the town. While we were there it was being renovated for tours.

Back at the caravan park, we were lucky enough to catch the $3.50 sausage sizzle (but unfortunately missed the weekly bingo night). The sausage sizzle was a big event on the social calendar in Carnarvon – all the old folks invaded the showers early and dressed up to the nines, and were seated and ready with their grape juice for the 5:30 kick-off. After everyone had enjoyed their sausage and salad, an elderly lady dragged out an old piano accordion and belted out a few tunes for everyone to sing along to. They enjoyed all the old favourites: Roll out the Barrel, Long way to Tiparary, Knees up Mother Brown and Highway to Hell (just kidding).

On the way out of the park the next morning, I bought a chocolate covered frozen banana. It was nothing to write home about, but it had to be done. It's called research.

Our destination was 70 kilometres north along the coast to uninhabited Point Quobba, surely one of the oddest place names in Australia, although I have to admit that there's a lot of competition. On approach, a large and cheerfully painted sign warns that 'King Waves Kill'. And boy do they have king waves. It wasn't a particularly rough day, but the waves smashing against the low volcanic cliffs were spectacular. The main blowhole sent a plume of water at least ten metres into the sky, and the waves sent huge amounts of foamy water skyward all along the coast. One wave nearly wiped us out, but I managed to get some good photos as I clumsily scurried away from the encroaching wall of foaming water.

From the road leading to Point Quobba, we drove south for a while into a curious little community of shacks and caravans spread for kilometres along the dunes. It looked like a few permanents were there along with a few dozen holiday-makers perched in some of the clearings atop and between otherwise pristine sand dunes. The camping fee was $1 per person, payable at an honesty box, and there were a few outhouses along the sandy track. This place looked to be a surfers' paradise and drew anglers looking for a fresh catch from the Indian Ocean. It looked like a great little, but crammed and somewhat bohemian, community.

When the track got too soft, we turned around and headed north to Quabba Station and the HMAS Sydney memorial. Before the HMAS Sydney was sunk by a German battleship in 1941, it managed to mortally wound the German ship. All the Aussies perished, but some of the German crew survived, providing the only record of the battle.

As we drove back, I was still transfixed by the ferocious Indian Ocean's massive waves pounding against the cliff face and spraying water high enough to be seen from kilometres away. I guess they had the whole ocean from South Africa to build up. In some places where I couldn't see the ocean, it looked like there were dozens of white frothy volcanic eruptions in the distance. It was a remarkable place and, for us, a worthwhile diversion.

We got back to the North West Coastal Highway and continued north over the Tropic of Capricorn to Coral Bay. When we arrived, the small village was absolutely packed with people and cars. There were no camping sites so we headed on up to Exmouth. We had decided on the Lighthouse Caravan Park, about 20 kilometres out of town, which looked to be the most enticing of the ones we drove past, and spent an uneventful evening amongst the caravan dwellers.

Exmouth sits at the end of a cape jutting out into the Indian Ocean. In 1818, explorer Phillip Parker King, son of the NSW governor, named Exmouth after a British Naval officer.

Much later, Exmouth and the surrounding area were strategically important locations in World War II and were raided by Japanese aircraft in 1943. In 1967, Australia and the US built a naval communications base on the outskirts of town. It's called the Harold Holt Naval Communication Station. What is this fascination we have with naming aquatic things after our drowned former Prime Minister?

A field of very tall skinny communications antennae illuminated the sky as the sun set and we drove through town. Amazingly, they had survived the cyclone that had struck not long before our visit. Most parts of town still bore the scars. A beach near our tent was littered with pieces of caravans dumped in the ocean by the fierce storm, the drive-in theatre screen was shattered, and there were still roofs being repaired and new buildings being constructed. No doubt the Ningaloo

Marine Park that stretches along the coast south of Exmouth for 260 kilometres also bore the brunt.

The road back to the highway from town was flanked by hundreds of one or two-metre high conical anthills rising out of the grass and scrub. The rest of the drive along the highway to Karratha was one of the most interesting we had done. Much of it was completely flat but with small pockets of hills or mountain ranges rising like pimples from skin. The earth was the richest red (as were all the roads, bridges and emus), almost maroon, covered with gibber. We saw our first bright red Sturt's Desert Pea plant on the side of the road, a resilient little bugger that was to become a common sight along the road where moisture seems to be most plentiful.

Along the highway, we drove into a small but menacing storm front. We could see it for about half an hour as we approached, it rained hard on us for five minutes and then we drove out of it into blue sky. We felt like we were in a cartoon and Wile E. Coyote was laughing at us from behind a boulder, under which he would soon be crushed.

We were still driving through huge unfenced cattle and sheep stations. With the exception of one paddock where all the sheep were huddled together, we saw no livestock. The enclosures are so big I don't know how the farmers spot their stock, but suspect it's most often by air.

We decided to spend the night at the town of Dampier, about 27 kilometres north of Karratha, before heading south-east to the Hamersley Ranges. We stayed at the only caravan park in Dampier in a very small tent area with several other campers. The park is across the road from the ocean, looking out to the 42-island Dampier Archipelago, to which Dampier is, of course, the gateway.

Karratha is just over 1,500 kilometres from Perth via Highway 1, the route that circles the entire country, or about two thirds of the way up the coast from the southwest tip. The Western Australian coast is certainly a great place to appreciate distance. The town is the Pilbara region's largest and takes its name from an Aboriginal word meaning 'good country'. It is, you guessed it, 'the gateway to the Pilbara'.

The Pilbara is about half a million square kilometres of mineral-rich dirt. Pilbara Iron Ore makes up over 5 per cent of Australia's exports and accounts for about a third of the world's production. It also has gold, oil, tin, copper, salt, natural gas and asbestos (that's another story). Fishing is also big at the coastal towns. Not surprising then that Pilbara means 'fish' in the local dialect, although words for hot, empty or dirt would probably have been equally apt. The region is seriously hot but encompasses some of the most spectacular scenery in the country.

The biggest event in Karratha is the annual Fe-NaCl-NG festival, signifying the region's major resources: Iron, Salt and natural gas. As usual, we missed it, but it sounded fun.

The next day we kept alive our proud record of being last to leave the caravan park. On the way out we drove past a turn-off to the curiously named East Intercourse Island. As it happened, it wasn't only the weather in Karratha that was hot. We drove into town to shop and do some banking and discovered that it is a hotbed of young outback beauties. It was unfortunate that we were minutes away from departing before it struck us but we enjoyed loitering for the engrossing and unfamiliar sightseeing experience.

Before we left, we tried cleaning the increasingly grubby windscreen, but the water evaporated before we could wipe it off. As we drove out of town, the horizon was shimmering with the heat. We couldn't help thinking how much of a contrast it was to icy cold and wet Tasmania only a few weeks before, and how big and diverse the country is.

After waiting for a 2-kilometre iron ore train to sedately cross the highway with a mesmerisingly repetitive click-clack rhythm, we took the Hamersley Iron access road south from Karratha. The dirt-stained train loudly crawled, rattled and squeaked along the dusty and sunburnt rails and stretched so far we couldn't see one end from the other. Being a private road, travellers have to get a permit to use it, but it's well worth it. The road was unsealed and in various states of repair with a couple of river crossings along the way. The surrounding land is mountainous and off in the distance, flattop mesas protrude from the patchwork of red and green.

We turned off the road into the arid 200,000-hectare Millstream-Chichester National Park. The park road was very narrow but sealed and the scenery quite impressive, again a red and green landscape with flat-top mountains sprouting all over the place and small pockets of purple, red and yellow wild flowers along the side of the road. Our first stop was Python Pool, one of the park's many freshwater pools towered over by tall and steep red cliffs. There were several people enjoying a swim in the cold water, but no pythons that we noticed. We soaked up the impressive landscape (but no water) and then returned to the access road and crossed it to continue to Millstream, where an old homestead, now a visitors' centre, is located. The drive between the access road and Python Pool showed off stunning views of the surrounding countryside. Other than the cloudless blue sky, the outlook was dominated by three distinct colours: on either side of the red road, the lowly undulating land was scattered with light green grasses covered in patches by darker green heath.

After looking around the displays at the visitors' centre, we got back to the car to find a flat tyre that we (i.e. Glen) had to change in the searing heat as the local kangaroos watched with stony indifference and kookaburras laughed. It was especially frustrating as it was after four o'clock and we hadn't chosen a campsite yet.

Back on the track, we stumbled upon one of the most sociable campsites to which we'd been. After cooking up our steaks and sausages on the free gas barbecue, we joined in on a game of Yatzee and chatted the night away with a young couple travelling in our direction, a German environmentalist from Denmark, WA, and a few other friendly folk. I was interested to hear from the German about some of the bizarre methods used by protesters to stop loggers from doing their destructive jobs. It's quite amazing some of the lengths they go to, like cementing themselves to the cars, the ground and/or each other, so that it takes days to get them out. And quite often it seems that the police and the rescuers are on the side of the protesters and offer support. And who wouldn't – the old growth forests are spectacular and too valuable to be chopped down, minced up and used to make paper to wipe our butts.

I was awakened early the next day by what seemed excessive campground activity. In caravan parks, most of the over-nighters shower in the evening so they can get an early start. In the bush, they just leave early. As has become my usual procedure, I woke just before seven, listened to the ABC radio news, stock market report, local weather and classic comedy, and then braved the pit toilet before taking my book into the sun with a warm cuppa and reading for a while, enjoying nature before Glen stirred. It was a pleasant and soothing way to begin each day's adventure and a heck of a lot better than facing the morning peak on Sydney's rail network.

When we eventually got rolling, we headed back to the Hamersley Iron access road. It was a rough drive as the road deteriorated into an increasingly rough track. The highlight was crossing the sizeable Fortescue River. There's no bridge for cars – just trains - so I wouldn't like to try it in the wet. For us the water was no higher than the tyres.

After about 130 kilometres, we made it to the iron ore-mining town of Tom Price. If you're going to name a town after someone, you might as well use his whole name to avoid any confusion. Apparently, you can just call it Tom after you get to know it. Tom Price is the highest settlement in WA and was built by Hamersley Iron in 1966 to house its workers. It's not far from Paraburdoo, another candidate for best town name. It's also not far from the incognito Mt Nameless. The population of Tom Price is almost 4,000 and the average age is only nine, a small fraction of the average temperature! There's not much else can you do in a small overheated mining town except breed.

We got the tyre fixed in town (it was our second nail), did some shopping and checked into the town's only caravan park. It was situated a bit out of town with massive red cliffs overlooking the park. We secured a huge campsite with power, among some friendly fellow travellers. Despite the searing days, it got down to about two degrees at night in the inland desert.

It could have been an earlier start the next morning, but we ended up talking to our neighbours for a while, as is often the case in caravan parks. We met so many people on the way and all the retirees were especially friendly and always keen for a chat. This morning's couple was trying out their new $14,500 trailer that folds out into a big tent and was towed by their new four-wheel drive, both of which they loved.

When we finally got under way, it was a short drive to Karijini National Park (formerly known as Hamersley Ranges National Park). The park straddles the Hamersley Range and at more than 600,000 hectares is the state's second largest. It is full of massive red rock gorges straddled by brilliantly white-trunked eucalypts that seem to be able to grow into or out of anything. The good weather we were enjoying since Perth continued and the deep blue sky was spectacular as we walked through some of the weathered red gorges of the park, surrounded by trickling and roaring waterfalls and peaceful rock pools.

We took the short and rewarding walk down into one gorge to Hand Rail Pool. In one direction, there was a narrow gorge with steep vibrant red walls dappled with stains of purple and hardy bush scrub and trees. In the other direction was a pool of crystal clear water replenished by a small waterfall and a wider gorge upstream. Dozens of bright red dragonflies hovered over the water.

Not far away was Oxer Lookout, with spectacular views in all directions from atop the junction of four massive gorges. There was no way our photos could reproduce the magnificence of the view, described in Lonely Planet as one of the most spectacular sights in all of the Australian outback. The trick is also to get there when the sun is overhead so most of the gorge walls are lit.

While driving the 60 kilometres across to the other main gorge and camping area, a huge goanna crossed the road in front of us. It would have been over a metre long. I chased it with my camera and managed to snap it perched on a log, feigning a branch. It was another memorable outback encounter, something that was to become increasingly common in coming weeks.

We went straight to the large and well set out Fortescue Falls campground. Within the campground there was a major road with several loops radiating from it. Each loop had tent, caravan, bus and trailer sites, each separated by a small stand of trees. It took us a while to find a vacant site we liked, but we found and secured a good one where the tents fit perfectly on either side of the car with the table and cooking setup at the back. Ahhhh, home again. The ground was hard and there wasn't much grass around. Glen tried sticking his key into the ground Tony Greig style, but it wouldn't go in. It was a good thing we carried a mallet to sink the tent pegs into such terrain. It was a pleasant shady site with a good distance to the next occupied site.

After dinner and after all our neighbours had gone to bed, we sat in the middle of the road staring up at the sky. It was one of the most remarkable skies I have ever seen. Having just had a new moon and there not being city (or any other) lights to spoil the view, we could see stars right to the horizon for 360 degrees. Looking through my binoculars, the Milky Way wasn't just a white cloud; I could actually make out individual dots of light. We were both in awe.

When underway the next morning, we checked out the gorges around the campground. Those included Fortescue Falls, into which we walked, and Dales Gorge, which rewards visitors with the refreshing Circular Pool among some shady ferns. The plains above the gorges and some of the gorge walls were lined with the brilliantly white eucalypts, many with strikingly contrasting blackened branches bearing the scars of past bushfires. Hardy fig trees also managed to cling to life and gorge walls in Karijini.

As we drove out of the park, we passed huge expanses of purple, yellow and a few red wild flowers interspersed with the spinifex. Picturesque ranges surrounded us, with red rocks breaking through the dusty green vegetation, in some places appearing from a distance like a sprinkling of red snow. Anthills two metres high, constructed with deep burgundy earth, were scattered along the roadside and into the distance.

Outside the park, we approached the Auski roadhouse and caravan park. The scene was quite breathtaking – the country in front of us was almost completely flat all the way to the horizon, the sun was positioned such that it was difficult to see any detail in the landscape and the roadhouse stuck up like a small island in the middle of a sweltering, shimmering ocean. Glen aptly described the scene as big sky country. Some call it 'the never-never'. Comedian Vince Sorrenti described the outback as the biggest scam in the tourism industry because there's nothing there! They say you'll never never know because there is nothing to know. Droll, but dead wrong. Reading the descriptions of the outback by some of the early explorers would also give you the wrong impression. I hope to be one of those setting the record straight, or at least presenting an alternative take.

We dined at the roadhouse, which offered 'trucker tucker' in the form of a truckers' Tbone. We settled on something a little less substantial.

We had planned to go to the country's hottest town, Marble Bar, for the evening. As with most places in northern Western Australia, Marble Bar's main attractions for the tourist are gorges. The down side is the heat. Back in the 1920s, Marble Bar endured 160 consecutive days of temperatures above 37.8 degrees Celsius (100 on the Fahrenheit scale). This compares to the annual average of about 125 days. Gold mining got the town started, with the most famous nugget in the area being the 413 ounce 'Bobby Dazzler'.

The town's name came from some prospectors who thought they'd found a marble bar, but it turned out to be jasper, a type of quartz, much to their disappointment.

Other than some interesting facts, our information on Marble Bar was limited and out of date, and it was 160 kilometres of dirt road to get there so we decided to continue up to Port Hedland for a night before setting out on the long journey to Broome.

A little closer to Karijini, in fact right on the outskirts, is Wittenoom, a former asbestos mining town. Asbestos mining began in 1933 and lasted 33 years when too many miners died and they decided the health risk was too great. Controversy still lingers, with court cases outstanding and authorities continuing to try to shut the town down. The residents are defiant though, arranging their own utilities and lifestyles. There are still warning signs around Wittenoom and nearby Wittenoom Gorge cautioning visitors that after nearly 40 years, airborne asbestos fibres still float around looking for lungs to infest. The maps in two of our tourist brochures didn't even show Wittenoom and seemed to avoid any mention of the place. We decided against making the diversion.

Being our 100th night, and having camped for the previous ten nights, we decided to splurge on a cabin with bathroom and TV, and break open our best wine. We would have been fine if a cyclone had swept through town – the cabin was strapped to the ground with wire cable. Washing off days of sweat, insect spray, dust and sunscreen in preparation for the next leg of our journey made the cabin worth every cent.

19. Kimberley Country

After a good night's sleep at Port Hedland, we hit what has been described as 'Australia's most boring stretch of road'. It's a fairly accurate description of the 600-kilometre trip from Port Hedland to Broome. There's not much to look at along the way, with only a few roadhouses to break the journey. We were driving into a strong headwind that noticeably reduced the performance of the Beast; not a good thing when buying high-priced outback petrol. The landscape varied between largely barren scrub country and densely wooded areas. Several patches of land had been deliberately burnt out as was increasingly common. We learnt that the fires were usually set by Aborigines, in keeping with their traditional land management, to encourage new growth. The road was lined with hundreds of anthills and there were more eagles and other birds of prey than we had seen anywhere else.

We'd been doing pretty well on the long desolate drives, but this one pushed the boredom threshold close to the limit. You can only ask so many Trivial Pursuit questions before patience wears thin. And at 101 days on the road, our CD collection was getting a little long in the tooth.

We stopped at the big Sandfire Roadhouse and parked beside three massive three-trailer road trains. This is the roadhouse from which, within days of our visit, an unprepared American tourist had taken upon himself to wander through the desert without camping gear, supplies and without telling anyone. After searches mounted by local emergency services and a special search team brought in from America, it took a television film crew to find the weary walker after his 42-day sojourn. Those who don't recognise and respect the dangers of the outback are lucky to survive.

As we set off, not far beyond the roadhouse a truck had crashed with a load of watermelons, which were scattered in bits and pieces around the road. People were scouring the area for unbroken melons. The anxious and excited looks on their faces gave the impression of striking gold.

We had driven into a region of the country known as the Kimberley, which covers an area about three times the size of England and has a population of 35,000. It has an amazingly diverse environment and gets very hot and very wet. The area was charted over many years and by several different explorers including Abel Tasman (1644), William Dampier (1687), Philip King (1818-22), George Gray (1837) and Alexander Forrest (1879). Quite a few explorers (like us) still challenge ourselves through some of the harshest terrain in the country.

One challenge was finding somewhere to stay in Broome in the midst of school holidays. Luckily we had thought to book ahead. There were several caravan parks in town and according to the sign outside the visitors' centre, all were full, as was the overflow park.

We stayed at jam-packed Cable Beach, a few kilometres out of Broom.

When we finally got there and squeezed our tents and table into the tiny faux grass campsite, we wandered to one of the most beautiful beaches I have ever seen. Cable Beach is broad, long (22 kilometres) and white, with pale clear water rolling onto the shore. The tides around the northwest can be a massive 10 metres. The beach is named for the communications cable that ran from Broome to Indonesia, and it has been anointed as one of the top five beaches in the world. In a cruel irony, swimming in summer is hazardous due to the deadly box jellyfish. I sat on a dune watching the impressive sunset go through its paces over the ocean. When we got back to the park we lashed out on a seafood basket and bought some more beer. It is interesting and annoying in Western Australia; you pay a premium of two or three dollars a slab over the room temperature price for chilled beer.

While scoffing our dinner, we enjoyed watching our new neighbours trying to erect their tents. One of them took an hour and a half to put up a simple two-man tent. Remarkable, and Chaplinesque. I had practiced in my back yard before departure to avoid just this kind of display.

The mobs of kids at the campsite ensured an early start the next morning. Travelling in school holidays can be a long way from ideal. Having really wanted to visit Broome, we drove back into town. Neither of us was sure why we wanted to see Broome, but like so many other Australians, we did. It's a pleasant enough town with uniform white buildings housing a variety of cafes, souvenir shops and the famous cultured pearl producer, Paspaley Pearls.

Broome is pearls. It's on the 'Pearl Coast' and is host to the annual 'Festival of the Pearl'. Broome is a multicultural town, thanks to the early pearling days when Indonesians, Japanese, Chinese and other Asians flocked in. These days Broome's Chinatown features a few Chinese restaurants, but otherwise it's just a big mixed-blood community. When settlers started diving for pearls in the late nineteenth century, Aborigines were already at it.

The town was named after the then Governor of Western Australia, not a reference to its sanitation.

We didn't really give it too much of a chance because of the tourist crowds, but sadly Broome was a bit of a disappointment. I don't know what I expected, but it didn't deliver. Apparently a lot of people don't share my view but Glen was on my side.

It was about a 220-kilometre drive to Derby, the first town to be established in the Kimberley, now an agricultural and mining centre and the administrative base for several Aboriginal communities.

On our way into the town, we stopped at the prison boab tree. The boabs are stumpy trees with fat trunks and very thick bark, and have the proportions of bonsai trees. They are unique to this area and tropical Africa and are quite a sight. The giant hollow prison tree was one of many used by early police officers to incarcerate Aborigines from outlying towns as they brought them into Derby's courthouse and/or gaol. This is real boab country, and I guess that's why Derby plays host to the annual Boab Festival, a feature of which is mud football. Typically, we missed the festival by only a few days.

We didn't spend much time in Derby. Again, we probably didn't give it the chance it deserved, but some serious outback exploration was around the corner and we couldn't wait to get into it. We picked up some more information from their tourist bureau, ate lunch at the bakery and picked up a couple of things from the supermarket that we forgot in Broome (we always forget something). On our way out of town, we bought a couple of blocks of ice from a house to which the tourist centre gave us directions. It was an honesty system where we took what we needed from a big cool room and left our money in the box outside. Fantastic.

There are two ways to get across the Kimberley at ground level: one is the continuation of the sealed Great Northern Highway. The other is the more northerly rough-as-guts Gibb River Road. We chose the more challenging and less travelled of the two. The Gibb is shorter, at 710 kilometres, but takes longer to drive, thanks to the mountainous corrugations and inevitable flat tyres as well as leading to some great beauty spots. The condition of the road varies considerably, depending on the weather and the length of time since it was graded. In the wet season, much of the road is impassable. In the dry, it is very dry and dusty. Preparation is extremely important because it's usually a long way from anybody who can help. Those who brave the Gibb are rewarded with stunning scenery, along with a very sore back. It was to prove the highlight of our entire trip.

Not far from Derby is the Gibb River Road turnoff, the beginning of the Kimberley proper, and we were both excited in anticipation of what lay ahead of us. The road was developed to transport cattle from outlying stations to ports and markets. These days many of its users are travellers like us. Signs warning of the road's dangers in both wet and dry abound. We bought ourselves a guide brochure with distance markers and a detailed map and we were even issued with a code of conduct.

Our map told us that Myalls Bore was on the way out of Derby. It used to feed a 120metre-long cattle trough, thought to be the longest in the Southern Hemisphere. That's a long trough.

The road was sealed for about 60 kilometres – not as good as it sounds; it was barely one lane wide, flanked by narrow shoulders. Amazingly, semi-trailers came hurtling down the road and the only way to stay alive was to pull over and wait. Dozens of reckless four-wheel drivers also barrelled along the road. I guess when you're near the end of the road coming the other way you just want to get off the bone-jarring dirt and rock and forget about your code of conduct.

Further up the road on the unsealed section, the graders were at work. It seemed that the road deteriorated reasonably quickly. Grading must be a really thankless, and endless, task. We eventually made it to our destination - Windjana Gorge National Park, a 20kilometre diversion from the main road.

The spacious National Park campground was shadowed on one side by imposingly high sheer cliffs of black and orange rock that took on various hues as the sun sunk slowly over the horizon. It was a wonderful situation. But as the sun dropped, so did the temperature, down from the 30-degree daytime winter warmth to a brisk desert chill.

We whipped up a couple of steaks and sausages for dinner, accompanied by a ripper of a Shiraz. Glen, preceded and followed this with a few beers. As he says, 'I can't help it if I like a few beers'. I can only commend Glen for the care he took with the beer. The drinking water might have been sitting in the sun gradually absorbing the desert heat, but the beer never saw a ray of light. And wasn't it worth it at the end of a long day of dusty, rugged, sweaty driving.

Thanks to a bustling campground, we both rose early, had packed away our stuff and were doing our first walk through Windjana Gorge by nine o'clock; quite an achievement for us. We were on holiday after all.

Windjana Gorge is a three-and-a-half-kilometre crevasse carved by the Lennard River through the Napier Range. The river wasn't supposed to be flowing during the dry season, but there was plenty of water for our visit; certainly enough for our first encounter with crocodiles.

The walk along the river was absolutely fascinating. The gorge walls stretch up 100 metres from the river with the odd eucalypt, fig and boab tree somehow growing precariously from cracks in the rock. It is quite a wide gorge, up to 100 metres across, allowing plenty of warmth for the freshwater crocs to sunbathe in on the beach.

Unlike the gorges at Karijini that you enter by walking down from the rim, you don't descend into Windjana. The river cuts through a narrow mountain range so the campsite is almost level with the river. Glen was glad not to have to struggle up a gorge at the end of our leisurely but sweaty stroll.

The gorge was spectacular enough but the highlight for me was seeing the crocs close up. The freshwater crocodiles are considered 'harmless' while the saltwater species are the ones of which you have to be particularly careful. As both inhabit the area, my preference was to keep a healthy distance from all of them. Unhealthily, I crouched three metres from one for a (brief) photo opportunity. 'Closer' says Glen, 'Closer!', much to the amusement of the few other walkers. The croc was slothfully taking in the sun just at the water's edge and didn't seem too interested in the gawking tourists walking past with snapping cameras.

As we delved further into the gorge, there was an increasing number of crocodiles, most of which were equally docile. Finally, we came across some action when we spotted two crocs either having a domestic or getting amorous. With crocodiles it can be hard to tell which. There was a display of open snouts and deep growling as the smaller of the two attempted a retreat. As we walked off, one of the other visitors was berating his wife for not taking a photo of this once in a lifetime opportunity rather than enjoying it herself.

On the return trip, Glen lost his footing on the trail and nearly went swimming with the crocodiles. I don't know who would have been more frightened, Glen or the crocs.

In the afternoon, we travelled south to Tunnel Creek National Park, about 30 kilometres further from the Gibb River Road. The main feature, Tunnel Creek, was another fascinating sight, where you take your torch and wade through cool knee-deep water along the 750m natural tunnel. In some parts, you have to crouch and in others the ceiling is about ten metres high. I had expected something low and narrow, but the more open parts were massive. Huge stalactites dangle from the ceiling like ornate chandeliers. About half way along the tunnel is a large hole where the roof has caved in and tree roots cascade down from the hill above to reach the water. The other end of the trees are home to Australia's only carnivorous bats, according to a fellow tourist. Five species of bats dwell in what has become known as the Cave of Bats. Thankfully, it wasn't until after the trip that I read of crocodiles residing in the permanent pools.

These two places added up to one of the most scenic days of the trip, a sensual feast. This was what the trip was all about. And just about every day in the Kimberley was as spectacular as the last.

When we got back to the campsite in Windjana, a Spanish armada arrived in a rental bus and immediately had an argument with the park ranger about not being able to start a fire. They weren't interested in hearing about a total fire ban. On the other side of our otherwise friendly and multicultural campsite, a German chap was having a shave using his rear vision mirror. I'm not sure why you'd bother out here. We certainly didn't.

Back on the Gibb River Road it was still a very rough ride over the ubiquitous corrugations and occasional pot holes, not to mention patches of the powdery soft and deceptively dangerous bulldust. We did quite a few river crossings, some small and a few bigger ones - very exciting for us city slickers. I waded though the biggest rivers just to make sure they weren't too deep for the Beast. I don't think Glen was eager to do the wading but was happy to volunteer his thongs. Up in the Top End I was happy for Glen to do the driving so that I didn't risk getting the car bogged up to the doors in a swamp or river. So was he. Driving through that terrain was hard work and mentally draining, so by the end of each day, Glen was exhausted.

After almost 100 kilometres, we arrived at the turnoff to Lennard River Gorge. Although the track was only eight kilometres long, it was so rough it took us 25 minutes from the road to the gorge. A few river crossings and some very rocky patches threw the Beast around, even at crawling pace in low-range four-wheel drive. The walk to the gorge was short and rough, but I was keen to try to get further into it. Lennard River is only a few metres wide with black and red rock stretching up about 30 metres above the river flowing though, with a small pool at one end. As we were admiring the view from the top, a family passed us and continued down to the river for a swim. I made it almost to the bottom but stopped because I didn't want to risk my backpack full of camera gear getting wet (that was the excuse I used anyway), and the last few metres were very steep and slippery. Glen was waiting at the top and we took a different but not much longer route back to the car. We were both pretty stuffed after the steep rocky trail and the relentless heat.

From there, it was not too far up Gibb River Road to Silent Grove and Bell Gorge, our next destination. There's a boab tree somewhere with a bell carved into it but we missed it. Not sure which came first – the name or the carving. Again, the track was rough with a few biggish river crossings, but nothing like the shorter Lennard River road. The large but pleasant campground at Silent Grove offered toilets and showers but we were keen to go further up the side road to Bell Gorge. There were only ten segregated campsites at the gorge, and we were lucky enough to bag the last one. They had a system whereby each campsite had a tag hung on a wall at Silent Grove and if there were no tags, there were no campsites. If everyone stayed overnight, there's no more the next day. The ranger confirmed that we were lucky to get the last one at the time of day we arrived, and it was well worth the effort. The sites were quite large and spread out, far enough away from neighbours to avoid disturbance. Each two campsites shared a flushing toilet. Luxury!

After setting up camp, we drove up to the gorge. A short rocky trail takes the weary walker to a beautiful spot with views up and down the gorge. The trail empties into an open area centred on a large pool of water sitting atop a ten-metre-tall terraced waterfall. The clear, still water reflected the pale green vegetation shading its edges and the blue sky above like a mirror.

We walked along the gorge rim for a while until Glen turned back for a swim. I continued on through the burnt-out scrub and bulbous boab trees but didn't want to go too far on my own and soon turned back for a dip. Glen was luxuriating in the cool tranquil waters of Bell River when I returned. The water was quite chilly and very refreshing. We both sat under a small waterfall that provided a perfectly reasonable natural spa. The scene was perfect – cascading water through several small and large pools, small shady trees rising from the water and around the water's edge, colourful gorge walls on the sides and mountain views through the end. Even the weather was perfect. A cocktail or two and scantily clad waitresses would have made the scene complete.

When sufficiently refreshed, we returned to the campsite for a quiet and early night with Spam-burgers and baked potatoes cooked on the fire. As on the previous evening, the sunset was a thin strip of very rich oranges and purples on the horizon, accompanied by an amazing symphony of birdcalls. The sounds gave a very Jurassic feel to the otherwise quiet campground.

I was woken during the night by a stirring in the bushes by my tent. The stirring was a couple of little furry critters, a bit bigger than a rat, hopping around the campsite and through the tall grass. According to the ranger we spoke with the next day, what I heard and saw were brown bandicoots. We also learned that the gracefully soaring birds of prey frequently circling overhead were brown kites, also known as Kimberley kites to the locals.

We moved on, delighted with another spectacular spot and hungry for more fascinations on offer in the Kimberley. The road from the Bell Creek turnoff got rougher and rougher, with a few river crossings and corrugations the size of sand dunes. Well, not quite. How the rest of the road could be worse (as it was supposed to be, according to our guidebooks), I wasn't sure. Along the road, we stopped at tranquil Galvans Gorge, which fed several small pools of shallow water with floating water lilies in flower.

Towards the end of the day's drive, we overtook four thrill-seekers on pushbikes. It's hard not to kick up a dust cloud, even driving slowly, so I can't imagine what would drive someone to do something like that in such a place and in such weather. Air conditioned comfort in the Top End is tough enough.

We made it to Mt Barnett Roadhouse at lunchtime and filled up with petrol, the most expensive of the entire trip, half again as dear as

Sydney. The roadhouse is on a cattle station owned and managed by an Aboriginal group, but there was no sign of any natives at the roadhouse. Also at the roadhouse, we bought overpriced ice, lunch (meat pies) and frozen meat and bread. I guess delivery isn't cheap in these parts. The bargain was paying $5 each for the campsite 7 kilometres up the road at Manning Gorge.

We quickly set up the tents in a shady and secluded spot and then hit the trail to Upper Manning Gorge. The trip was 3 kilometres each way and took about an hour to get to the gorge, where we had a refreshing swim. The rocky walking track was marked with faded aluminium cans stuck on trees and the odd arrow painted on a rock. We both had a dip in the ponds under the broad cascading waterfall, and sat around for a while admiring the scenery while drying off in the sun. Compared to some of the gorges we had seen, Manning was quite wide with relatively low walls. There were several pandanus and other trees hanging over and in the water and a number of small cascades. It was again a tranquil spot and very refreshing. As the temperature dropped we headed back to camp under the long shadows of the setting sun.

The campsite was huge so we managed to procure a good spot not too far from the below par pit toilet (BYO toilet paper) but away from the main concentration of campers. Both of us preferred roughing it a bit to avoid the noisy throng. Despite the searing heat during the day, it dropped down to about 10 degrees when we eventually turned in for the night.

It was a long day's drive from Manning Gorge, with poor Glen at the wheel the whole day as we continued east. As with Cordillo Downs, the constant jarring of the rough road must have done something to our tumble-dried stomachs (not to mention our backs and bruised kidneys) because neither of us was very hungry. We didn't stop for lunch until three (and all we could get was a packet of chips) at Jack's Waterhole. Neither of us could be bothered unloading the stuff to make sandwiches.

The drive of about 250 kilometres was tough going. It varied between moderate to severe corrugations, patches of bulldust, small sharp stones jutting out of the surface, large rocks stuck in the road and soft sand stretches. Our speed varied from crawling pace to about 80kph. Only the last 20 kilometres had recently been graded and even that was very rocky. At about 2:30 the road got its revenge and we had a major tyre blow-out taking a sharp corner. There was no hope of a patch job on that sucker; it was history.

As Glen set about replacing the tyre, it allowed more time to sit back and take in the quiet atmosphere. The landscape was rugged and mountainous, scattered with spinifex and tall grasses, boabs and eucalypts. I'm sure there were other trees but botany isn't my forte.

With replacement tyre attached and the Beast repacked, we pushed on at a slightly slower pace. We negotiated several more river crossings, including the Pentecost, about 30 metres wide but not very deep, and not far from our destination.

As we drove towards El Questro Station where we had planned to set up camp for the night, we were confronted with the spectacular Cockburn Range. The bluff of the flattop range gently changed through shades of orange as the sun set behind us. At one stage, the cliffs were a brilliant red. Even the wooded mountains became purple-red as the sun set and shadows became longer.

We finally made it to El Questro cattle and tourist station. It covers one million acres of land and while they still run a few head of cattle, tourism is the main business, in common with most of the stations along the road. El Questro, however, is on the grandest scale. The top accommodation in the homestead went for well over $1,000 per night. We settled into the main campsite at $10 each, a price that former Midnight Oil singer and now member of parliament Peter Garrett and his family seemed comfortable with as they pitched their tents not far from us. There was a shop and bar near the campsite, and we enjoyed a hearty meal while chatting to the eclectic staff.

By the way, *El Questro* doesn't actually mean anything. There are various stories, but no one really seems to know where the name came from. The station is owned by an English chap who, so the story goes, was given £1 million for every year of his life at his 21st birthday. He brought his stash out to Australia and married a girl from Melbourne. He then paid an astonishing $1 for each of the one million scenic acres of land at El Questro. Imagine having a couple of mountain ranges in your back yard. And these are some of the most picturesque ranges in the country, not to mention all of the spectacular gorges. Thankfully, the owner realised the tourism potential of the place and before long had it open to the public with three or four types of accommodation and plenty of outback activities.

A variety of birds, particularly cockatoos and geese, in concert with children and general activity, got us up early the next morning. A warm shower felt fantastic and then we battled for one of two washing machines and had some breaky while the washing machine was battling with our very dusty and crusty clothes. A leisurely morning seemed in order after our hard previous day so while Glen snoozed in his tent, I read by the river until the geese, crows and flies got to me and I moved up to the bar area. I ended up spending most time just watching the passing human (and other) traffic. A horse and a two-foot long lizard strolled through the bar area along with two very cute baby donkeys that wandered around the place acting like pet dogs. They slept in the campground and never left each other's side. I was slightly more nervous when a bull sauntered through the beer garden, but he didn't bother anyone.

After lunch, we took the Chamberlain Gorge cruise which was well worth the surprisingly high charge. Although only a short trip up river (1.5 kilometres each way), it lasted for about three hours, and included a history of the station and rundown of the flora and fauna of the area.

At the end of the river, we piled out of the boat to see some Aboriginal rock art. The first artistry we saw was by Aborigines who used to live in the area and was the most intricate and vivid I have ever seen. Also in the area were several examples of Bradshaw paintings, named after their discoverer Joseph Bradshaw in the late nineteenth century. No one knows who has painted these figures. It wasn't the Aborigines, as the ornate stick figure structure is quite different from any Aboriginal art and indeed was painted over by many Aborigines in a kind of ancient graffiti. The main authority on the paintings believes that they could date back to a species of humans that became extinct before the Aborigines even came to Australia. The mystery continues.

Saturday night was the weekly BBQ at El Questro so we paid our $18.50 for a good steak and great barramundi and an enticing damper as well. The damper recipe they used had self-raising flour, milk and honey – quite different to the recipes we were familiar with.

After dinner, we were treated to a display of lasso and whip cracking by a bloke who looked either Aboriginal or Afghani. We tried to find out, but he would only say that his origin was Queensland. He also recited a couple of his own poems, told us how much he loved Australia and sang a song or two. It was all a bit corny, but fun nonetheless. Then came Boonga, an Aboriginal guy with a guitar, who sang some classics as well as a few of his own numbers. Included in his original repertoire were *Grader Drivin' Man* (sung to the tune of Jimmy Barnes's *Working Class Man*), *My Mate Flagon*, *I Never Gone To Bed With An Ugly Woman But I Sure Woke Up With A Few*, *El Questro* and a staff favourite, *Ugly Old Mole*. If only Peter Garrett was around to join in.

We were really loving El Questro, were still exhausted and still had plenty to see, so we decided to stay another night. I was keen to do a horse ride but Glen wasn't a fan of horses so I booked for one on a ride around the station. A couple staying at the highly priced homestead were booked on the ride, so it had to be checked whether a lowly camper would be allowed to tag along on the trip. I could, and did.

The ride was gentle and enjoyable. We meandered through the bush along and across the river and back to the campsite. I tried to go for a canter through a dried-up creek bed at the encouragement of our guide Brooke, but unfortunately my horse Troughy (having fallen in a trough as a youngster) had different ideas and we were very soon back with the others. The English couple who were staying in the very luxurious homestead seemed to enjoy themselves, and proclaimed almost everything to be 'smashing'.

Of interest along the way were a giant boab tree, a couple of goanna burrows, a freshwater croc sitting in the river we crossed a couple of times, a pheasant (I didn't even know we had them), and a green ant nest. Brooke made me suck on one of the green ants to get a vibrant minty taste that stung my chapped lips. The locals, so the legend goes, get a bunch of the ants and mix them with water to produce 'Kimberley Kool Ade'. The taste and sting lingered for ages.

After the ride, I wandered up to a campsite where I had seen Tim Bowden, ABC TV presenter, historian and author. Both Glen and I had read his *Penelope Goes West*, a book describing his journey from Sydney to Margaret River, as we headed along the same route. After I saw him, I was determined to tell him how much I liked his book and his TV series on Antarctica, even if I had to disturb him and his wife at their campsite. He was very amiable, happy to sign my copy of the book, and interested in a chat.

The two young donkeys continued to wander the camping area. They were indeed the cutest asses I'd seen in a long time, absolutely irresistible. Several hundred feral donkeys are shot each year around these parts. During a donkey cull, a couple of the resident foals ran into a hunter's arms and he couldn't bring himself to shoot them, so they became pets of the resort.

For dinner, we cooked up a chowder and had a bottle of Chardonnay and then a couple of ports around the small campfire Glen had fired up. I played a few tunes on my old blues harp to the apparent enjoyment of the group camping next to us, who donated some wood for our fire so I would keep playing. Some people have no taste in music.

As usual, the black and white magpie geese and tourists got us up early so we moved on.

About 30 kilometres from the El Questro campground is Emma Gorge, still within El Questro's boundaries. The walk is about 45 minutes each way over a very rocky but well signposted trail past a serene pool large enough and safe for swimming. Further on is the spectacular gorge, over which tower more high red rock walls and a couple of waterfalls plunging to the pool of tranquil cold water below. On the way there, we bumped into the couple with whom I was horse riding. They had their own private ranger to lead them through the figs and pandanus trees. Smashing.

After the stinking hot walk, we continued driving to the end of the Gibb River Road, only another 22 kilometres. Driving again along the relative smoothness of Highway 1 was welcome, but the end of such an engrossing adventure was disappointing. Luckily northern Australia had plenty more to offer, so we'd only just begun.

It was only a short trip to Kununurra, where we pitched camp in a caravan park right on the shore of Lake Kununurra. After setting up and taking in the view from our prime campsite, we went back into town to replace the blown tyre. We also visited an excellent local butcher to stock up for dinner. The butcher sold venison, crocodile tails, kangaroo steaks and tails, emu steaks (sold out), camel steaks, buffalo steaks and a variety of other game and seafood. Most of the interesting stuff was very expensive and neither of us was skilled in cooking camel so we stuck to a couple of traditional but very good T-bones.

Kununurra town is a pleasant place; a large outback town with enough amenities, great weather and friendly people. The name comes from the Aboriginal word for 'the meeting of big waters'. It's the eastern gateway to the Kimberley and sits on Lake Kununurra and the Ord River. In the 1940s, the area was assessed to have agricultural potential. Ten years later, the Ord River Irrigation Scheme was launched. The Ord River Dam was built and it created Lake Argyle, one of the Southern Hemisphere's largest man-made lakes and several times bigger than Sydney Harbour. Not far from Kununurra is the Argyle Diamond Mine, the largest of its kind in the world and staffed by the townsfolk.

Aborigines are prominent among Kununurra's population of 6,000, chilling out on their blankets in the town park, and all seemed friendly and peaceful.

In a reversal of the normal chain of events, Glen got up early the next morning and fished for an hour or so before I rose. He caught some puny fish, including one barramundi that had to be returned to the lake. There was nothing big enough to eat in his haul, but he did better than we'd done on the trip thus far.

We were on our way south to Purnululu National Park, better known as the Bungle Bungles. Highway 1 may be the main road that traverses the country, but it narrows to just one lane in several places. Thankfully, there were bridges to cross some of the larger rivers. We stopped at Turkey Creek roadhouse for a quick bite and saw our first snake for the trip: a big and venomous brown snake well and truly squashed on the road.

The track into the park was narrow and very rough and took us almost two hours to traverse. It had all the Gibb River Road had to offer and more in terms of bone and car jarring travel. At the start of the trail (through Marble Downs Station), there was an information bay advising of the dangers along the road. It also warned that there were dingoes around the campsites so lock up your food and rubbish.

By the time we got to the Kurrajong campground it was after four so we found a secluded spot not far, but far enough, away from the wafty pit toilet and set up camp. Through the trees, we could see the bright red Bungle Bungle Range slowly changing colour as the sun set.

The next day ranked up there with Windjana/Tunnel Creek as one of the most spectacular days of the trip. The walk through the famous domes of Purnululu was one breathtaking vista after another and justified the jolting four-wheel drive only trip to get there. I was in awe as we wandered through the massive beehive-like striped mounds.

Purnululu was at the top of our list of must-see destinations. The landscape has been carved out by wind and water from the 360 million-year-old range to create the spectacular formations that appear in so many calendars, postcards and documentaries. The remarkable beehive patterns are made up of silica (the orange stripes) and lichen (the black) layered over millions of years. The name Bungle Bungle is thought to come from the name of the bundle bundle grass found in the Kimberley region. Amazingly, the place was only declared a national park in 1987.

From the walk among the domes, we continued to the spectacular Cathedral Gorge. At the end of the trail one is confronted with a massive red rock cave in the form of a natural amphitheatre. The place was awesome – probably 50 metres in diameter, partially covered with the rock wall curving in like a giant shell. There was a large lake in the middle of the cave, blanketed with a layer of algae, making the water appear like a sheet of green glass. There was absolutely no movement that we could see and when we chucked a rock into the water (it had to be done), it was swallowed up and the gap in the greenness quickly closed. We also felt the need to test the acoustics of the amphitheatre with a few piercing whistles. We were impressed, as no doubt were our fellow tourists. We sat quietly for quite a while just soaking up the atmosphere.

Stopping briefly for lunch back at the campsite, we continued on to Echidna Chasm. The return walk through the chasm was only a little over an hour through a gradually narrowing gorge but stunning from beginning to end. The walk took us along the dried riverbed (as did some of the drive there) past hundreds of Livistona palms, which, like figs, seem able to grow anywhere. The walls of the chasm were strikingly red and seemed to reach up to the rich blue sky. As we progressed up the gorge, the walls became closer and closer, eventually almost to shoulder width. There was some serious rock hopping involved, but we made it to the end of the chasm where we took the obligatory photos before slowly clambering back.

From the chasm, we drove directly to Walanginjdji Lookout to check out the reputedly awesome sunset views. A group of jocular English and Irish backpackers had struggled up the mountain to watch the sunset. The lookout offered a fantastic view of the western side of the Bungle Bungle Ranges which, typically of this area, turned all shades of red as the sun set over the opposite horizon. After that remarkable show and after everyone else had left, we were on our way down the track when we were confronted by a massive full moon rising over the range. The moon appeared several times larger and brighter than usual and stopped us in our tracks as it rose over the red mountains and meandered upwards into the night sky. What a pity everyone else missed out.

Little did we know the show wasn't over. When we got back to the campground to rustle up some soup for dinner, as the moon climbed higher in the sky and we casually gazed up to the stars, we were treated to a lunar eclipse. Reflecting on what an amazing experience we were having, all we could do was laugh. What a pity so few Australians will ever truly experience the outback as we have.

The trip from the campground back to the highway the next day was two more bone-jarring hours. It was a welcome relief finally getting to the highway and I took over the wheel from an exhausted Glen.

The remainder of the day's driving was plain sailing until we hit one of the many bushfires we saw across the plains. This one was larger than others we had seen and was lapping at both sides of the road. The fires in general didn't seem to be too fierce, partly because they appeared to be frequent, but also because there wasn't that much to burn. The undergrowth burns well but doesn't produce a big flame and the leaves of the trees are barely singed. We could still feel the heat as we drove rapidly through the thick of the fire after stopping and watching a few other cars running the gauntlet. As we stopped on the other side for a photo, we noticed hundreds of birds of prey circling above the burning bush. They were lucky not to be fried or hit by the cars speeding through the flames, but looked to be feasting on a smorgasbord of barbecued insects.

When we made it back to Kununurra, we found a spot on the lake not far from our previous site. As we cooked dinner, a crocodile glided up to the shore a couple of metres from our tents. Thankfully, it stayed in the water. Then our neighbours who had come to check out our guest told us about the water python and green tree snake they had spotted right near our campsite earlier in the day. Oh dear.

We were again treated to a show as the moon rose bright orange over the reflective water and then slowly faded to white. Smoky air in the distance contributed to another picturesque sunset.

The evening was typically social, with neighbours from all walks of life coming up to the water and having a chat. The site next to us was vacant so it was popular with people standing by the shore sipping their wine and soaking up the atmosphere. One old bloke threw a line into the water after dark and within a minute or two had pulled out a catfish. That was all he caught, but it was a decent size – better than everything we (i.e. Glen) had caught since we left Sydney.

You are never alone in Kununurra. The next morning, I went to the toilet under the watchful gaze of a gecko and a big green frog.

We had hoped to do a tour of the Argyle diamond mine, but at $220 and a short flight away it was a bit steep. In the morning, we took the car for a clean. Not the best use of our dwindling finances, but Glen was getting worried about his clothes getting dirty all the time. I couldn't wait to tell the guys at the pub back in Sydney that Glen was worried about dirty clothes in the outback. The car definitely looked cleaner afterwards, but washing off the dirt revealed hundreds of tiny pits in the paint. Glen didn't seem too concerned; it was worth the damage to experience the Top End properly.

With the Beast sparkling in the hot sun, we checked out the Kununurra Rodeo, having at last landed somewhere on the right day for an event. We arrived in time to see the camp draft. This is where the horse rider has to break out a bull from a small herd and then draft it around two poles and through a gate.

The rodeo was quite a spectacle, with plenty of people to watch through the haze of dust. There were a lot of big hats, big horses, big bulls, big buckles, big spurs, big women and a lot of men in tight jeans drinking milk. There was also a lot of dirt and cow poo.

After the big day out at the rodeo, we tried our luck fishing in Lake Kununurra and caught bugger all, as usual. We wound up when the croc returned. As we dined, a fearless peacock strutted around our tents. We felt like we were camping in a zoo.

It had been an amazing two weeks travelling through the rugged red country of northern Western Australia. We felt privileged to have enjoyed such an experience. What could possibly come close to the wonder of the Kimberley?

Oh yeah, the Northern Territory, and that was just around the corner...

20. Touring The Top End

There's no speed limit on the country roads of the NT. As a local said to me later, 'if we had a speed limit, we wouldn't get anywhere'. We took the point, but with the load we were carrying, we weren't able to build up too much speed and were happy cruising somewhere between what we were used to and what the locals were used to.

At a moderate pace, we got to Katherine along the Victoria Highway, another component of National Highway 1. We checked in at the Low Level Caravan Park, just next to the Low Level Nature Reserve. The park was quite big (and low), and had heaps of grass to plant a couple of tents on. At $14 for our two tents, it was a bargain relative to the higher priced campgrounds of the west.

The Northern Territory is about 1.3 million mostly empty square kilometres, and that's what I love about it. It has 170,000 inhabitants, about one quarter of whom are
Aboriginal. This compares to New South Wales, which is 802,000 square kilometres and is home to more than six million Australians. The 'NT' is split into two regions – the Top End and the Red Centre, each of which has a spectacular assortment of natural features. The Territory's capital city, Darwin has an average maximum temperature in January of 32 degrees and in July, it chills all the way down to 30 degrees.

A Dutchman by the name of Carstensz found himself at the Top End in 1623 in a boat called *Arnhem*, the origin of the name for Arnhemland, a large chunk of northern NT now set aside as the country's biggest Aboriginal reserve. Abel Tasman came along about 20 years later and Flinders charted the coastline during his 1802 circumnavigation. The Brits didn't show much interest until Sir Stamford Raffles thought it might be a strategic location for a settlement. So in 1824 Captain JJ Bremer travelled up from Sydney to establish a settlement as part of New South Wales. On behalf of the Empire he took possession of the land between 129 degrees and 135 degrees east, the former still the Territory's western border. As usual, the settlement was a disaster and promptly moved after only a few days. Learning little from their mistakes, the second British settlement didn't work out either so the civilian and convict settlers moved on again. Believe it or not, the next settlement was also abandoned. I think after that they gave up and left.

A few years later HMS *Beagle* was filling in the gaps in Matthew Flinders' charts and sailed into a port, which the captain J. L. Stokes named Port Darwin after his former shipmate, Charles. Explorers Leichhardt, Gregory and Stuart braved the tough inland conditions to learn more about the northern regions of Australia. After Stuart ventured up from South Australia in the 1860s, the Northern Territory was placed under South Australian control.

Several more explorers tried their hand at the harsh land, mostly less successfully than Stuart. Later, the overland telegraph line and a railway line were built from the south coast, and in 1911 the Federal Government took control of the Territory. The South Australian-settled Palmerston was renamed Darwin by the Federal government and chosen as the capital city. Between 1926 and 1931, the Territory was split in half for administrative purposes and the halves named Northern Australia and Central Australia. It wasn't until 1978 that the Northern Territory finally gained self-rule under its current system of government. The Commonwealth still controls a few issues such as Aboriginal land rights and uranium mining and, more recently, euthanasia, but otherwise the Territory rolls along at its own pace.

The town of Katherine is the 'Jewel of the Territory', 'the Crossroads of the Outback' *and* the 'Gateway to Gulf Country'. That's a lot to live up to. It's the third largest town in the Territory and is handy to some spectacular sights, in particular Katherine Gorge.

While Leichhardt had already discovered the Katherine River, it took Stuart's visit to give it a name. In 1862, he named it after Catherine, the daughter of his benefactor James Chambers. The name was misspelled at the time and no one's bothered to change it since. Tourism and a big air force base nearby have resulted in a steady increase in Katherine's population, now more than 11,000.

We had hoped to do a canoe trip up the Katherine Gorge, but trying to book the day before was not time enough in the winter dry season. I was keen to cruise up the Katherine Gorge whether it was under my own steam or someone else's and Glen was happy to laze around the caravan park reading, doing the washing and swimming. So I booked myself on a four-hour cruise.

The gorge was spectacular, but we had just come from a batch of spectacular sights and this one probably didn't quite match up to the Kimberley gorges, especially with the hordes of tourists at Katherine. The Gorge is actually a network of several big gorges, and visitors have to rock hop from one boat to the next. My cruise covered three of the thirteen gorges. We saw a massive gallery of rock art which was interesting but couldn't match the Chamberlain Gorge at El Questro. We saw a few crocodiles, but again, Windjana will be the highlight of our croc spotting experiences. Unfortunately, there was a flood in the Katherine region a couple of years before, which had washed away several of the previously sandy beaches. 'This used to be...' was an oft-heard part of the commentary. If only we'd come to Katherine before the Kimberley to compare it with, I'm sure it would have impressed more. Still, it was a stunning outback experience and worth the visit.

After the cruise, Glen and I checked out the dulcet tones of a campground guitarist named Bevan, who had attracted an audience of travellers around the aptly named Big Fig. Sadly he didn't know 'my mate flagon' or 'I never gone to bed with an ugly woman but I sure woke up with a few'. He did, however, know numerous John Williamson tunes, as did the old-timers in the audience, who sang heartily along.

In the evening, it was back to the water for an enjoyable night cruise and riverside dinner. Our tour guide, Mike, was made for this sort of thing and obviously knew his way around Katherine. He wasn't half bad on the didgeridoo, harmonica and guitar as well. There was plenty of croc spotting, but mainly small freshies, which could barely be seen along the shore lined with dead ghostly white and grey trees. We were told along the way that the way to tell freshies from salties is that if you get eaten, it was probably a saltie.

Steering clear of the crocs, the 20 of us had a feed on a sandy clearing after the half-hour boat ride. The BBQ dinner was a hearty surf and turf mixture and most (including us) brought a bottle of wine. During and after dinner we all sat around the campfire and listened to Mike sing a few John Williamson songs with the didge, guitar and mouth organ. I managed to belt out Waltzing Matilda on my harp but when I got to the guitar I completely stuffed up the Beatles' Blackbird, my favourite tune which I have played for years. I was obviously out of practice but naturally blamed the guitar. My attempt at playing the didge was also quite shameful. Overall, the tour was worthwhile although more time around the campfire would have been pleasant. I guess our companions had to take their pills and get to bed so they could be up and out of the caravan park by sparrow's fart the next day.

Sure enough, we were woken at sparrow's fart by all the eager caravanners on the next day, so we got ourselves up and when packed and ready, we took the relatively short drive to Litchfield National Park. We chose a longer scenic drive from Hayes Creek to Adelaide River, which winds through the hills and passes through numerous floodways. It wasn't particularly scenic and most of the vegetation had been burnt out. The highlight, which made the trip worthwhile, was a giant termite mound that we estimated to be seven metres tall. It was amazing. It made the car look like a model car and us, ironically, like ants.

Along this part of the Stuart Highway, we drove past the remnants of several World War II airstrips, now dilapidated and barely noticeable.

We stopped at Litchfield's main service centre, the small town of Batchelor, predictably described as 'Gateway to Litchfield National Park'. There wasn't much to the place, but a couple of signs on the community notice board gave us a laugh: 'Any dogs found on lot x will be shot on sight'. Below that one, someone else had added another note: 'Any dogs found on lot y will be forwarded to lot x'. No matter what adversities are faced, the dry outback humour shines through.

The town hosts a large college for training Aboriginal teachers and is next door to Rum Jungle, Australia's first uranium mine site. According to the Northern Territory News, which happened to have a story on it while we were there, the name comes from late in the 1800s. The legend says that an early gold miner accidentally smashed a cask of rum into a natural spring and after enjoying the tainted water for a while his co-workers dubbed the area the Rum Jungle, although there are several other equally suspect stories floating around. Uranium was found there in the late 1940s and a mining operation established. The mine closed in 1971, which was a blow to Batchelor because it supplied most of the labour. These days, between the college, tourism, horticulture, agriculture it soldiers on.

Driving into the park, we were greeted with a fire awareness sign proclaiming that 'we like our lizards frilled, not grilled'. Don't we all.

Litchfield is 650 square kilometres of flattop mountains, sheer cliffs and lush water holes. Back when the NT was the *Northern Territory of South Australia*, a group of explorers, including Frederick Litchfield, traversed the area naming several of its features. Mining of tin and copper took off in the 1860s and later giant cattle properties moved in. The National Park wasn't declared until 1986. Litchfield, of course, has many and varied species of plants and animals, but one of the common species of tree in the park would have to be my favourite example of floral nomenclature of all time – the *woollybutt*.
There's that sense of humour again.

Not far into the park is an amazing congregation of narrow two-metre tall headstone-like termite mounds all facing the same direction. The alignment is thought to be due to the ants minimising the surface area of their large homes that is exposed to direct sunlight (nothing to do with magnetic alignment as has previously been postulated). Now that's a bunch of smart ants.

We checked out a couple of campgrounds which were small but crowded, and settled on the four-wheel drive campground at Florence Falls where there were only six sites amongst the ferns at the end of a short rough track. We were a few metres from the small, fast flowing Florence Creek and took advantage of its refreshing waters in the Top End heat for a dip. Refreshed, we returned to the car and looked despairingly at both sets of keys locked inside. Oops. It didn't take long for Glen to manoeuvre a piece of scrap metal under the window and release the latch, but by then we were both ready for another swim.

Multitudes of birds flitted around the campsite; among them, quails darting through the scrub, and striking Red Backed Wrens perched over our tents threatening to unload dinner. There were also plenty of green ants to munch on (I made Glen reluctantly try one). The congenial neighbouring middle-aged lesbians from Düsseldorf swore that they saw a metre-long lizard running right past my tent earlier in the day but there was no sighting during our presence. As at Bell Gorge in the Kimberley, bandicoots kicked into action after the sun went down, noisily scavenging for food and water.

The small camping area gradually filled up and unfortunately the group next to us stayed up late drinking and talking, detracting from the otherwise utopian ambience. Before turning in for the night we cooked up a spag bol avec live bugs. It's all protein.

When we got our lazy butts up and moving in the searing heat the next day, we drove up to the tourist mecca of Wangi Falls, the park's main attraction. A waterfall and large pool at the bottom full of people trying to beat the heat. We did the walk to the top of the falls. Unlike some of the places we'd been where we felt like we were the first people there, this pleasant walk was over a clear track with steel stairs and a couple of boardwalks and carried a fair bit of foot traffic.

After a quick bite of lunch at the kiosk, we visited Tolmer Falls. The waterfall was flowing and there weren't quite as many people as at Wangi, helping to make it more enjoyable. Near the end of the track was a stark burnt-out patch of land scattered with large ancient cycad ferns with long creamy coloured fronds. The contrast of the fronds against the blackened trunks and burnt ground was striking. Again, I felt like I had wandered into a black and white movie.

Back at the campground for a swim there was a pleasant English couple camped next to us and the campground was much quieter than the previous night. We sat up quite late listening to the soft breeze in the trees, the water rushing over the small rapids and the bandicoots hopping through the tall grass. It was almost too good to be true. It was one of our most memorable evenings of the trip – although they were adding up.

The next morning, I talked Glen into doing another waterfall walk, this time Tjaetaba (don't ask me how you pronounce it) Falls. We did the walk to a pleasant little waterfall but it didn't quite live up to the postcard photo I'd seen which I guess was taken during or just after the wet season when the waterfall is in full flow. The peacefulness was soon shattered by a busload of loud young Americans with bad haircuts and worse clothes. We were too spoilt in the Kimberley with only a limited number of adventurous people around.

On that loud note we left the park and headed north. It's only a short trip to Darwin, so we stopped at Palmerston, the 'fastest growing town in Australia' to have some lunch. I wasn't sure to whom the slogan was marketed. I can't imagine they were trying to attract tourists with a gem like that. Before we were engulfed by the amazing expanding town, we drove on and lashed out on an air-conditioned caravan park cabin just outside Darwin. Camping would have too closely resembled sleeping in an oven in that heat.

Darwin's 100,000 people live in the country's most remote city. It's closer to Jakarta than any Australian state capitals, and Bali is a short hop away. The persistent Japanese bombing raids during World War II, when 243 people were killed, scarred Darwin's troubled history. They were the first enemy attacks on Australian territory since European arrival. Disaster hit again on Christmas day 1974 when Cyclone Tracy swept through the city, killing lots of people (different sources estimate between 50 and more than 100) and wiping out most of the buildings. Since then the city has rebuilt and continues to grow and develop in the face of adversity. I guess a drink helps gets them through.

Darwinians drink more beer than just about anyone else on the planet, and then use the empty cans in the annual beer can regatta.

Darwin is like a large country town with the trappings and buildings of a capital city. Every Australian state capital has an open mall and Darwin's is on Smith Street, around which the city is centred. We wandered around town for a while and strolled down to the underground oil storage tunnels from World War II in the wharf district. For a cost of $4, we walked through a couple of the tunnels, one of which had more than a hundred wartime photos of Darwin.

The heat and humidity in Darwin toward the end of the winter dry season were almost unbearable. Walking one or two blocks resulted in a self-basting sweat bath.

After a quick bite at the Golden Arches (our first in three weeks) we drove up to the Darwin Museum. I was most interested in the extensive range of Aboriginal art and the Cyclone Tracy room. We also tried matching up some of the animal specimens to the more lively versions we'd seen along the way, not to mention the flatter ones. The Cyclone Tracy room featured some news footage from Christmas day in 1974 and several photos of the devastation caused by the furious storm. There was also a dimly lit room where an audio recording of the cyclone was played. It was a chilling experience but I'm sure nothing like the real thing, wondering if you're going to be alive when it's all over. The photo in which someone had painted 'Tracey [sic] you Bitch' on the back of a crushed car said it all.

Having sweated off a few kilos in Darwin, we hit the Arnhem Highway south to Kakadu National Park. After so long, it seemed odd saying 'today we're going to Kakadu'. I talked to a mate back in Sydney on the way there and he couldn't get over the day's schedule.

It's a short drive from Darwin to the world heritage park, which is also Australia's largest national park. I had heard so many mixed reports about how wonderful or overrated Kakadu was so I was anxious to see and decide for myself.

On the way in, we had to stop the car for a huge goanna to stroll lazily across the road.

There wasn't too much of interest on the highway that runs through the northern part of the park so we continued to the campground near Ubirr (*Oo-beer*). There are two roads into Kakadu, one running east and a more southerly one running north east, which meet in the north-eastern corner of the park at Jabiru. The road continues a bit further, stopping at Ubirr, which sits beside the East Alligator River. The other side of the river is Arnhem Land, the giant Aboriginal reserve, which requires a permit to enter.

We found a large campsite nestled between two vacant sites and set up camp. As usual, a squillion ants and plenty of birds were around, including a kookaburra which Glen virtually picked up while trying to shoo it off his tent, upon which its sharp claws were clenched.

After setting up the tents and having lunch, we spent more than half an hour trying to lasso the high-up dead branch of a tree. It looked perfect for the campfire and we were determined to get the damn thing down. After we were bathed in sweat and had finally retrieved the rogue branch, we drove a few kilometres up the road to Ubirr and its gallery of art. Ubirr's rocky outcrops provided the perfect canvas for an amazing array of Aboriginal painting and offers fantastic views around the park. A wide diversity of artistic styles is on the rock walls, down to the earliest form of graffiti, with paintings over paintings. We stumbled across a couple of ranger talks by a young Aboriginal girl who gave a brief but interesting perspective on the art and its artists. It was only a short scramble up a mountain to a spectacular 360-degree view of the park's floodplains, the huge Arnhemland escarpment and rocky terrain. That, combined with the art was a great experience.

With the oppressive heat and humidity, we didn't accomplish too much over the day, and returned to the campsite early. We heard a lot of movement in the spear grass around the site after dark but we couldn't actually see any critters except for the occasional small bat flitting around the fire. The mosquitoes at night were worse than the persistent bird-sized flies during the day. Not only are they as loud as a buzz-saw, they carry some nasty exotic diseases. Nonetheless, coated with insect repellent, it was a very pleasant evening under the stars in Kakadu National Park.

Another day of oppressive heat followed. The footprints and bullet-shaped brown calling card on our table suggested a small guest overnight. The heat kept us awake all night, along with the birds and mosquitoes. I managed to slaughter the two or three mozzies that slipped into my tent but the noise of those outside that were trying to get in was painfully loud and persistent. There was also a very loud bird haunting us before sundown, which we had hoped would shut up at night. It didn't. Another conspicuous sound was the call of the barking owl. It sounded amazingly like a dog (we recognised the call at the visitors' centre later in the day).

From Jabaru we drove to the Mardugal campsite. There was a lodge with caravan park-style campsites near famous Yellow Waters billabong, but the nearby National Parks site looked much more comfortable and homey than being squeezed into an ordinary caravan park. So we found a large site and sweated it out setting up camp.

After a bit of a rest, we took the one kilometre walk from the camping area. The track led to a serene spot on the river with a lonely picnic table under the shady trees. We looked but couldn't see any crocs, but noticed a big monitor lizard cautiously watching as we passed.

We drove the short distance to the spectacular Yellow Water wetlands and strolled along the steel boardwalk that meanders over Kakadu's most famous and spectacular feature. We came across a waterbird that had just speared an unlucky fish with its sharp beak and was trying to get it down its long but narrow throat. The fish was about half again as thick as the bird's neck and it took a long time just to get the whole fish past its head. It seemed like a lot of painful effort for a feed.

At the end of the trail, we finally saw a big saltwater croc being more active than most, as it glided stealthily through the water. On the return walk, the bird we had seen earlier was still having trouble with the fish, which was now halfway down its neck. We couldn't bear to watch and returned to camp.

Thankfully, it was a cooler night at the more southerly campground and there were fewer of the parks 4,500 insect species, but the tourists were greater in number and volume.

We should have chosen the 6:45am Yellow Water cruise like all the other campers around us who saw to us getting an early morning. Consequently, we were at the boat quite early and scored a 'window' seat each. The cruise was sensational and comprehensively showed off the Kakadu I had been waiting for and that everyone has seen on TV or in Crocodile
Dundee. The majestic wetlands and mirror-like backwaters around the South Alligator River were so peaceful and just as though they were

out of a promotional nature documentary. The cruise went for two hours and rather than a set commentary, the guide gave descriptions of the fauna and flora as it appeared.

The bird life was astounding; we were in awe at the abundance of species. In fact, one third of Australia's bird species can be found at Kakadu. The cruise passed a number of different environments, including a swamp filled with semi-submerged paperbarks (a melaleuca rather than its close cousin the eucalypt). The young trees float on the water until they are strong enough to send down their roots through the soil. Other interesting flora included the huge aquatic pandanus, the fragile looking snowflake water lilies (the flowers bear a remarkable resemblance to a large snowflake), and the spectacular lotus lilies whose large pink flowers only open for a day at a time. Animals we spotted included the very colourful Rainbow Bee Eater, a small blue Kingfisher, wild horses and some cattle (bred by the local Aborigines, seemingly in conflict with the environmental health of the park). A few saltwater crocs glided through the still water and sunbathed on the riverbank with their cavernous and lethal mouths gaping open as though they were waiting for lunch to stroll in. The two hours were gone in an instant, so it was time to bid farewell to Kakadu.

Our question was now answered. Did Kakadu stack up to the hype? Absolutely.

With the Yellow Water visual feast fresh in our minds, we hit the road out of the park and headed south along the Stuart Highway. We had thought about staying at the well-known Mataranka station for the night, but Glen was keen to continue south to make the next leg to Tennant Creek a little shorter, a decision which turned out to be quite fortuitous.

21. The Reddest of Centres

As we drove south down the Stuart Highway, we passed a miniature tornado-like willy-willy spinning a tube of black ash from burnt scrub into the sky over the remains of a recent bushfire. Still talking about how we could embellish the tornado story with the folks back home, we stumbled on a gem of a place called Larrimah, a small town about 80 kilometres south of Mataranka.

We checked out two of the caravan parks in the small village, but settled on pitching our tents at the back of the pub.

After forking out $3 each and bending numerous tent pegs in the rock-hard but grassy ground as we set up the tents under the watchful eye of Andrew (a peacock), we headed back to the bar, reputedly the highest in the NT. Although we started with a couple of very tasty beers, the menu boasting 'good home style grub and country hospitality' was enticing: sardines and ice cream on toast ($20), boar's tits on toast ($20) or sump oil soup with croutons ($10). I opted for the barbecued fresh barramundi, which was superb despite my general ambivalence about eating fish. The menu also highlighted the availability of 'fine wine' and we noticed a selection of reds in the fridge. Well it does get hot in the outback.

At the entrance to the bar, we were greeted by a large Pink Panther several metres tall, blowing the froth off an NT draught. Over the door hung a professionally printed sign reading, 'Telecom Australia Official Watering Hole – Larrimah Pub'. Apart from the usual beef jerky (which was really buffalo jerky), and beside the nuts were packets of croc jerky. There was a dartboard with two darts and an old tyre as a frame, a sticker advertising Wheredafukarwi Tours, walls lined with beer cans, and several vehicle number plates from around the world including SEX007, and BLOWER.

Larrimah was on the train line that transported troops during World War II and the pub housed a lot of memorabilia including some interesting telegrams relating to troop movements through the town. We took part in a competition to hit a small stick hanging from the ceiling with a 50-cent coin. Regardless of the outcome, the silver goes to the School of the Air, and there is no prize other than knowing that you've helped another worthy outback cause. One of the main characters of the bar was Zoe, an aging toothless bull terrier. I rarely have time for any dog unless it has character, but Zoe was bursting with it and hung around us until we left. Zoe and Andrew's relationship wasn't a close one, neither invading the other's turf.

The real characters were, of course, the locals. Conversations were enlightening. A couple of farmers were talking about the shortage of water on their parched farms, one of them being in particularly short supply. The other, a stranger until then, said that he had brought in 50,000 litres and could spare some for his new mate. A delivery would be made the next day. 'No worries mate'. That's the outback for you.

The 'campground' was a large patch of surprisingly green grass out the back of the pub. The topsoil was only a couple of centimetres deep, under which lay the peg-bending rock. Our campsite was about 100m from the Stuart Highway and the nearby service station ensured that the sounds of road trains stopping and starting lasted through the night.

I managed to consume a massive homemade meat pie for brekkie the next morning before we pushed on. It sounded like the famous Daly Waters Pub was worth a visit so we turned off the highway to check it out. Scores of bank notes hung from the walls, along with various items of clothing including signed g-strings and bras, and heaps of other bric-a-brac. The most remote traffic light in Australia faced the front door of the pub, not that it actually did anything, and nearby petrol bowsers offering petrol a couple of cents cheaper than the highway roadhouse protruded from the orange dirt. At least you could fill up your tank before getting yourself tanked in the pub. We did neither because we had a full tank of petrol and were keen to continue towards central Australia.

The terrain around Daly Waters is fairly flat and barren and gets more so the further south you go. We passed several pushbike riders on the road. It was amazing how many there were in the muggy heat and with so far between facilities, particularly water. How did they do it?

Tennant Creek, our destination for the night, is a mining town and most of what it has to offer the tourist is mining-related. A few touristy places - museums, galleries, parks - were in and around town to try to keep people there for more than a one-day stopover on their way to Darwin or Alice Springs, but I'm not sure of their success rate. We made the most of *our* one-day stopover anyway. Most coach tours come in late afternoon and leave again after breakfast, missing all of the gold mining memorabilia.

Enticed by favourable recommendations, I went on the 'Dot Mine' tour in the evening. Old overalled Col Bremner took us though a vintage hand-dug gold mine, but the highlight was sitting around the campfire with an enamel mug of good billy tea listening to Col's history of the area and enthusiastic bush poetry recital. He had been doing the same thing for nine years and some of the historical spiel sounded a bit that way, but it was interesting nonetheless and the bush poetry was great. There was a brightly speckled blanket of stars overhead and the only sounds other than Col's voice were crickets and the after dinner churning of stomachs. The Europeans who didn't really follow what was going on talked through most of the presentation.

There's a rumour that Tennant Creek was started when a couple of blokes with a truck full of beer broke down and decided to hang around for a while, consumed their cargo and decided to stay for good. Col reckoned the story was fanciful, and offered the more likely story of the telegraph station coming through in 1872, and a couple of prospectors being pointed in the right direction by the telegraph station occupants. They struck gold and the town grew from there. Personally, I prefer the beer story.

It wasn't until 1931 that gold was discovered in the area. The town quickly grew to 500 people and in 1950 the telegraph station, then used mainly as accommodation for linesmen, was sold to a local prospector and used as a homestead. In the mid-1980s, the station was handed back to the government and is now managed by the Parks & Wildlife people. Gold mining remains the lifeblood of Tennant Creek.

After taking in a couple of mining-related attractions, including an old working gold stamper and museum in a newish complex with the tourist office, the next day, our first stop out of town was 100 kilometres down the Stuart Highway. The Devil's Marbles are an amazing series of outcrops of huge rounded red granite boulders covering a large expanse of the similarly red desert. I wasn't anticipating too much on the excitement scale, but once confronted by the natural array of red rock spheres, I was in awe of the sight. The rocks range from about a metre in diameter to several metres and many are precariously balanced atop one another as though they had been purposely placed there. We wandered through and over the rocks, took some photos (no doubt taken by thousands of people over the years) and performed luncheon in their shadow under the brilliant blue sky. A lone leather-clad biker with a stereotypical beard got me to take of photo of him and his Hog in front of a large ball of rock. It was a great shot of the proud rider, which I wished I had taken for myself as well.

The rocks were formed by the surrounding earth being weathered away, leaving the balls of granite balancing on what is now the ground. According to Aboriginal legend, they are eggs of the Rainbow Serpent, one of the most important Dreamtime spirits.

Back on the highway for a mostly nondescript southerly drive to Alice Springs. Along the way, we passed Wycliffe Well, which claimed to be the UFO capital of Australia. We drove past a couple of lanky green aliens filling their flying saucer with gas, and made a note to stop there on the return trip.

As the landscape became dryer, redder and more barren and the air less humid, the number of trashed, burnt out cars by the side of the road fell and the number of trashed birds and kangaroos increased dramatically. We nearly collided with a huge eagle while I was at the wheel. Usually they were good at getting out of the way, but this one must have been enjoying its road kill feast too much and lost concentration.

We also passed Ti-Tree, reputedly home to Australia's most central pub. We didn't see it. Neither did we see the monument at the base of Mt Stuart marking the middle of the country.

Alice Springs is nestled beside the MacDonnell Ranges, through which the Todd River (on the occasions when it runs) has sliced. It was on the shores of the Todd that Alice Springs began its life as a telegraph station. The Alice, as it is known, is the slowly beating heart of

Australia, and we felt right at home as we approached the towering red mountain range.

It was hot further north in mid-August, but it was also humid. The weather report said that the humidity in Darwin was 90 per cent and in Katherine 99 per cent. Now that's humid. Down in the arid country where we were it was much drier heat and much colder at night. It was forecast to be 2 degrees for our first night in Alice Springs so we wimped out and got an on-site van at a caravan park just over the Todd River from the thriving metropolis of Alice Springs (a slight exaggeration).

Our first day in the Alice was spent around town. We'd managed to crack a couple of roof racks somewhere along the way and had to airfreight in a couple of replacements, which would keep us there for a couple of days, so there was time to relax.

We wandered around town, which is really just Todd Mall and its immediate surrounds. It was pretty deserted except for tourists, Aborigines and police. After walking the length of the mall and looking in a few galleries which seemed overpriced compared to the more remote galleries and shops along the Stuart Highway, we asked a couple of tan-clothed police where the Aboriginal Cultural Centre was. Both looked blank. You'd think they would know, but both sounded like Kiwis. Eventually they sorted out what we were talking about and pointed us in the right direction.

One of my favourite things on the mall was the small damper and billy tea barrow perched on the edge of the mall. The barrow housed a couple of small fires to heat the billies for tea and cook the damper bread.

Todd River and Mall were named after Sir Charles Todd, postmaster, astronomer and overland telegraph engineer. His wife's name was Alice, after which a spring was named.

Oh, and the town.

The cultural centre, owned by the local Aboriginal clan, was manned by some friendly Aboriginal staff who encouraged us to take a didgeridoo lesson at their school in the centre. I was keen and joined in. There were about ten of us, including a couple of young European blokes who were very good and kept taking over the class. I was having difficulty getting the knack of what was required to make it sound musical. My attempt sounded more like Glen after a big night of curry and beer. It wasn't until after the class that I really started to get the hang of the instrument. I bought a beautifully painted didge to annoy the neighbours with and we both bought a couple of clap sticks adorned with Aboriginal designs.

Finally we got to the impressive Alice Springs Desert Park not far from town. The handsomely built and planned park featured an informative display of the flora and fauna found in different desert environments. We solved a few mysteries by identifying some birds and plants we'd seen through our desert travels. Sir David Attenborough says it's the best of its kind on the world. The highlight of the Park for us was the huge nocturnal house - by far the best I have ever seen - showing off the animals we had heard jumping around our tents at night, and some, which thankfully, we didn't come across in the wild.

The next day was a full one exploring the West MacDonnell Ranges, described by our brochure as 'a treasure trove of nature's best handiwork with not just one or two important features, but a dozen'. Well well. We drove west from Alice along Namatjira Drive into the West MacDonnell National Park to the end of the bitumen and then 25 kilometres further up a gravel road to Redbank Gorge. It was a little like Windjana but with narrower redder walls and no crocs. The river was dry for the 1.2 kilometre walk up the riverbed, and then there was a small pool from which the river extended beyond our view further up the gorge. It was well worth the rough road to get to it.

From Redbank, we started heading back toward the Alice. Next in the long line of gorges and chasms was Glen Helen Gorge, carved by the Finke River. It was a short walk from the car park to the large pool at the head of the gorge, but without swimming across the pool or climbing along the gorge walls, we couldn't get inside the gorge. It was a pleasant view past the pool over some tall reeds through the wide red walls, but not terribly exciting relative to some other gorges because of the lack of access.

Next in line was the spectacular Ormiston Gorge. It was a short steep walk to the Ghost Gum Lookout, which had a great view up the vast gorge, which on one side was shadowed by a red sloping wall that must have been well over 200 metres tall. The view was spectacular and probably the highlight of the day. The trail continued down into the gorge but the heat and time encouraged us to head back. Back in the car park, we saw a scrawny dingo scavenging for morsels left behind by tourists, seemingly unconcerned by leering photographers and a steady flow of traffic entering and leaving the car park.

The swirling colours of the Ochre pit further up the road were attractive but not as impressive as the pits we had seen earlier on the Birdsville Track. Again, we had been spoiled by the more remote and less visited outback sights, although each one is a different experience.

A small nature reserve is centred on Ellery Creek. It's a short walk to a big waterhole aptly named 'the Big Hole', shadowed by towering red cliffs. It looked quite inviting for a swim and a few people were refreshing themselves in the icy water. Another tranquil and photogenic scene.

Back on the road, the pastel coloured ranges to the north looked like a false movie backdrop in the hazy distance. Glen thought they looked like the background from Blazing Saddles. With this image and Glen's dazzling flatulence, we could have re-shot the film there and then; all we needed was the supply of baked beans and a sheriff. On the southern side, the closer and smaller red and pastel green range looked like it was begging to be painted. In fact, it looked like it *was* actually painted. This is the country that famously appeared in watercolour on the canvases of full blood local Aborigine Albert Namatjira and several of his relatives.

The alternative to driving through the ranges is to endure the 220-kilometre Larapinta Trail which runs from Alice Springs to Mt Sonder, just past Redbank Gorge. Maybe next time.

After a shower and brief rest, we got a cab into town and dined at the Overlander Steakhouse. It was a bit pricey for our meagre budget, but the menu had to be experienced. I had smoked emu and kangaroo for entrée, both of which were very tasty, followed by camel steak, which was also quite gamy but tender. Glen had the 'Drover's Blowout', which included soup, damper, emu, crocodile, kangaroo, camel, barramundi and apple pie. We were identified by the flag on our table representing our place of origin, and there weren't many other Aussie flags around. After dinner, there was a bit of a singalong for which they dragged up a bunch of reluctant tourists onto the stage to play wobble boards for *Tie Me Kangaroo Down* and *Give me a Home Among the Gum Trees*. Entertaining if you're not the one making a fool of yourself.

After dinner, we returned to Bojangles Bar in which we had enjoyed a beer or two earlier in the week. It was the most crowded bar we'd seen on the whole trip. There was a country folk band bashing out the Ausse classics like *Click Go the Shears* and *Give me a Home Among the Gum Trees* (again). A definite theme was beginning to emerge in this town. The bar was decked out saloon-style right down to a barrel of peanuts near the bar, resulting in a floor covered with discarded shells. Unfortunately, the band didn't play for long after we arrived and people started vacating so we moved on to the casino's Irish bar at the recommendation of the bar staff at Bojangles.

The casino bar was very quiet when we got there and a duo played a very eclectic selection of not very good music. So we wandered out into the small gaming area and I put $50 down on the $2 roulette table. In all other casinos I have visited, I have had to fight my way to the cheap tables, but in Alice all we saw were $2 tables and we strolled right up to one of them and started betting. I had a lengthy losing streak and was down to $4 when a combined effort of choosing the right numbers and lower odds splits quickly brought me back up to double my original bet so I cashed out. Glen had a quick flutter on the pokies, not fairing so well until 'one last go' paid out $60. With our newfound wealth, we headed back to the bar where the restaurant staff had gathered, and gradually managed to give the casino back its cash.

We spent a while in deep conversation with a white Zimbabwean about the common challenges faced by black Africans and Australian Aborigines. It was an interesting and insightful, if somewhat garbled discussion, which kept going until the bar closed a bit after 3am.

Everyone else dispersed immediately at closing time, leaving us stranded. We waited for a cab outside in the crisp Alice night air with about twenty amiable Aborigines. They were a rowdy bunch but who wouldn't be at 3am. They made some jokes about the cop car cruising the streets ('the black fellas' taxi'), and that the Aboriginal term for social security was 'sit down money', but gave us no trouble with the exception of one bloke who had had a few too many and didn't care for our presence. I don't think the others cared much for his. Eventually we got a cab and headed back home.

Our planned trip to Stanley Chasm and Simpsons Gap the next day was thwarted by the car service taking longer than expected and the time taken replacing the roof rack brackets that turned out to be worse than we had thought. We were both buggered and neither felt like heading back out to the range so we had a quiet arvo and an early night before heading off on the next leg of our journey. Both sleeping for twelve hours, we missed the 10 o'clock checkout but got going not long after.

We visited the visitors' centre a few days earlier to get the $2 permit to travel along the Mereenie Loop to Kings Canyon through Aboriginal land. The Loop is a series of roads linking Alice Springs and Uluru via the West MacDonnell Ranges and Kings Canyon. It includes the Lasseter Highway and Luritja Road, which are both sealed, and the gravel Ernest Giles Road and Larapinta Drive.

It was a comfortable drive on the sealed road to Hermannsburg, birthplace of artist Albert Namatjira. The settlement was established as a Lutheran mission in 1877 and an Aboriginal school set up a couple of years later. His and other paintings are still hanging in the mission's little museum.

From Hermannsburg the gravel road began and gradually deteriorated. Along the road there were a few intriguing signs, including a couple with directions painted on rusty old car bonnets (a common sight in the outback). Another, approaching some bends in the road, was painted on the side of a 44-gallon drum and read, 'Lift um foot' and then after the turns, 'Puttum back down'.

There's one designated lookout along the road, which was the only place we were permitted to stop on the Aboriginal land. The rocky lookout was high enough to allow sweeping views across the sand and desert shrubs to the distant mountain ranges. It's not far from there to the crowded and boisterous Kings Canyon Resort campground, often full of coach tour buses. About 40 kilometres further south is the quieter and friendly Kings Creek Station, where we decided to set up camp.

The station ran 400 head of cattle, which were about to be mustered, and about 3,000 camels. Sunset camel rides or helicopter rides over the typically red George Gill Mountains were available but comfort and expense ruled both out. Like El Questro, the station is about 1 million acres, although it used to be double that size until a successful native title land claim was made. A similarly sized station in the region had recently been completely reclaimed by its traditional owners, according to one of the campground staff.

Just after we had set up camp, we drove down a nearby unmarked track to collect some firewood. We stopped on the side of the track and walked through the strikingly red powdery earth and the scattered baked green desert vegetation to find some wood. It was an amazing feeling walking over this isolated land marked only with an extensive patterned array of animal tracks (and our footprints). I felt like the first astronaut to record my footprints on the crimson surface of Mars.

When we returned to camp, a rough old bloke walked up to us and asked about the Mereenie Loop. His travelling companion was keen to try it, but our visitor wasn't too keen on towing the old caravan out there. We must have heard 50 'fucks' and several other swear words from the toothless old troubadour in the brief conversation, not to mention a few 'boongs' and 'coons'. Later in the evening he walked past again and muttered that our fire was a 'black fella fire', whatever that meant. We took it as a compliment. He shuffled off mumbling several other things under his breath. He didn't seem like the happiest of campers.

After dinner, we invited our neighbouring campers, who didn't have a fireplace, to sit by ours, BYO wood. The wife was an outback doctor and had plenty of interesting and horrifying stories of her medical experiences to tell. In return, I regaled them with some pretty ordinary didgeridoo playing before hitting the sack as the desert night temperature dropped close to zero.

The king of canyons is the prime feature of Watarrka National Park, which, as the crow flies, lies a bit northwest of midway between Alice Springs and Uluru. In preparation for the long walk over and through the canyon, we cooked up some snags for breakfast and to take with us on the hike. It's a 20-minute drive back to the canyon and then the walk begins from the canyon floor. There are two options: a short level walk along the creek, or a long, steep, rocky trail up and around the canyon. We chose the latter for starters.

The canyon significantly exceeded my expectations. Having seen so many beautiful and spectacular canyons, I wasn't sure if and how this one could match up. But I'm here to tell you that it did.

The tabletop surface of the canyon consists of a vast landscape of layered Bungle Bunglestyle dome formations on a smaller scale. The whole place is red, broken only by the intermittent green and bright white of the ghost gums and various other resilient trees and grasses.

The ghost gum gets its name not just from its white trunk, but from a powder it secretes, creating a ghostlike apparition during summer nights. Everywhere you look is another photo opportunity. Much of the southern wall of the canyon is a strikingly smooth surface that looks as though it has been rendered with red cement while leaving the surrounding wall pockmarked and more visibly layered.

There were quite a few people on the walk, but apart from some obnoxious Germans, few enough that the atmosphere was not affected. The trail loops around the V-shaped canyon offering various aspects of the rough terrain, and ends in a steep descent back to the riverbed.

Back down at the canyon floor, the rock-strewn creek walk through the trees was pleasant, offering a vastly different perspective on the massive canyon. The view upwards at the end of the trail towards the end of the canyon made the short and shady riverside walk worthwhile.

By the time we got back to camp, exhausted, we had a short while to relax by the fire, cook up some pasta and hit the sack before heading for the *big rock* the next day.

We were the last to leave the campground (nothing new) and drove directly to Yulara, the village that services Ayres Rock, now known by its Aboriginal name, *Uluru*. On the way west, we passed Mt Campbell, a monolith that must catch out hordes of tourists (like us, at first) in mistaking it for its more famous neighbour. After some consideration, we decided we had been fooled and continued on our way.

When we finally did see Uluru off in the distance, it was so amazingly red it made what I thought was the red earth we have been driving and walking over look a dull orange. And it was big. Big, red and very sacred to the area's inhabitants.

The Yulara campground was predictably expensive and crowded, although we staked out a pretty good spot close to some trees so that we wouldn't be surrounded by other campers. We had yet another flat tyre so after repairing it we didn't attempt to do anything other than drive around the resort complex and settle in for another night of close-to-zero temperatures.

The Irish travellers camped next to us woke Glen early with their rantings, and Glen woke me with his retort of 'shut the fuck up!'

Notwithstanding my other grievances, the campground showers were first class, which was a welcome change. Mind you, we were increasingly familiar with significantly fluctuating shower temperatures, drizzling showerheads and our clothes and towels being drenched.

We decided to do Kata Tjuta (formerly known as The Olgas) before its slightly more famous cousin 32 kilometres away. On the drive, there we were again amazed at the sight of Uluru, and then by the similarly shaded but more expansive Olgas. They cover an area larger than Uluru, but are clustered together as though they were once Uluru's big brother, since weathered down to form a bunch of smaller domes.

On the way, we had to pull over for an Ambulance heading for the rock – another tourist bites the dust trying to ascend the unforgiving monstrosity against the often expressed desire of the local Aboriginals.

The seven-kilometre walk through Kata Tjuta (meaning 'many heads' to the local Anangu people) was spectacular. The 36 domes are larger than Purnululu (Bungle Bungles) but fewer in number and more uniform in colour. The largest is Mt Olga which hits the 500metre mark. The domes consist of what we believed to be conglomerate rock, which looks like big clumps of eroded fruitcake. Various terrains along the walk took us through the Valley of the Winds, numerous sizeable trees such as red river gums, ghost gums, melaleucas, bloodwood and desert oak (and dozens of other types of plant prefixed with 'desert' or 'bush'), along with the ubiquitous spinifex.

After traversing the domes, we came back to the campsite for a shower and then headed to Uluru to check out the famed rock sunset. Scores of people were lined up in front of a seemingly endless row of cars. It would have brought a tear of joy to Mr Kodak's eye. The event was remarkable. The rock changed shades subtly, almost unnoticeably, while the sun set behind us and our shadows grew longer. The range of hues was to be more obvious when I later lined up the series of photos I took as the sun set.

The show was over and the next day was going to be the climax of the trip – it was time to hit the rock.

The morning came and it was the last day of the trip proper, or so we thought; everything else will be on the way home. It was a strange feeling after more than four months of almost non-stop travelling. But what a place to finish!

It felt like we had only just left, yet when I think back on everything we had done, it felt like we had been travelling for a year. Tasmania seemed so long ago. The jumble of sensations and memories proved the point of a largely beautiful and diverse country.

Giles and Gosse (who thought Uluru was one of the most impressive things he'd ever seen) wandered through the area in 1872 mapping it for future prospectors and graziers to usurp land occupied by the natives. Uluru named Ayres Rock after Sir Henry Ayres, the outback-loving South Australian Premier. The new and old settlers clashed, as in most parts of the country when white men showed up and hung around, and while there were attempts to settle and school the Aborigines in European style, they largely returned to the land they had lived off for thousands of years.

In 1985, freehold title to Uluru and the surrounding National Park was handed back to the traditional owners, many of whom are still involved in the Park's management and tourism. At the ceremony, the Governor General thoughtfully observed that Uluru does not merely sit at the centre of our continent, but also at its heart. In 1987, Uluru-Kata Tjuta National Park was added to the United Nations World Heritage List for its natural value. Seven years later, it was re-listed for its cultural value.

We made it to the rock just on ten o'clock and tagged along on the free ranger tour of a small section of the trail around Uluru. The non-Aboriginal ranger gave a fascinating commentary about the spiritual and cultural background, the history of tourism, the local Aboriginal community of about 300 and management of the park.

The local community still lives a relatively traditional lifestyle even though they are clothed, live in houses, use rifles instead of spears and drive beat up old cars, they still adhere to traditional beliefs and keep their law strong with ceremonies and teaching of the younger generation.

The traditional owners request that visitors don't climb Uluru. While thousands of people ignore the request, the increasing Park visitation rate has been accompanied by a drop in the number of climbers. Maybe one day no one will climb it but just enjoy it from its barren surrounds. Unfortunately, when the government handed back the land to the Aborigines in 1985, one stipulation was that tourists would still be able to do the climb. It is very steep, there are numerous warnings, about one rescue every fortnight and most people do it merely so they can buy the t-shirt saying 'I climbed Ayres Rock'. I preferred the sticker for sale at the cultural centre, which said, 'I didn't climb Uluru'.

The 9.5-kilometre level walk around the perimeter of Uluru is fascinating and by most reports provides a better perspective than the walk up the rock. The appearance from a distance of a relatively smooth chunk of rock sticking up out of the desert is quite deceiving. From close up, it looks more like a mountain range made up of undulating plated patchwork rock (not conglomerate rock like Kata Tjuta) pockmarked with caves, and slowly weathered by waterfalls (all dry during our visits) and enlivened by pools of water. Some of the upper caves are so large and filled with such intricate formations they look like small ancient cities built into the rock, but are virtually invisible from a distance.

I was continually pleasantly surprised as we rounded each corner by another spectacular view of mottled and scarred red rock against the deep blue sky. Every view was worth a photo but I limited myself to one roll of 36 exposures in addition to a few digital shots. There are several individual sacred sights around the perimeter, for either women or men, where photos are not permitted. Many of these areas still host ceremonies on occasion. One occurred a couple of weeks before our visit and a section of the trail was closed for three hours so that the participants would not be in view of anyone.

On the way back to the campground, still in awe, we stopped at the impressive cultural centre, which gives a detailed explanation of the cultural and spiritual significance of the area and about the people who live in the park now. They show an interesting video about the controversial handover of the Park to the Aborigines by the Hawke government in 1985. The centre also houses a couple of shops with what we thought was overpriced merchandise, although the quality was good and the money went directly to the local people. By then our legs were wobbly enough so we went back for an early dinner. Thankfully the temperature that night in the desert wasn't quite so low, but still frigid.

After bidding farewell to Uluru we hit the long flat barren road to Alice Springs. We passed several decaying dead cows by the road, and kilometres of fences attempting to keep animals inside paddocks you can't see the other side of, nor can you see water or fodder of any substance. It must take months and a lot of money (and patience) to build these endless fences. They must be worth it though, judging by the number of splattered stock providing sustenance for the huge wedge-tailed eagles and omnipresent crows. We also saw a large pack of roaming camels that appeared to be outside the bounds of any of the outback's massive stations. You never know what you're going to come across in the middle of nowhere.

Back to the Heritage Caravan Park at Alice and we lucked out with a caravan the size of a house. I couldn't see how anything other than a semi could pull the thing anywhere. There was a bit of free 'entertainment' at night, in the form of a pudgy old Sri Lankan, singing golden oldies to a cheesy backup CD. The young foreign tourists didn't seem to be taking too much notice but the grey nomads were lapping it up like there was no tomorrow. They were all lined up in their chairs with their little dogs on their laps, tapping their feet. They kept snugly warm in Grosby slippers, home knitted ensembles keeping the rest of them (including heads) toasty, and wine cask bladders to keep their insides warm. We stayed as long as we could before retiring to the van to thaw.

Before beginning our homeward journey, the morning's news bulletin told us about another croc attack on an unsuspecting fisherman. There was also a fish attack in the Territory over night, seriously injuring some unwary local. Must have been a big (and angry) fish.

22. The Home Stretch

Back on the long flat barren road between Alice Springs and Tennant Creek, this time northbound. It was boring enough the first time! Boring is relative though. Would I rather have been driving through the outback than doing anything else? YES!

We saw several willy-willies near the road, whipping up all manner of dust and loose vegetation. The biggest was crossing the road as we drove past so we got splattered with dust and buffeted by blowing spinifex. Hundreds of putrid dead kangaroos lay beside and on the road.

We stopped for lunch at the Ti-Tree roadhouse at which several of the locals were gathered in the 'Grog Yard' out the back with all the orphaned kangaroos and wedge tailed eagles being nursed back to health.

Our curiosity about Wycliffe Well, the UFO capital of Australia, got the better of us and we stopped at the roadhouse/motel/caravan park to check it out. There was a voluminous register of people who claimed to have seen a UFO in the area and several press clippings on the wall, not to mention the little green men at the petrol bowsers and the cosmic paintjob on the outside of the roadhouse. They were constructing a large lake to accommodate fish for guests to catch their dinner. A space oasis in the desert, indeed.

Tennant Creek was just how we left it. We left it again, just as we found it.

The next day's drive east to Mt Isa was about seven hours through more flat and uninspiring scrubby countryside. The road from Three

Ways (just north of Tennant Creek and where we turned right for an easterly bearing), the Barkly Highway, is our very own route 66, but without the kicks. Much of the drive is through the Barkly Tableland, a flat expanse not known for its trees but covered in Mitchell Grass, one of the most productive arid-zone grasses. Often we could look all around and not see a single tree. On occasion, we could barely see the vegetation on the horizon though the shimmering heat radiating from the hot surface. This is the land where Leichhardt went missing after upsetting a tribe of Aborigines. They killed him and his travelling companions, although the exact location remains a mystery despite numerous searches. Barkly was the next European explorer to come though the area. When he and his party were surveying the area in 1878, they ran out of water, dug into a dry sandy riverbed and found some. It was from this experience that the Plenty River and Plenty Highway (an unsealed road that cuts through to Queensland further south than the sealed Barkly Highway) got their names.

We stopped frequently at the abundant rest stops throughout the outback. It was nice not to be in a rush and to stop and soak up the environment, listen to the crows, smell the dust and blooms and see, well, not much. Often there were handy travel tips scrawled over the picnic tables, water tanks and any other surface that could be written on. Complaints about all the toilet paper lying around were common and there were often tips on cheap petrol or bad food up the road.

After the unlimited speed highways of the NT, it was a drag crossing the border into Queensland, where the state limit of 100kph was the lowest in the country. Not only that, much of the highway to Mt Isa was only one lane wide, so once again we had to dodge dead roos, mammoth lizards, road trains, potholes and caravans while crawling along.

Camooweal, just over the Qld border, is a small town with a few roadhouses and a sign reminding eastbound travellers to put their watches forward five years and 30 minutes. Some might suggest that the opposite would be more appropriate.

Mt Isa is the biggest city of north-west Queensland and home to one of the largest silver and lead mines in the world. Mt Isa seems to like being called 'The Isa', as if there were others with which to compare. Apparently the name was declared by 1920s prospectors and is a variation on the Mt Ida gold mine in Western Australia. The smokestack at the lead smelter is Australia's tallest freestanding structure and dominates the skyline. Copper and zinc are also mined in large quantities at The Isa, and the town of more than 20,000 swells annually when it hosts the country's largest rodeo. Yee ha!

Mt Isa doesn't look much chop, and the reports we heard from travellers going in the opposite direction weren't big on praise for the place. One night was enough for us, although we did have a decent pub feed not far from our lodging.

The drive out of Mt Isa is through the rugged Mt Godkin Ranges, quite a change from the flat tableland on the way in. We drove through Cloncurry, birthplace of John Flynn's Royal Flying Doctor Service. It's a mining-turned-pastoral town at which copper was discovered by a search party trying to track down Burke and Wills. When the price of copper went south, farmers moved in and took the miners' place as the town's lifeblood.

Travelling southeast along the highway, we stumbled upon McKinlay, otherwise known as Walkabout Creek, Mick Dundee's stamping ground. Prior to the Crocodile Dundee movie, the Walkabout Creek Hotel was known as the Federal Hotel and was about to celebrate its hundredth year of business. After the movie, they moved the pub from the only street in town to the side of the highway. I admit, however, that it's what caught our eye. It just didn't look right and distinctly lacked atmosphere, although the barmaid was very friendly and informative. The Croc Dundee theme is not overly exploited, but obviously a good point of interest in the township of about 20 people. I wondered how they felt about their pub being moved. At least it was only around the corner.

While there, a bloke enjoying the veranda's shade (and a cold brew) asked us if we'd been to Purnululu (Bungle-Bungles) in the past month or so. He recognised the car and was keen to share travel tales. He and his wife had traversed the Tanami Track and told us the story of Rabbit Flat, the main outpost along the track. When they arrived with plans to stay, the proprietor of the roadhouse told them to drive about 100 kilometres further up the rough road and bush camp because he couldn't guarantee their safety at the roadhouse. Very sad.

Back on the road, we were dodging the colossal road trains hurtling along in both directions. They were massive – 53.5m long, according to the road signs. Some of the copper trucks had at least six trailers.

Tumbleweed was prolific along the road, occasionally whipped up into an arresting but harmless twister. In addition to the standard assortment of road kill, crows, eagles, emus and kangaroos, we spotted a flock of elegant brolgas delicately tiptoeing around in one of the paddocks we drove past.

Further down the road we drove through Kynuna (population 18), which surprisingly has a surf lifesaving club (but no surf) and an annual surf carnival that we missed by a week (typical!). Sounds like your classic Australian outback tongue-in-cheek festival. Any excuse for a party. It is also home to the Never Never Caravan Park, the Jolly Swag Van Park and the Blue Heeler Hotel adorned with a neon blue heeler dog.

One hundred and sixty more kilometres southeast, we arrived at our destination of Winton and settled on the very friendly caravan park in town for the night. We got a small rundown caravan for about twenty bucks. At five o'clock, we sat in on a talk about what Winton had to offer, and frankly we were amazed. How this little place hasn't received more attention I don't know. Rather than our original plan of getting some sleep and leaving the next morning, an extension seemed a good idea to soak up the atmosphere of this aesthetically uninspiring but activity-packed town.

After cooking up dinner, we visited the equally friendly Tattersalls Hotel. As soon as we walked in the locals started chatting to us. We ended up talking for some time with a contractor for Telstra who did a bit of opal hunting in his spare time. Sounded like a pleasant life. He gave us a surprisingly fascinating insight into outback telecommunications and the constant advances in technology. He also had an opal mining story or two to tell.

Later in the evening, a local walked into the bar and all present called out 'Norm'! It was bizarrely like being in an episode of the TV sitcom *Cheers*.

We started the following day in the small town strolling down the main road, reading the informative history boards outside historically significant buildings. Just a block from the main road was Arno's wall, a wall around an eccentric (they always seem that way) opal miner's house, built of a bit of everything. We walked up and down the wall and saw a couple of motor bikes, sewing machines, lawn mowers

299

numerous car parts, various heavy farm equipment a cement mixer, vacuum cleaner, crockery a concrete Aborigine and of course the kitchen sink, all roughly cemented together. Unfortunately, Arno was not around for us to see if his disposition matched his wall.

Back on the main road, we visited the Corfield & Fitzmaurice Store, a National Trust classified craft shop and gem display. It had a fascinating display of more than 6,000 minerals, gemstones and fossils – not something that would normally capture my interest but there was something about it that drew me in. The excellent fossils were largely from this dinosaur-rich area. Not far from town is Lark Quarry, where dinosaur tracks dating back 93 million years have been fossilised in the mud. For those of us who don't have time to get out there, the museum has a life-size replica of the prints and the dinosaurs that are believed to have made them.

The minerals and gems in the collection were a full palette of colours and shapes. Some of them naturally formed near perfect geometric shapes as though they had been cut. On the other hand, it was surprising to see how attractive asbestos can appear when it has been cut and polished. It was also interesting to see the deadly substance in its natural state (behind glass). It was by far the most interesting display of rocks I have ever seen; well worth the $5 entry fee.

Back out on the main street, we strolled past the town rubbish bins, which were composed of wheelie bins placed inside large plastic dinosaur feet. The public toilets were labelled rams and ewes.

We then spent a few hours in the amazingly hi-tech Waltzing Matilda Centre. It claimed to be the only museum in the world dedicated to a particular song. It's in Winton because the famous Australian anthem was written and first performed in the area by Banjo Paterson. Upon entering the museum, the swagman's ghost gave a moving description of the song and its meaning to Australia and Australians. A lot of people think it should be our national anthem. It more or less was, briefly. At the Helsinki Olympics when Marjorie Jackson won a gold medal, Waltzing Matilda was accidentally played as the Australian national anthem. More recently, there was considerable controversy when the organisers of the 2003 Rugby World Cup would not allow the tune to be sung in response to New Zealand's haka. Of course the spectators sang it anyway.

The museum also featured thoughts by many famous Australians on what the song means to them. Another room provided numerous interpretations of the song from around the world. Performances on offer were from Dame Edna Everage, John Collinson (an unknown Queenslander who was the first to record the song), Gwadu, an exotic New Guinea group singing in pidgin English, David Evans and Thunder Down Under offering a heavy metal version, Bill Haley and his Comets singing 'Rockin Matilda', Sten and Stanley – a Swedish folk duo, and the more authentic Bushwhackers and Slim Dusty.

Apparently, at a meal attended by Churchill, Menzies and deGaulle, the three leaders retired to a room in which Waltzing Matilda was being played on a gramophone. Churchill began singing along and exclaimed, 'that's one of the finest songs in the world'! He obviously had his usual few cognacs under his belt.

Also at the museum were rooms full of historical junk, a history of the area's contribution to war, information on the local Aboriginal tribes, a good library, an art gallery and a detailed history of Qantas, which held its first board meeting in Winton.

It had been a surprisingly insightful and educational day.

After regaling our neighbours with my dubious didgeridoo playing, we went to a BBQ at the caravan park. There were about 30 or 40 people gathered around the campfire to feast on local character Gloria's stew, curry, rissoles and chops. And the highlight - her yarns. The meal wasn't bad but the stories were fun and mainly true, perhaps with a furphy or two thrown in for interest or a laugh. The jokes were corny but some of the audience members were falling off their stumps with laughter. There was traditional billy tea as well as some good bush poetry. We sat with the manager of the caravan park and a lady from the Tatts Hotel, and after the 'show' Gloria came up for a chat with us and told a few more stories. We found out that she butchered her own meat for the daily BBQ feast, and that you didn't want to piss her off.

Poetry seemed to play a large part in Winton, partly thanks to Gloria, mainly because of Banjo Patterson and also because of the annual poetry competition. Winton is also famous for giving the world the longest road train in history. It had 34 trailers.

Longreach is a quick 190 kilometres down the road and was our next stop. It claims to be the home of Qantas (as does Winton), and houses the impressive Stockman's Hall of Fame. It's a large museum of Australian history, paying particular attention to the outback. I don't think there would be a better place for a foreign (or local) visitor to get a feel for Australia's background and the outback way of life other than to cover most of it themselves.

The area is home to many thousand more sheep and cattle than humans, and is where Captain Starlight and his bushranger gang rustled 1,000 cattle before driving them down to South Australia to be sold. In memory, the town hosts the bi-annual Starlight Stampede. Its other major event is Diamond Shears, the country's leading shearing competition.

But none of that was enough to keep us in town. On the advice of the lady at the Longreach tourist bureau (housed in a replica of the original Qantas booking office), we left Longreach for the 25-kilometre drive to Ilfracombe, a small settlement further on down the highway. It seemed to consist of several farms, a general store and a pub that doubled as a caravan park. We went into the bar to hand over our $10 camping fee (second night free) and were displeased to be served by a Pommie tourist. It just seemed a shame out in the middle of the outback to be waited on by a foreigner who really didn't know much about the history or geography of the place.

The pub is curiously called the Wellshot Hotel. In 1873, a Glasgow based New Zealand-Australian land company acquired land in the Ilfracombe area and named the million-acre property Wellshot, after a Scottish estate. Ilfracombe's claim to fame is to have the largest flock of sheep ever to be mustered: 43,000 in 1886. As the *Let's Go guidebook* says, 'now you know'.

After checking in, we were shown to a site by the very friendly Noel, who lived in a caravan with his wife in the small park out the back of the pub. After chatting to him several times, we returned to the hotel. The hotel had a bunch of battered old hats hanging from the ceiling (what pub doesn't in the outback?), as well as hundreds of five and ten dollar notes stuck to the ceiling. They were meant to be for the museum that stretches alongside the highway but I think the pub keeps them there and writes a cheque to the museum. There was also an interesting display of cattle branding symbols on the wall, and as usual, the beer fridge was covered in stickers from around the world. The main topics of conversation among the locals seemed to be bull bars and shearing.

We both ordered a big juicy rump steak from the menu and after dinner went outside to the $9 stockman show. It is put on by one of the brothers who own the property and consists of an impressive whip demonstration, an amazing working dog exhibition rounding up ducks and then sheep and finally with an explanation of horsemanship. Just before moving back into the pub for a brief talk on its history, a 16-year-old local rode a bucking bronco for well past the eight second minimum. Better him than me.

We stayed in the bar until it closed, chatting to a couple of blokes from Sydney who were seeing how far they could drive in a week. I'll take four and a half months any time thanks.

Another long boring drive followed. When I say boring, it wasn't really that bad. We managed to keep up spirits over these trips, and at the time it seemed preferable to sitting behind a desk in a stinky, crowded noisy city. We passed through a couple of small country towns, including Barcaldine, famous for a big shearer strike which led to formation of the Australian Workers Party, the precursor of the Labor Party. We also drove through Blackall, home to the world record sheep shear (and close to the famed Black Stump). In 1892, Jacky Howe sheared 321 sheep in eight hours with a set of hand shears. The record still stands for hand shears and wasn't beaten with mechanical shears until 1950. So great was his feat, that the blue singlet typically worn by shearers is known as the Jacky Howe.

Another local town, Barcoo, also has its claim to fame. *Lonely Planet* points out that *The Macquarie Dictionary* includes the phrase 'Barcoo spew', which means vomiting from excessive heat. I couldn't confirm this, but when examining my dictionary, I discovered the terms *Barcoo dog* ('a device made with tins...which produces a loud noise and is used to drive sheep'), *Barcoo rot* ('chronic streptococcal skin infection') and

Barcoo salute (swatting flies away from your face). From where did this presence in the Australian vernacular emanate?

Travelling east along the Capricorn Highway until we hit Barcaldine, we took a hard right and headed south along the Matilda Highway. Now we were really heading home.

We were impressed to hear that Charleville had a brewery and ten pubs by 1900. We had planned to stay at an historic pub, but decided that we would end up spending too much money (again), so we opted for a $9 campsite at the caravan park.

The next day's drive took us through Cunnamulla. This is in the heart of serious sheep country, with a heck lot of the woolly buggers about. The town's been around for a long time, and used to be one of Cobb & Co's stagecoach stops. Back in 1880, its bank was robbed by a bloke named Joseph Wells. Joe thought he'd done well until he tried to get away, when he couldn't find his horse. The townsfolk weren't too happy about having their savings nicked so they trapped him in a tree, which is now the town's main attraction. If you're really keen, you can head 60 kilometres west to the opal mining town of Eulo, home of the world Lizard Racing Championships, which we of course missed by a matter of weeks. There's a great little pub, and the town also features the *Destructo Cockroach Monument*, erected in memory of a racing cockroach that came to grief under a spectator's boot.

Driving through the big flat open sheep country of inland southern Queensland and northern New South Wales, we must have seen as many emus as sheep. It was amazing how many of the big gangly birds there were, hanging out in flocks of between two and fifty. Only one ran in front of the car (luckily we missed him) and surprisingly few were splattered on the road, especially compared to the hundreds of kangaroos. Like the roads, the number of dead and smelly roos improved significantly once we crossed the border into NSW.

Just over the border along the Mitchell Highway is Barringun, formerly a town with a few pubs and other businesses but now down to one pub and a shack/roadhouse. We stopped at the pub and chatted with the owners of 22 years. The old, very country pub has stood there since at least the 1870s and looks like it from the outside. It is small and oozes character. A younger bloke came behind the bar and we spent a while talking to him about the country and its problems, particularly drastically dropping sheep prices and the chronic lack of rain. The reason for the rain conversation was that it had just started to rain as we crossed the border. As we sat in the pub, we could smell the rain about to fall, and then it fell. Paddy behind the bar was praying for a decent dump and we were happy enough to see some rain again after the dryness of the previous couple of months.

When we eventually made it to Bourke, we weren't encouraged to stop. The caravan park at which we had intended to stay had closed down. The next one looked run down and was for sale, as seemed to be the case with several of the businesses in town. Neither of us felt like camping in the rain and the pubs didn't appeal either, so we continued through twilight in search for lodging.

About half an hour up the road, we came to Byrock, a small Tidy Town community with a clean looking pub by the highway. We paid $50 for a pleasant small room and had a few drinks and good steak at the bar. We chatted to a truckie for a while. After driving through truck territory for so long, it was timely to learn a bit about the road trains that traverse the country and the solitary life these drivers live. He also gave us his two cents' worth about the area's racial problems. Another local chimed in on the conversation, which gradually turned to back yard butchering. That was my cue to go to bed.

The highway southeast to Nyngan was long and straight. The same could not be said about Nyngan, although we were disappointed not to see stoned hippies drifting along the footpaths, as we had naively expected.

We continued south, getting depressingly close to home. Had we only just left home or had we been travelling for a year? It felt like both.

Where better to spend our 140th and last night than the vineyard-rich town of Mudgee? We checked in at a place Glen had stayed at previously and settled on a homely wooden cabin to close the journey. With little time to spare, we toured the town and visited a few wineries, making one or two purchases along the way. Back at the cabin, we had a drop or two with dinner and toasted our great country and the trip of a lifetime.

The End

Made in United States
Orlando, FL
22 January 2024

42790534R00189